Thatcheris

For Citlali, Lyn, Rowena and Vanessa

Thatcherism

A Tale of Two Nations

BOB JESSOP, KEVIN BONNETT,
SIMON BROMLEY AND TOM LING

Polity Press

First published 1988 by Polity Press in association with Basil Blackwell.

Editorial Office:
Polity Press, Dales Brewery, Gwydir Street, Cambridge CB1 2LJ, UK

Basil Blackwell Ltd
108 Cowley Road, Oxford OX4 1JF, UK

Basil Blackwell Inc.
432 Park Avenue South, Suite 1503,
New York, NY 10016, USA

British Library Cataloguing in Publication Data

Thatcherism: a tale of two nations.
  1. Great Britain. Politics, 1979–1987
  I. Jessop, Bob
  320.941

  ISBN 0-7456-0669-5
  ISBN 0-7456-0670-9 Pbk

Library of Congress Cataloging in Publication Data

Jessop, Bob.
  Thatcherism : a tale of two nations.

  Bibliography: p.
  Includes index.
  1. Conservative Party (Great Britain) 2. Labour
Party (Great Britain) 3. Great Britain—Politics
and government—1979–   . I. Title.
JN1129.C7J45   1989   324.24104   88–26284
ISBN 0–7456–0669–5
ISBN 0–7456–0670–9 (pbk.)

Typeset in Ehrhardt 10 on 11½ pt by Photographics, Honiton, Devon
Printed in Great Britain by Billing & Sons Ltd, Worcester

Contents

Preface

It is said that 'the devil has all the best tunes'. Whether or not this is always true, radical writers have certainly called the tune in describing and explaining Thatcherism. This tune sometimes comes perilously close to a hymn of praise for Margaret Thatcher's strategic sense but it is usually sufficiently restrained to convey the extent to which her success also derives from sheer good luck and the incompetence of the opposition. But we should also be aware of the dangers of falling into a defeatist fatalism. Gramsci once called for 'pessimism of the intellect, optimism of the will'. Since 1979 the left's problem often seems to be too much of the one, too little of the other. It was this impending defeat of the left in the 1983 election which motivated us to write our first article on Thatcherism and our continuing despair about the left's approach to Thatcherism that has prompted our further work. In contributing to the debate on Thatcherism we have tried to introduce a note of scepticism about its coherence, strength and durability and a note of warning about too precipitate a collapse into a 'new realism' which accepts the Thatcher agenda without question. At the same time we have tried to establish the material bases for the emergence, consolidation and recent changes in Thatcherism and to suggest that the left must fight Thatcherism on an economic and political terrain significantly different from that of the old, but not yet forgotten, postwar settlement.

The purpose of this book is to broaden the discussion of Thatcherism. We were always unhappy with the precise form which our first article assumed: it tried to combine a reasoned and friendly critique of the work of Stuart Hall with an alternative, more polity-centred account which both qualified and complemented his work. Many people failed to see that our criticisms were addressed more to methodological problems in Hall's approach and the one-sided strategic conclusions which might follow from them than to the substance of his analyses in the areas to which he applied them. It might well have been better to have separated out these two strands of argument rather than combine them in one article. Thus our subsequent work moved away from a confrontation with Hall's work to develop our own approach and to present a more rounded account of Thatcherism. We have now taken this approach further by presenting a considered analysis of the most important and influential alternative interpretations of Thatcherism as well as developing some of the emerging theoretical and conceptual foundations of our own approach.

Part I of our book presents a general critique of definitions, periodizations and explanations of Thatcherism. This serves to put both our own work and that of Stuart Hall into its broader theoretical and political context. Part II reproduces our original articles from *New Left Review* together with Stuart Hall's reply to our first critique. These articles are presented in their original form (with all their faults) since they were interventions into particular conjunctures. Readers must judge for themselves how much of these accounts still seems valid today. We believe that these changing analyses of a changing phenomenon can be integrated into a multi-dimensional, but nonetheless coherent, account. We try to develop this account in Part III of the book.

We gratefully acknowledge the invaluable help and encouragement we have received from many friends, colleagues and students. This has helped us survive the Thatcher years intellectually and learn to analyse them, if not to love them. Richard Drane helped bring us together in the task of examining Thatcherism and also contributed to an early version of our first article. The editors of *New Left Review* encouraged us in our work and, in particular, Robin Blackburn and Patrick Camiller provided creative editorial advice on all three articles. We are grateful to them for permission to reproduce these articles from issues 147, 153, 165 of the review. Stuart Hall has always been more of a friend than a foe and has been a major source of inspiration in our own work. He has very kindly given his permission to reprint his reply to our first article from *New Left Review*, 151; it also appears in his book *The Road to Renewal: Thatcherism and the Crisis of the Left*, published by Verso in 1988. The active and enthusiastic support of all at Polity Press, especially David Held and Pip Hurd, has given this book tangible form faster and more efficiently than we ever dared hope.

Finally, as ever, we are each in our different ways grateful to those close to us for their tolerance of our academic and political obsessions, their acceptance of the pressures to which our work on this book subjected them and, most of all, their loving support. This book is dedicated to each and all of them.

Kevin Bonnett, Simon Bromley,
Bob Jessop, Tom Ling

Cambridge

List of Abbreviations

AES	alternative economic strategy
AP	authoritarian populism
AS	authoritarian statism
CBI	Confederation of British Industry
CLP	Constituency Labour Party
CND	Campaign for Nuclear Disarmament
DoE	Department of the Environment
DES	Department of Education and Science
DTI	Department of Trade and Industry
EC	European Community
GDP	gross domestic product
GLC	Greater London Council
GOP	globalization of production
IMF	International Monetary Fund
KWS	Keynesian welfare state
LDC	less developed country
LEA	Local Education Authority
MNC	multinational corporation
MSC	Manpower Services Commission
MTFS	Medium Term Financial Strategy
NEDC	National Economic Development Council
NHS	National Health Service
NIDL	new international division of labour
NUM	National Union of Miners
PR	proportional representation
PSBR	Public Sector Borrowing Requirement
PWS	postwar settlement
SPD	Sozialdemokratische Partei Deutschlands (German social democratic party)
TGWU	Transport and General Workers' Union
TULV	Trade Unions for a Labour Victory
UDC	Urban Development Corporation

PART I

Coming to Terms with Thatcherism

1

The Nature of Thatcherism

Margaret Thatcher has given her name to the age in which we live. Whether you abominate her, as many people do, or are transfixed with admiration, that much you cannot deny her. Thatcherism is unique: not perhaps as a set of ideas, but as the only 'ism' attached to the name of a British prime minister. (Young and Sloman 1986)

The elements of what we now, in absurd flattery of its heroine, call Thatcherism, have long been present in the liberal wing of the Conservative Party, though dormant since 1931 ... But in combination and in the exuberant insistence with which they have been proclaimed and implemented, these ideas represent a significant shift away from the postwar settlement. (Golding in Bull and Wilding 1983)

Thatcherism is a reasonably coherent and comprehensive concept of control for the restoration of bourgeois rule and bourgeois hegemony in the new circumstances of the 1980s ... The central elements in the Thatcherite concept are the reorientation of Britain's foreign policy and the redefinition of its place in the world; its attack on the position of the trade unions and the Labour Party (Thatcher aims to eliminate 'socialism' as a serious political force); the restructuring of the role of the state in the economy; and finally a reordering of the balance of power between different fractions of capital in Britain. (Overbeck 1989)

In the end the Thatcher experiment seemed to be a rather naive experiment in social engineering, through which it was hoped that the behaviour and attitudes of the unions would somehow change and that this would make life easier for entrepreneurs. (Keegan 1984)

Thatcherism is essentially an instinct, a sense of moral values and an approach to leadership rather than an ideology. It is an expression of Mrs Thatcher's upbringing in Grantham, her background of hard work and family responsibility, ambition and postponed satisfaction, duty and patriotism. (Riddell 1983)

The Thatcher government proclaimed . . . that the new national philosophy should be based not on altruism but the eager and unfettered pursuit of self-interest: the politics of greed. (Loney 1986)

Thatcherism comprises classical liberalism laced with misogyny and proto-feminism. (Campbell 1987)

Thatcherism is a novel and exceptional political force . . . Its novelty lies, in part, in the success with which this 'populist' appeal was then orchestrated with the imposition of authority and order. It managed to marry the gospel of free market liberalism with organic patriotic Toryism. 'Free market, strong state, iron times': an authoritarian populism. (Hall and Jacques 1983)

I want to reaffirm the government's commitment to a sensible policy of prole-crushing and wog-control. (Attributed to the (fictional) Home Secretary by Steve Bell)

After three years at Essex University I'm fed up with people trying to define and explain Thatcherism. It's only the Conservative Party led by Mrs Thatcher. (Essex graduate, 1988)

As these quotations illustrate, there is widespread disagreement – not to mention some scepticism, cynicism, and sheer boredom – about the nature of Thatcherism. This book is as much concerned with how Thatcherism has been analysed as it is with Thatcherism as such. It examines a wide range of approaches to Thatcherism at different stages in its development and addresses some crucial questions about how one should analyse complex historical phenomena. These approaches range from abstract theoretical accounts to detailed empirical studies, from the grand visions of political parties and their ideological spokesmen to the everyday stories of journalists and the newspeak of the Tory press, from the hopes and fears of establishment figures to the considered opinions of ordinary voters and citizens. All these approaches are relevant to our concerns since they have all helped to shape the nature of Thatcherism and/or responses to it.

Clearly this book cannot be exhaustive but it does try to serve five main purposes: firstly, to examine some influential competing accounts of Thatcherism since its rise to prominence in the late 1970s; secondly, to pose the main issues involved in the analysis of conjunctures and the periodization of social phenomena; thirdly, in this dual context, to present the main contributions to the debate over the authoritarian populist character of Thatcherism and the alternative analysis presented by the 'Gang of Four' in *New Left Review* and *New Socialist*; fourthly, to relate these accounts of Thatcherism to some key theoretical issues in the social sciences, such as the relation between structure and agency, society-centred vs. state-centred theories, the relative autonomy of the

state, class analyses and feminism, and so forth; and, fifthly, to draw
some general political conclusions about Thatcherism and the appropriate
ways to resist its neo-liberal hegemonic project and strategy for social
transformation. Part I concentrates on the first two aims; Part II presents
the main contributions to the debate over authoritarian populism and
one alternative approach; and Part III is concerned with a general
overview of Thatcherism and with some broad theoretical and strategic
conclusions which might follow from our analysis.

What is Thatcherism?

Thatcherism sometimes seems to have acquired almost as many meanings
as there are people who mention it. Thus a book on Thatcherism is
bound to disappoint some readers' expectations because it will omit
some aspects they consider important. Hopefully the present review will
cover enough ground to minimize disappointment. Since it is impossible
to deal with the full range of meanings, however, we will concentrate
on just six broad approaches to the origins, nature and significance of
Thatcherism. Two of these combine agnosticism about Thatcherism's
existence with a hard empirical look at recent British history; the other
four accept that something which can be called Thatcherism exists and
relate it to recent changes in the Conservative Party or government
under the Thatcher leadership. But the precise definition varies from
one to another. Since other terms could serve equally well or better to
identify broader social trends, we do not discuss analyses which equate
Thatcherism with more general social changes without regard to the
impact of Margaret Thatcher and her party. The six approaches we do
consider are outlined in the next paragraph and then more fully examined
in subsequent pages.

   Firstly, one could abandon 'Thatcherism' as an analytical term and
just define concepts and study topics without referring to it. Secondly,
one could treat uses of 'Thatcherism' as a topic for analysis in their
own right without committing oneself to an independent definition.
These represent the agnostic approaches. Some positive definitions
could also be given. Among such definitions four broad approaches
stand out. Thus, thirdly, one could define 'Thatcherism' in terms of
Thatcher's personal qualities. Fourthly, one could examine 'Thatcherism'
in terms of the Thatcher style of political leadership. Fifthly, one could
define 'Thatcherism' in terms of the policies pursued by the Conservative
Party under Thatcher. And, sixthly, one could define it more broadly
in terms of the changing strategic line of the Conservative Party as
organized under the Thatcher leadership.

Six Approaches to Thatcherism

The first option means refusing to adopt 'Thatcherism' as a meaningful term, whether to describe events and/or to explain them. Instead one would simply specify distinct topics for analysis and explore them in other terms. Thus one might study, say, the development of electoral ideology in the Conservative Party 1975–9, industrial relations policy 1979–83 or changes in manpower policy 1984–8; and one might then explain these developments primarily in terms of, for the sake of argument, rational choice theory as applied to party competition, the crisis of corporatist relations among business, organized labour, and government and the search for an alternative, or the development of the training policy community respectively. In itself this approach would not help us to decide whether such a phenomenon as Thatcherism really exists and what it might involve.[1] But, since there are alternative accounts of Thatcherism suggesting that it is a single and coherent phenomenon, serious empirical work along these lines would help to demystify them by revealing the uneven development and emergent contradictions of so-called 'Thatcherism' in different areas.

The second approach could also be useful, for it would reveal the wide range of meanings of Thatcherism and their role in organizing accounts of the phenomena so described. This sort of enquiry need not be just a dry academic exercise concerned to enumerate alternative definitions: for different interpretations will influence the responses of different forces to so-called 'Thatcherism'.[2] This could help us understand such varied phenomena as the growth of the 'new realism' in the trade union movement, the transformation of the Social Democratic Party under David Owen into a party supposedly representing 'Thatcherism with a human face', or the rise of political tendencies in other countries advocating the 'Thatcherite' road as a solution to their own domestic problems. This approach is particularly relevant to understanding the recent development of the Conservative Party itself under Thatcher. For 'Thatcherism' has become part of the party's self-identity as well as something Thatcher herself now talks about quite openly and with no pretence of false modesty. In addition various tendencies and factions within the Conservative Party (as well as think tanks closely associated with it) have begun struggling over the future development of the 'Thatcherite' programme and several politicians are already manoeuvring to inherit Margaret Thatcher's mantle of leadership.

The third approach would identify Thatcherism with personal attributes of Thatcher, such as her beliefs, political philosophy, suburban attitudes, Victorian morality and so on. This approach assumes that there is something special or even unique about Thatcher which justifies focusing on these qualities and associating them with a specific 'ism'.

It also implies that this 'ism' is better deciphered from Thatcher's conference speeches, personal statements of faith and interviews than it is from the policies and actions of her government.[3] Even then there is scope for debate over exactly what these qualities comprise; and, depending on one's psychological views and/or hermeneutic skills, different versions of Thatcherism can be constructed.[4]

The fourth approach focuses on issues of political personality and leadership style. It suggests both that there is something distinctive about Mrs Thatcher in this regard *and* that her political style has major political consequences. This approach has the advantage of looking more directly at the political significance of Thatcherism than the third approach with its emphasis on direct personal qualities.[5] Although the precise words and phrases used vary from study to study, a broad consensus clearly exists on the Thatcher style. Among the most commonly cited attributes are: the resolute approach, conviction politics, rejection of compromise, missionary zeal, aggressive radicalism, a governess style, overbearing manner. Despite its greater concern with the political dimension of Thatcherism, this approach runs the same risk as the preceding view of trivializing discussions of Thatcherism, for both reduce Thatcherism to issues of personality. It also implies that the principal (source of) discontinuity in postwar British politics since 1979, if any, is a change in political style. This might be as limited as the shift from Callaghan's avuncular populism to Thatcher's authoritarian populism but style would still be of the essence. Even if the latter theoretical point were true (which we will later contest on several grounds), it would not explain why this particular style of leadership emerged when it did, how it has survived, nor what consequences it has had. These are all interesting and important issues which we review in subsequent chapters. An adequate understanding of these requires us to go beyond questions of style in order to assess both Thatcherism's context and content.

The fifth approach sees Thatcherism as the distinctive set of policies pursued by the Conservative Party under the Thatcher leadership. Thus early accounts of Thatcherism often reduced it to monetarism or equated it more generally with the commitment to 'free market, strong state'. In this context the policies typically cited include: control over the money supply, reductions in the public sector, encouraging private enterprise, freeing the labour market and restoring the authority of government.[6] In contrast to the agnosticism of the first approach mentioned above, this approach accepts that there is a distinctive Thatcherite set of policies. In turn this implies that the 1979 election marked a significant break in government policies. If the policies of the Thatcher governments basically continued those of preceding governments (whether those of the Wilson–Callaghan Premierships or Heath's neo-liberal policies of 1970–2), any mention of Thatcherism would serve to obfuscate rather than illuminate contemporary politics.[7] If continuity outweighed discontinuity across the divide of the 1979 election, it would be more appropriate to examine such definitions in terms of our second approach, that is, the ways in which accounts of 'Thatcherism' have organized political perceptions and actions in the 1980s. A related problem with this approach is its implication that, since the 1979 divide, there has been little fundamental change in Thatcherite policies. At most they would have developed incrementally and been implemented in trial-and-error fashion. If there have been major discontinuities in the development of government policies since 1979, however, then we would have to examine why and how government strategy has changed. This would lead us to the last approach to be considered here.

This sixth approach is not directly concerned with explicit references to 'Thatcherism' in political discourse nor simply with the series of policies pursued by the Thatcher governments. Instead it focuses on the development and specificity of the emergent strategic line pursued by Thatcher and her various circles of political and ideological supporters. This strategic line may have been modified in recent years as Thatcher and her colleagues have come to adopt Thatcherism as their self-identity. But it must also be studied in itself, regardless of any explicit references (which could well be misleading) to Thatcherism. In these terms the sixth approach examines the personal impact of Thatcher on the strategies and policies of the Conservative Party and the influence this has, if any, on the restructuring of different spheres of society. Different versions of this approach focus on different fields of action, different objectives and different strategies. Besides studies of the economic and/or political strategies of Thatcherism, this approach also includes analyses of its hegemonic project and the associated discursive strategies used to promote it. Stuart Hall's work on 'authoritarian populism', key aspects of Andrew Gamble's work on Thatcherite political strategy, and our own researches into Thatcherism can all be located within this approach.[8] In applying it one should always focus directly on actual strategies and policies in all their *ad hoc* and emergent character. Indeed, as we hope to show below, it would be quite wrong to assume that the strategic line has ever been fully developed, internally consistent, unchanging and adequate to the tasks set by Thatcher and her allies.

If this approach is to be fruitfully applied its core concept cannot be limited to fully elaborated strategies. Indeed, since strategic objectives are often pursued in the face of various dilemmas, risks, uncertainties and complexities, strategy is often emergent and pragmatic – adopting trial and error techniques, learning by doing, and changing along with circumstances. But these qualities do not justify extending the concept to purely hypothetical 'as if' strategies were no-one actually engages in strategic reflection or conduct. Thus it is best to consider strategy as a complex and continuing process which involves: selecting and ordering objectives; deciding on a pattern and sequence of actions deemed appropriate to attaining these objectives; monitoring performance and progress; and adjusting tactics and objectives as strategic interaction proceeds.

Three general points are worth stressing in relation to this approach. Firstly, strategy inevitably has a temporal dimension: the relationship between objectives and actions across different time horizons is crucial to strategic calculation. Secondly, in assessing the coherence of strategy, we should not require logical consistency out of time and place but simply consider how far different elements fit together over time and in different areas in pursuing the primary strategic goals. Thirdly, nothing in the above discussion should lead one to conclude that strategies will succeed. Indeed, since the relative success or failure of a given strategy typically depends on unacknowledged and changeable structural and conjunctural conditions, strategies are bound to fail in at least some respects. This suggests that we should pay more attention to the differential capacities to retain the long-term strategic initiative than to the success of any one short-term political strategy.

Finally, in examining Thatcherism as a strategic line, we should not reduce it to the impact of Thatcher as a personality and/or as the advocate of a political philosophy. This would be as one-sided and meaningless as to treat Thatcher as the passive instrument through which some grand economic logic or historical mission is realized. We need to avoid both extremes in discussing the relative contribution of great women (or men) and historical circumstances to decisive changes. Thus Thatcher should not be treated as if she were a truly independent, fully consistent, and self-willed historical agent – even if media hype and her own personal conviction often suggest otherwise! Equally we should not deny Thatcher's significant and undeniably personal impact on the development of Britain and the world: this would imply that, faced with the same circumstances, any leader would have acted in the same way because, to purloin a phrase, there is no alternative. This would be just as misleading. Fortunately, as will soon become apparent, there is no real difficulty in avoiding this essentially false dilemma.

Our Own Approach to Thatcherism

It should be clear from the following analysis that we adopt all six approaches in different contexts. This does not mean that we are agnostic about Thatcherism. Indeed we are polytheists in this regard: we believe in many Thatcherisms. This belief stems both from *a priori* theoretical arguments and from our *post hoc* reflections on the changes in the strategic line adopted by Thatcherism as well as its application to different areas.

In some cases we argue, in line with the first approach, that concepts such as 'Thatcherism' have been used too loosely and applied too widely. We recommend that they should be disaggregated so that the uneven development and complexities of the phenomena to which they refer can be highlighted. This can be seen, for example, in our first critique of authoritarian populism (or AP) as an interpretative device: this suggested that AP can be studied in eleven different spheres and that its relevance will vary across them. In other cases we adopt the second approach. Thus we will consider how specific interpretations of Thatcherism have affected academic analyses and political strategies or have fed back into the development of Thatcherism itself. Indeed it is an important part of our argument that socialist strategy has been seriously handicapped by the interpretations of Thatcherism developed on the left and/or taken over uncritically from other sources.

In looking at Thatcher's personal qualities we could clearly define a set of values and predispositions whose influence on British politics could then be assessed. On its own this would be inadequate in defining Thatcherism. But this third approach could certainly help in assessing how far the general strategic line of Thatcherism depends on and/or is linked to Thatcher's personal qualities. Likewise, when we look at the more 'Bonapartist' aspects of contemporary political life, revealed by the drift towards strong leadership, authoritarianism and a rather plebiscitary politics, we will certainly look at Thatcher's distinctive political style. But we also argue against both approaches that neither Thatcher's personal qualities nor her political style can be taken for granted. Indeed much effort has been invested in continually reworking both her image (ranging from her voice through her wardrobe to her sexuality) and her imagery (from housewife through iron lady to fishwife). In addition we must also examine the precise conditions in which this form of leadership has flourished and refuse any suggestion that one can understand contemporary British politics simply as a *folie de grandeur* or a product of the so-called 'resolute approach'.

In line with the fifth approach we also consider the policies pursued by the Thatcher governments. But we are less convinced than many other political scientists that there is a consistent set of policies which run through all three governments and which can be used to define the nature of Thatcherism. Thus sometimes we will examine these policies in a neutral, agnostic sense, studying which measures have been taken in specific areas since 1979. And sometimes we will consider whether it is strategic coherence which explains temporal discontinuities and logical inconsistencies within and across different policies.

But our chief interest in Thatcherism is organized around the sixth approach, namely, the strategic line. For only when this has been examined can we begin to answer questions about Thatcherism's functions and impact in British society. Some have argued that

Thatcherism is a reflection of petty bourgeois resentment and alienation stemming from the trend towards big business, big labour and big government associated with the Keynesian welfare state; that it represents a distinctive 'British road' to the next long wave of capitalist economic expansion based on flexible specialization and new forms of individualized consumption superseding the previous long wave based on mass production and mass consumption (sometimes known as Fordism – discussed in more detail in chapter 7); or that it is merely a continuation of politics and business as normal. Only if we have an independent definition of Thatcherism can we assess such claims: otherwise they are stipulative definitions incapable of critical evaluation. Thus, although we also consider it in other terms, our analysis will focus on Thatcherism in the sixth sense.

In adopting this wide range of approaches, we might seem guilty of inconsistency. Obviously we deny this. But then we would, wouldn't we? For different approaches reveal different aspects of the phenomenon and together they bring out its uneven development and complexity. Thus we will examine specific policy areas. We will treat Thatcherism variously as a political and ideological construct which serves to organize experiences of life under Thatcher and/or helps in shaping strategies and conduct in the seventies and eighties. We will also examine the impact of Thatcher's personal qualities and distinctive political style on the approach and policies of her government(s). Above all, however, we will consider the changing strategic line of the three Thatcher governments and the relative unity or disunity this imparts to the policies they have pursued. For it is the strategic line which has given a distinctive cast to Thatcherite policies and introduced a sufficient degree of discontinuity in postwar political economy as to justify an exploration of Thatcherism. It is the changing strategic vision which has given direction and coherence to the policies in the face of strategic dilemmas, policy failures, emerging contradictions and resistance. And it is the changing strategic vision which enables us to see Thatcherism as the vehicle through which a distinctive economic strategy, new state form and hegemonic project are being developed for Britain.

Stages of Thatcherism

Clarifying possible meanings of and approaches to Thatcherism in this way is only a start. It leaves unanswered some key questions about the prehistory and genesis, the continuous or discontinuous development and the even or uneven impact of Thatcherism, however it might be defined. Since we believe that Thatcherism is best examined historically, that it has changed considerably through time, and that its consequences have been uneven, it is clearly important to distinguish specific stages and phases in its development and to explore the timing and extent of its penetration into different areas of social life. These aspects, too, pose theoretical questions. How can one define the origins of Thatcherism, on what criteria can one divide it into stages, and how can one assess what difference it has made in various areas during specific periods? Crucial though such questions are, they have rarely been addressed in theoretical terms in studies of Thatcherism. Yet Thatcherism is a complex phenomenon whose genealogy, development and unity are far from easy to analyse. Accordingly we address some of these issues here.

The Future is Made and Cannot be Predicted

As a dynamic phenomenon Thatcherism's past history has been continually reconstructed as different aspects come to appear important. Thus to explain the 'rise of Thatcherism' implies that we already know the nature of Thatcherism; moreover, as it (or our understanding) changes, such reconstructions will change too. Indeed, only when a distinctive Thatcherite strategy and regime have been consolidated can we examine the successive stages in its emergence and subsequent development. Moreover, if Thatcherism has changed and continues to change, lessons drawn from earlier stages may later mislead us. Likewise, if its impact is uneven, it may be wrong to generalize from one area to another. And, in so far as the nature of Thatcherism is never fully and finally fixed and its significance will always depend on contrasts drawn with other phenomena, any analysis of its various stages and effects will always be incomplete and uncertain.

These theoretical comments help us understand why early accounts of the Thatcherite phenomenon referred less often to Thatcherism as such than to authoritarian populism, monetarism, the doctrine of the social market economy and strong state, the emergence of petty bourgeois reaction to the postwar settlement and so on. In these early days no clear Thatcherite phenomenon could be discerned because it had not yet articulated a distinctive *and credible* project, acquired any clear form or established its dominance in organizational and institutional terms. Indeed the somewhat diffuse focus of early accounts is significant because it suggests that there was nothing inevitable about Thatcherism: the various currents which combined to produce Thatcherism could, in different circumstances, have led in other directions. They also help us understand how many commentators could confidently predict a U-turn in Conservative policies once the so-called 'realities of power' had become evident: for they were reading Thatcherism through the lenses of the postwar settlement, corporatist bias and the earlier policy reversals of the Heath government when it abandoned neo-liberalism to return to corporatism and dirigisme. It is only with hindsight that we can reconstruct the 'rise of Thatcherism' out of all the disparate tendencies and developments in the 1960s and 1970s and begin to ask (and investigate) why the expected U-turn never came.

Had Edward Heath's deal with Joe Gormley managed to prevent the 1973–4 miners' strike, had Sir Keith Joseph not committed political suicide by some ill-judged proposals on birth control for the underclass in 1974, had Jim Callaghan opted for an 8 per cent wages guideline before the Winter of Discontent set in (to cite just three relevant factors), it is unlikely that we would all be talking about Thatcherism as a natural and inevitable feature of today's political scene. Similar problems are evident in the obituaries for Thatcherism written at various times since Margaret Thatcher became Prime Minister in 1979. Thus, to take three different examples, the summer of popular and establishment discontent with her leadership and policies in 1981, a different outcome of the Falklands war, or a victory for the Tory MPs who wanted to consolidate past victories rather than the neo-liberals who wanted to press ahead with more radical policies in 1985–6, would each have produced a turn in the Conservative line. Likewise policies which seemed to have been ruled out in earlier stages can be resurrected (for example, reorganization of the NHS, introduction of student loans); and others, which seemed to be successful, have been dropped (for example, continued legislative attack on the unions) as the government's strategic line and priorities change or the conjunctures in which they are pursued unfold in new directions.

Precisely because the future is made and cannot be predicted, we must be sensitive to the ways in which structure and agency interact to make history. Thus, whilst it is worth distinguishing successive stages of Thatcherism, they should not be treated as unfolding according to iron laws of history: capitalist laws of motion, the dynamic of electoral cycles, an inevitable trend towards authoritarian statism, or whatever. Nor should we make the mistake of reducing the development of Thatcherism to the wilful realization of an individual or collective project conceived out of time and place. Thatcherism is neither a natural necessity nor a wilful contingency. It is the complex, contradictory, unstable, inchoate and provisional product of social forces seeking to make their own history – but doing so in circumstances they have not chosen, cannot fully understand, and cannot hope to master.

On Thatcherism and its Stages

We have already reviewed six basic approaches to Thatcherism. None of them treats the Thatcher era or Thatcherism as if they were stable and unchanging and one could easily establish chronologies of actions and events for the phenomena which they consider important. This sort of exercise should not, however, be confused with periodization. For, whilst chronologies are essentially one-dimensional, focus on temporal coincidences and adopt a narrative approach, periodizations operate in several time dimensions, focus on conjunctures and presuppose an explanatory framework. Thus a chronology orders actions and events in a unilinear, calendrical time; classifies them into successive stages according to their occurrence in one or another time period (defined simply through the calendar and/or some socially relevant marker such as business cycles or intervals between elections); and thereby gives the basis for a simple narrative. Conversely a periodization orders actions and events in terms of multiple time horizons; classifies them into stages according to their conjunctural implications (as specific combinations of constraints and opportunities) for different social forces; and, since both these procedures involve consideration of how actions and events are generated as the complex result of multiple determinations, they operate with an explanatory framework as well as providing the basis for a complex narrative. We believe that the sixth approach is best placed to develop useful periodizations, but relatively simple divisions of Thatcherism into stages (chronologies or periodizations) can be produced using other approaches. We can show some of the problems involved here with three different examples.

Our first example comes from Anthony King's division of Thatcher's prime ministerial stewardship in her first government into three stages.[9] Until autumn 1981 high inflation and unemployment led to deep unpopularity in the opinion polls and weakness in the Cabinet. Then a Cabinet reshuffle strengthened Thatcher's position and her opinion poll ratings began to rise as inflation fell, the money supply was brought under control and spending cuts were secured. This period of uneasy compromise was followed by the third period as the Falklands war changed everything and enabled Thatcher to gain control of the whole government. This enhanced power did not, however, end the isolation which affects all prime ministers: thus Thatcher's continued hold on office still depends on her ability to deliver the political goods.

Although this approach could also be applied to more recent political fluctuations, it is actually too narrow even for its own limited aims. On the continuum from chronology to periodization, King's account is already some distance away from pure chronology. It clearly involves more than a simple chronology because, firstly, it assumes certain causal linkages between prime ministerial popularity, prime ministerial power, and government performance and, secondly, it is oriented to the balance of prime ministerial and Cabinet power. At best, however, the factors it identifies provide only a partial explanation for Thatcher's survival as prime minister. After all, although she was in a minority during the first phase, she managed to avoid any U-turn; the ever-imminent counter-attack from the 'wets' never came; she soon regained control after the Westlands, Libyan and Land Rover affairs; rapidly dispatched the 'consolidators'; and, most recently, has survived an open dispute with her Chancellor on exchange rate policy. In short, neither Thatcher nor Thatcherism have, it would seem, faced any serious challenge from opponents within the Cabinet, the Conservative Party, or Parliament.

This suggests that other factors must be sustaining the Thatcher line besides the iron lady's personal popularity and/or the short-term performance of her government. Given the traditionally flexible system of powers within which all prime ministers operate, other relevant factors we might cite include the following three. Firstly, the broader political conjuncture (with its crises in the party political and corporatist systems) which has neutralized or paralysed effective opposition; secondly, the previous economic impasse and the present economic transition which have made it difficult for forces to develop and organize around a clear-cut alternative economic strategy; or, thirdly, the continuing long-term shifts in the political agenda and common sense which enable even an embattled prime minister who is temporarily on the defensive to set the terms for a counter-attack. Each of these factors makes a fundamental strategic difference to the exercise of the traditional powers of the prime minister and, once we allow for Thatcher's own strategic objectives, they help to explain what is happening. It only makes sense to see particular defeats as signs of political weakness if Thatcherism is reduced to the ideas in Thatcher's head or the various policies she tries to promote. Once we consider this issue from a broader structural and strategic viewpoint, however, tactical defeats and reversals could be perfectly compatible with the more or less consistent pursuit of political and economic objectives. This would seem to be the case for Thatcherism.

Some of the advantages of extending the analysis of power into the wider state system and adopting a strategic theoretical approach can be seen in Bill Schwarz's conjunctural account of the Thatcher years. He too implies that there have been three main stages of Thatcherism. The first extends from its gradual conquest of the Conservative Party and mobilization of support before the 1979 election through to its effective command of the state machinery. In describing this stage he focuses on the crisis of the postwar settlement, the successive steps in the rightward drift of Conservative opinion, the hegemonic project developed by the Thatcherites, and the measures taken to consolidate power. The second stage, beginning in autumn 1980 and lasting until the spring of 1982, involved the combined attempt to break the old social democratic regime and pursue a distinctly Thatcherite economic strategy. The eventual failure of this experiment with free market economics and an enterprise culture provoked a drift towards authoritarianism and a resort to legal and police powers which undermined Thatcherism's attempt to establish a new hegemonic consensus. Although the Falklands war provided a brief respite from this creeping disintegration and helped the Conservative Party to win the 1983 election, it did not fundamentally change the nature of the third period. This has witnessed a loss of strategic coherence, political drift and protracted intellectual exhaustion. The measures taken against unions, local government and other targets substituted mindless attacks for longer-term strategy and this was reflected in the spectacular setbacks and banana skins of the second Thatcher administration. These alleged failures led Schwarz to conclude that the Conservatives were likely to lose the 1987 election on the issue of unemployment.[10]

What is interesting about this periodization is its incisiveness about the prehistory of Thatcherism as a hegemonic project and its vapidity as an analysis of the Thatcher administrations. Schwarz gives a better explanation for the volatility of prime ministerial popularity than King because the range of forces he introduces into his account is not essentially restricted (as is King's) to voters, parties and leaders. But he never investigates the structural sources of their power or the nature of the conjunctural opportunities they were able to exploit. In this sense his conjunctural analysis lacks real structural depth. Thus his account of the rise of Thatcherism takes for granted the crisis of the postwar settlement and then explores how the new right mobilized against it. As history it is interesting. But he continues to focus on the changing balance of forces in the second and third stages without looking beneath the surface to examine the complex structural changes which were recomposing social forces and transforming their underlying structural power. Moreover, since his focus shifts uneasily between Thatcherism's narrow economic policy strategy and its broad hegemonic project, Schwarz never really examines how the Thatcherites themselves have reorganized the state apparatus or restructured the more general conditions in which market forces operate, with the result that their own power was reinforced and the opposition weakened. In reducing this to mindless attacks or the resort to coercion he neglects its long-term strategic significance. And, in identifying Thatcherism with the strategic objectives it set itself in its first stage, Schwarz tends to ignore its movement away from short-term crisis-management to a long-term economic, political and intellectual project more attuned to the changing realities of global capitalism and Britain's place within it. Thus his periodization breaks down on the issue of multiple time horizons as well as its one-sided, neo-Gramscian concern with the changing balance of forces as reflected in the relative importance of coercion and consent. What is missing here is a real concern with the decisive economic nucleus of hegemony or the structural sources of power.

A focus on class forces and class struggle informs our third example of periodization. Writing from the viewpoint of the revolutionary left, Peter Green argues that Thatcherism is best studied as a ruling class offensive against the gains of the working class.[11] This in turn implies that it is best periodized in terms of the steps in the class struggle. Accordingly he suggests that each of the first two terms of Thatcherism

included an offensive stage and then a consolidation stage which
prepared for the next election. The first offensive began in 1980 and
lasted until early 1982 and consisted in deliberate government measures
to accentuate the impact of the global recession and to defeat unions
and local authorities. From early 1982 until the 1983 election, however,
fiscal policy was relaxed and pay rises could exceed inflation. Then
came a second offensive which lasted until the spring of 1985 and
involved further spending cuts and a renewed attack on unions, local
authorities, state support for private sector lockouts and, of course, the
year-long miners' strike. The ensuing consolidation phase may have
been marked by banana skins and drift (as noted by the media and
many commentators) but it also saw a limited recovery in output and a
government-engineered consumer boom. It is tempting to extend this
analysis to the third term with its renewed radical offensive now spreading
well beyond the economic field to restructure civil society and the state
to further roll back the gains of the postwar settlement.

This approach does at least recognize that Thatcherism is more than
a set of policies or battery of personal prejudices. But it reduces the
strategic significance of Thatcherism to the pursuit of a general economic
class offensive in the interests of capital. Thus Green makes no real
attempt to explain the institutional and organizational links between the
interests of capital and the nature of political power and little concern
with the restructuring of state institutions. He also treats phases of
political paralysis or disorientation (of the kind emphasized by Schwarz)
as nothing more than periods of consolidation in the economic offensive.
Equally amazing is his neglect of struggles over intellectual or moral
hegemony. Clearly, in contrast to Hall or Schwarz, Green would not
make much sense of Thatcher's claim that 'economics are the method;
the object is to change the heart and soul'.[12] In this sense his attempt
at periodization fails because it penetrates so far beneath the surface of
economic and political life that it loses touch with reality and, even in
his own terms, is unable to explain how the underlying economic
tendencies are mediated (and at the same time transformed) in and
through political and ideological struggle. In this sort of approach the
specificity and complex overdetermination of conjunctures vanish before
the historical logic of capital.

Our Periodization of Thatcherism

Our own periodization of Thatcherism has been influenced both by
these general considerations (which will be taken up again in the
concluding chapters) and by our particular concern with the changing
strategic line of the Conservative Party and of governments under the
Thatcher leadership. It is organized around the changing circumstances
in which Thatcherite strategy has been developed, specified and applied.

Thus we take account of the changing strategic terrain on which Thatcherism operates as well as changes in the strategic line the Conservatives have adopted. This does not rule out other periodizations for other purposes and we shall look at some alternatives later.

In broad terms our periodization begins with a threefold location of Thatcherism in the *longue durée* of the mode of growth in Britain, the economic and political dynamic of the postwar settlement, and the changing political scene in the last 15 years. Thus Thatcherism must be related to the long-run relative decline of the British economy over the last hundred years and the mode of growth with which this came to be associated; it must be related more directly to the emerging crisis of the specific form of Britain's insertion into the global economy after 1945 and its associated social democratic mode of economic and political regulation; and it must be related to the organic crisis of British society which once again became acute in the mid-1970s. This does not mean that Thatcherism can be fully comprehended purely as a reaction to past failures. It has a Janus-face. Hence it must also be viewed as a project for the future. We should consider how it relates to emergent trends in various spheres of social relations and, indeed, tries to shape and conform such trends in and through its own project and thereby gives them a coherence they might otherwise lack. It is in this context that we will also consider whether Thatcherism is preparing the ground for new modes of growth and regulation more attuned to current changes in the capitalist system. In adopting this approach to periodization, with its forward look as well as its concern with the past, we must clearly relate Thatcherism to the contradictions and dilemmas of the old system, to the problems inherent in any transition period and to the contradictions and dilemmas of the emergent system. The relative importance of these three sets of issues will clearly change over time and these changes will help us to analyse shifts in the strategic line of Thatcherism since 1975.

We then distinguish three main stages in the strategic development of Thatcherism in the complex war of position and manoeuvre. These stages are: (a) the development of Thatcherism as a social movement defined by its opposition to the postwar settlement and the policies being pursued to sustain it; (b) the period of consolidation culminating in the first effective control by Thatcherite forces of the Conservative Party, the Cabinet and the political agenda; and (c) the period of 'consolidated Thatcherism' in which this control has been (re)deployed to pursue a long-term transformation of British society. We also distinguish three sub-stages of each main period.[13] Since we give a fuller analysis of these stages in introducing Part II and in later chapters, we will focus here on the basic principles underlying this periodization.

As our chief interest in Thatcherism is its changing strategic line, we obviously think it important to periodize Thatcherism in terms relevant to the complex dialectic between structure and strategy. The first stage lasted from the emergence of Thatcherism as an oppositional force until it won formal control of the machinery of central government. The key issues in this stage were how the Conservative Party came under Thatcher's leadership, the steps taken to win popular (especially electoral) support for the party, and the strategy adopted for winning support from various elite groups and organizations. The growth of Thatcherism was facilitated by both class and partisan dealignment in the electorate and a profound political disorientation and ideological ferment in the Establishment. Moreover, considered as a social movement, Thatcherism was flanked and supported by new pressure groups, think tanks, an ideological reorientation of the mass media and the passage of some key social democratic intellectuals to the new right. At the same time there was a profound crisis in the organizations and groups which had served as standard bearers for the postwar settlement. This was particularly marked among trade unions, the Labour Party, and leftwing intellectual circles. In turn this political and ideological crisis gave greater space for petty bourgeois resentment to be voiced against the trends and problems generated by the postwar settlement.

The next stage comes with formal control of the machinery of central government. The Conservative Party won a majority in the Commons and Thatcher appointed a Cabinet drawn from all the sectors of the Party. However, as many commentators have noted, formal control is far from identical with real control. Thus we define the second stage in terms of the struggles for real control of the Party, Cabinet, and the machinery of government, for more stable electoral support, and for broader-based support from the Establishment. Since the demands and interests of the different groups involved were often in conflict and since the requirements of the politics of support and the politics of power are clearly different, this was a period when contradictions and strategic dilemmas were particularly acute. We deal with the problems involved below and date the effective consolidation of Thatcherism in the spring and summer of 1982.

Thereafter a third stage began: that of consolidated Thatcherism. It is only in this third stage that a coherent Thatcherite project has begun to emerge to remake the British economy, state, and civil society. This is associated with greater concern for structural consolidation rather than the sort of conjunctural manoeuvres of the second stage. Whereas the latter was concerned with buying votes, time and political space through concessions and more or less skilful exploitation of short-term opportunities, the third stage of Thatcherism is interested in striking deep structural roots to secure the survival of the Thatcherite project beyond short-term policy failures and fluctuations in support. In this context we can see steps taken to eliminate yet more parts of the state system associated with the postwar settlement; to Thatcherize the civil service and administration; to reduce the political independence of TV and radio, educational institutions, and the churches; to create new channels of representation and intervention; to consolidate a new social base through a fundamental recomposition of class forces rather than merely exploiting temporary disaffections and discontents. And so on. We will discuss these issues in more detail in Parts II and III.

Distinguishing stages in this way involves far more than simple issues of chronology or how best to organize a complex historical narrative. For we also argue that the dynamic of Thatcherism has differed in each stage in several crucial respects. Thus it would be quite illegitimate to generalize conclusions from one stage to other stages both in terms of historical understanding and in terms of the appropriate political response. Among the crucial areas where these stages differ we can mention: the electoral and social bases of Thatcherism, the relative primacy of the politics of support and the politics of power, the role of favourable short-term conjunctural factors as opposed to long-term structural shifts in facilitating pursuit of the Thatcherite project, the movement from short-term economic interests to a broader project of social reorganization, and so forth. In turn this suggests that different theories may correspond to different stages of Thatcherism and so a periodization may help us to understand the strengths and weaknesses of different approaches. We begin to address this problem in chapter 2 and will return to it in the concluding section of our book.

The Consequences of Thatcherism

A related set of problems concerns the uneven development and impact of Thatcherism: once it emerged (whenever and however this occurred), Thatcherism could be divided into very different stages according to the particular topic under investigation. Thus different phases would be distinguished depending whether one looked mainly at ideological, political, educational, welfare, party political, corporatist or other interests. Alternative phases would also suggest themselves if one looked at Thatcherism's links to different social forces or, again, at its impact in different spaces – national or international, local or regional. Indeed it is no exaggeration to claim that some of the heated disputes over the nature and relevance of Thatcherism are rooted in differences over the periods and the focus chosen for investigation.

Concluding Remarks

In this chapter we have defined six broad approaches to the study of Thatcherism and briefly commented on their strengths and drawbacks. It has not been our intention to promote some approaches and bury others: instead we wanted to highlight the advantages and disadvantages involved in each and the results which can be expected from using one or other approach. Thus, although we have a clear preference for one approach, other approaches will also be used to round out or qualify the lessons gleaned from the strategic-theoretical approach favoured here.

A second aim of this chapter has been to introduce a periodization of Thatcherism which we will employ not only in developing our own approach but also in contextualizing and criticizing other approaches. We believe that many hotly contested issues in the debate over Thatcherism could be resolved if due attention were paid to questions of periodization as well as to the uneven impact of Thatcherism.

2

Theories of Thatcherism

In our first chapter we discussed two possible agnostic approaches to Thatcherism and then declared ourselves polytheists. For we believe in many Thatcherisms. Sometimes it might seem that we are also pantheists. Once a phenomenon such as Thatcherism emerges and seeks to remake society in its image, it becomes ever more difficult to imagine an institution, relation or event which has not been affected. This is a measure of the dominance (if not necessarily the hegemony) of Thatcherism in contemporary Britain and its capacities to influence the agenda in many different areas of social life. That Thatcherism often seems to be omnipresent does not mean that it is omnipotent (far from it): indeed, if it seems to be everywhere, this could easily stem from its many different meanings, so that it is not really hard to find signs of 'its' presence in many different places. However, whilst playing 'hide and seek' with Thatcherism might prove an amusing parlour game, it could also dull both one's senses and one's critical faculties. Thus it is particularly important to be clear about the implications of different definitions and approaches so that appropriate lessons can be drawn in both theoretical and strategical terms.

Who Theorizes Thatcherism?

Although we try to offer a balanced review of relevant theories and will also criticize most of them, some readers might conclude that we give Marxist accounts too much attention. If so, this could well occur because it is leftwing theorists who have been most directly and explicitly concerned with Thatcherism. We agree with Kenneth Minogue when he writes that 'Thatcherism' as an expression is largely the creation of Thatcher's enemies and we would add that, like other terms which originated in political abuse, it has since entered into everyday usage and even become a badge of pride for Thatcherites. We are less inclined to agree with Minogue, however, when he explains how the term was coined because, being intellectuals, her enemies would hardly be satisfied with merely disliking a person when they really disapproved of everything she stood for.[1] Instead we are more inclined to agree with Brian Walden, an ardent admirer and confidant of Thatcher, that disillusioned (his word, not ours) Marxists have provided the best analyses of Thatcherism and its works.[2] In turn we believe that this is because, whether disillusioned or not, they work with a scientific realist method which, when properly applied, gives their analyses greater depth and enables them to provide more detailed conjunctural analyses.[3]

Certainly the analyses offered by social democrats and the traditional right have been far less incisive about Thatcherism. It seems that the Labour Party and trade union leaders have been so deeply wedded for so long to the traditional patterns of parliamentarism and the postwar settlement that until recently they did not really grasp the magnitude of the break with that settlement intended by Thatcherism. Traditional rightwing politicians are also divided on the meaning of Thatcherism, largely because they find it hard to counter Thatcher's claim that 'there is no alternative'.[4] Indeed Thatcherism itself was constructed from a synthesis of old and new tendencies within the Conservative Party and successfully included many economic liberals and diehard Tories whilst excluding the right progressives (who later acquired the typically Thatcherite soubriquet of 'wets'). Moreover, while the 'wets' tended to view Thatcherism as an irrational project which would soon run aground, the 'new right' tended to see it as so self-evidently sensible, given the alternatives, that its emergence and triumph hardly needed to be explained. Thus the new right often seems to oscillate between quietly celebrating the achievements of Thatcherism to date and ostentatiously fretting about backsliding on future radical measures.

For a long time the liberal centre simply portrayed Bennism and Thatcherism as the complementary, extremist twins on the left and right of the political spectrum respectively.[5] This relieved it of the need to undertake any serious analysis of their relative strengths as radical solutions to Britain's crisis. The eruption of the social democrats into the centre simply confirmed the emerging crisis in the party system as the Social Democratic Party started out on the middle road back to 1945 before gradually veering right and on to the Thatcherite future. Even after the fusions and splits in the Alliance, its leaders still seem unable to understand the nature of Thatcherism and its contribution both to their meteoric rise and subsequent fall.

Apart from left theorists, the other people who have been most concerned to dissect Thatcherism also belong to the 'chattering classes': journalists, political figures and other talking heads. Many of their analyses are concerned mainly with the everyday story of Thatcherism and, where they dig beneath the surface, they often draw on leftwing theorizing. *Marxism Today* has played a crucial mediating role here: it ranks several top labour correspondents and political commentators (and, indeed, a handful of Tory MPs) among its contributors as well as many more among its readers. But, whatever the factors which link the chattering classes, there are obvious family resemblances in their analyses. Thus, if we do focus mainly on leftwing accounts, it is not for want of looking for others.

Scratching at the Surface

For many commentators Thatcherism does not really exist – except perhaps as a misleading term of political discourse. The advantages and disadvantages of such scepticism have already been discussed and we now examine different ways to describe and explain the Thatcherite phenomenon. We begin with analyses which deal mainly with its surface manifestations and then examine those which try to discern its deeper meaning and/or causes. Our own approach belongs in the latter part of this crude dichotomy but there is also much to be learnt from analysing the more immediate and practical aspects of Thatcherism. To facilitate the discussion of a complex and disparate set of analyses, they have been loosely grouped around three broad sites of analysis and explanation: the economic, juridico-political and ideological.[6] This reflects important institutional as well as disciplinary boundaries but it can also be misleading where studies range across several fields of analysis. In moving among these levels and sites of analysis we will draw on studies from the right as well as the left and also consider feminist studies in a separate section. But we start with three approaches largely concerned with the intellectual origins and practical impact of Thatcherism.

The Thatcher Economic Experiment

One of the most common interpretations, especially during the first Thatcher government, is the treatment of Thatcherism as a monetarist economic experiment. This has produced some excellent 'knocking copy' from critics and sceptics,[7] as well as some highly superficial and tendentious analyses of how the government's strategy to master inflation succeeded. Following the abandonment of monetary targetry, however, attention has turned towards more general issues of economic strategy. This is beneficial because it widens the scope of analysis and encourages a more institutional and comparative approach. Even the government came to share these concerns once it recognized that 'monetarism was not enough' and that rigidities on the supply-side must be removed before any real long-term economic recovery could be secured. In turn this has shifted attention from such technical issues as targets, instruments and statistical manipulation towards more important questions of economic and political strategy.

This broadening and deepening of debates about 'Thatchernomics' is most welcome and helps to overcome some of the risks involved in the earlier discussion of Thatcher's economic experiment. This threatened to equate Thatcherism with monetarism and to reduce its genesis to a story of how monetarist doctrines came to supersede Keynesian ideas and policies. It also meant that many commentators tried to judge Thatcherism's early success in terms of its record in economic targetry. Even in economic terms this was misleading, since it distracted attention from the ways in which the economy was being restructured rather than just tested to destruction. The government itself joined in this game and manipulated statistics, corrected forecasts and changed targets in order to put the best possible gloss on its record. During the first two or three years, the record seemed unfavourable and the experiment was often pronounced a failure. More recently, however, the record is more ambiguous and early critics have either been silenced or else obliged to shift the grounds of attack.

A related problem is that such debates involved an almost fetishistic concern with empirical indicators which provide at best only indirect evidence about the real economy. In a period when radical changes are occurring in the world economy together with Britain's place inside it, this was still further complicated by changes in the mechanisms which connect the underlying movement of the real economy with its immediate experiential forms. Thus there was real uncertainty in knowing what was happening and how economic developments might be subject to some degree of control. The government tried to turn this to advantage by invoking an unquantifiable (but positive) 'Thatcher factor' to justify its own optimism and to inspire confidence in a depressed business community. Moreover, whether or not such a conjunctural factor exists, structural changes have been even more important in undermining the old economic certainties. Two examples must suffice to make this point. Firstly, in response to the government's own measures as well as to fundamental changes in the financial system, the links between the money supply and the rate of inflation have also changed so that old models no longer apply. Secondly, as firms adopt new methods of production, they can react more flexibly to demand. It is therefore harder to judge when the economy is overheating and running up against supply constraints. These sorts of shift in the real economy mean that discussions about economic policy and strategy cannot be restricted to questions about economic records, targetry and techniques. They must also address fundamental questions about underlying mechanisms in the real economy and how these help to determine both the actual course of economic development and the fluctuations in any corresponding empirical indicators. In short we must penetrate beneath the surface to see how its movements are linked to changes at deeper levels of the real economy. This in turn requires us to adopt a much broader approach to political economy with due regard to the links among different spheres of society.

Obviously there is considerable scope for disagreement on such questions and any answers will depend on the approach adopted towards the real economy and its laws of motion. We should not anticipate our own arguments here but it is worth noting that these problems are not limited to the macro-economic level. Similar difficulties arise for such micro-issues as international competitiveness or industrial relations. Current economic changes here must be related to the overall reorganization of the capitalist economy currently under way as well as to the Thatcher government's general policies and specific measures. If this is not done, the real impact of Thatcherism cannot be assessed.

The Thatcher Factor in Politics

Analogous problems occur in analyses of Thatcherite politics. Because Thatcherism is self-evidently a political phenomenon it has been most often discussed and analysed by those with a professional interest in politics. In many cases the Thatcher party and government have been treated as just another object for applying the concepts and analytical methods of orthodox political science. Thus some studies have examined the sources of electoral support for Thatcherism and/or constructed scales of Thatcherism to chart shifts in public opinion about the government and its policies. In this way they treat it just as though it involved nothing more than business as usual for party politicians and political scientists alike. It is among proponents of this approach that agnosticism (or model-induced ignorance) about the existence of a distinctive Thatcherite phenomenon is most marked. Since studies along these lines are highly focused and use the general tools of the political science trade, it is relatively easy to decompose Thatcherism into researchable topics so that one can no longer see the novel configuration of the wood for the usual sort of trees. This is not to disparage such work (on which our own studies have often been parasitic) but merely to recommend that political scientists sometimes take a more panoramic view and consider whether Thatcherism might not be different in some respects.

In other cases the Conservative Party and government led by Mrs Thatcher have indeed been defined as 'anomalies'. Analysing them might require a more critical reworking of established paradigms, models or theories but, hopefully, their basic features could still be explained in these terms. Thus other studies have examined how the party has won elections whilst adopting a conviction politics stance which conflicts with earlier assertions about the end of ideology and also contradicts orthodox views on party competition. Similarly there is an interesting debate as to whether Thatcher has broken with normal patterns of prime ministerial and Cabinet government or has merely shown the flexibility of the unwritten British constitution whilst remaining within its conventions. In this sense the novelty of Thatcherism is defined by the paradigms, models or theories of orthodox political science and treated as an intellectual puzzle without regard for its broader social implications.

For our purposes in dealing with Thatcherism, there are two main problems with these sorts of analysis. The first is simply a matter of empirical focus, the second concerns the broader set of concepts with which orthodox political science operates. Regarding the first problem, particularly in the early years of the Thatcher government, there was a one-sided concern with the quantitative dimension. This was similar to the concern about economic targetry noted for the economic experiment. Since it is easy to measure votes and opinions, spending and taxation, numbers of civil servants, and so forth, there is a vast body of work recording continuities and discontinuities in these respects. And such information is often useful in demolishing the pretensions and mystique of Thatcherism: showing the difficulties faced by the incoming Thatcher government in controlling public spending, reducing the overall level of taxation, redirecting resources or steering the ship of state in new directions. But, whilst it is true that the Thatcherites have not managed to change things as much as they had wanted, real and important shifts have certainly occurred. The problem is knowing how to assess them and, in particular, to judge whether incremental shifts amount to a qualitative break.

This is where the second problem occurs. For much of the Thatcher revolution in the political system and the machinery of government has been experimental, short-term, *ad hoc*, gradual and marginal to the main structures of power. Moreover the pertinence of any continuity or discontinuity in the state apparatus and its operation will depend on the context in which they are supposed to function. During a period of social transformation the criteria for making these judgements are not self-evident and, in many cases, they are nowhere to be found within the orthodox political science field. Indeed, in contrast to continental traditions of political analysis, with their long-standing concern with the state and its relationship to civil society, British political science has been slow to theorize the nature of the state. This is not the place to discuss why the state has been neglected nor the most appropriate ways in which it might be analysed. Instead we merely want to emphasize that, unless the recomposition of the state is brought into focus, the real political significance of continuities as well as discontinuities (and, indeed, the very meaning of these terms) cannot be assessed. And this requires us to move beneath the surface of political life to examine the dynamics of different forms of political representation, modes of policy making, forms of intervention, and, even more importantly, the changing social bases of the state and the general projects which endow the state with some internal coherence and broader social significance.

Political Theory and the New Right

One other approach worth a brief mention here is the concern with the social, political and economic theories supposedly associated with Thatcherism. A wide range of studies exist which engage in little beyond more or less critical exegesis of the new right theories of intellectuals such as Milton Friedman or Friedrich von Hayek; the work of think tanks such as the Institute of Economic Affairs, the Adam Smith Institute, or the Centre for Policy Studies; or the personal political philosophies of Thatcher and her immediate colleagues. These studies are usually illuminating and often incisive but they can only provide elements for a more complex genealogy of Thatcherite ideology. They also leave unexplored the relation between ideology, policies and the consequences of Thatcherism. This in effect reduces Thatcherism to its intellectual history, which could be doubly misleading. In many cases ideas are taken up because they serve political purposes rather than because they carry real intellectual conviction. Most recently, for example, Nigel Lawson has derided the 'teenage scribblers' in the City who have been questioning the wisdom of his 1988 'give-away' budget to the rich and his management of the exchange rate. Not ten years earlier these same scribblers (Lawson himself among them) were the decisive organic intellectuals of the Thatcherite economic revolution. Related to this is the problem that important shifts have occurred in new right ideas since Thatcherism embarked on its radical phase after 1986. In which direction, if any, the chain of causation runs in these cases is unclear. Properly to explore such issues requires a much broader and deeper analysis of the struggle for political, intellectual and moral hegemony.

On Digging Deeper

Focusing on people, ideas, policies and events can generate more or less convincing descriptions of the Thatcherite phenomenon. When we seek answers to its deeper significance they are less helpful. For this we need analyses with ontological depth, that is, the theoretical capacity to penetrate beneath the actual course of events to the more fundamental mechanisms and causal powers which generate these events in specific circumstances. In making this claim we are not suggesting that knowledge of these mechanisms and causal powers is itself sufficient to unfold the secrets of Thatcherism (let alone the meaning of life, the universe and everything). Instead we are claiming that events are the complex product of many different causes and circumstances and that any adequate account must establish the mediations between their underlying causes and their more immediate causes. We will consider some of the resources available to this end and how it can be achieved later in this chapter and in the final part of our book. But now we turn to some studies which have precisely attempted to dig deeper to reveal the true significance of Thatcherism.

Three Economic Explanations

Many theorists have tried to find the significance of Thatcherism in its economic policies and/or the economic interests it serves. This is particularly clear in analyses which focus on its commitments to monetarism, the social market economy and neo-liberalism, and their impact on the economy and other spheres of society. They explain the activities of Thatcherism in one of three ways: in relatively instrumentalist terms, through its active promotion and domination by economic interests; in terms of the functional correspondence between these economic policies and the ideology and interests of specific economic groups; or in terms of the autonomous pursuit by the Thatcher government and its allies of policies which happen to serve the needs of these economic interests. It should be noted that these economic interests are not always identified with the capitalist class: they can also be linked to intermediate classes or, indeed, with sections of the working class. Nonetheless most of these interpretations stress that it is capitalist interests which are advanced in and through Thatcherism. And, within this context, they see these interests either in simple instrumentalist terms or else in a more sophisticated fractionalist and/or collective capitalist framework. Let us consider an example of each.

Paying the Piper, Calling the Tune

Simple instrumentalist accounts seek to establish a direct relation between the Thatcher government's economic and social policies and the specific capitalist interests which profit from them. Thus John Ross suggested that there was no real mystery to Thatcherism. The government's policies simply continued the traditional Conservative promotion of the interests of 'a great complex of firms based on foreign investment, banks and suppliers of the internal working class market'.[8] He insists on this economic dimension in order to criticize arguments that the relation of companies to the Conservative Party, or a phenomenon such as Thatcherism, is simply based on 'ideology' or 'purely political' considerations. In support of this claim Ross cites some impressive-looking statistics to show that, rather than accurately reflecting the overall shape of the British economy, financial contributions to the Conservative Party actually mirror the profit levels and the structural economic shifts which occurred during the first Thatcher government. Those who paid were, in short, those who gained.[9]

He concludes that:

> Certain sections of the capitalist class have gained enormously from the Conservative Party in general and Thatcherism in particular and continue to finance the Tory Party to a high degree. Other economic sectors have ceased to gain as much as before and are withdrawing their level of funding. Only someone who is very naive, or deliberately wants to obscure reality, can believe that these trends are 'accidents'.[10]

Thus Ross reduces Thatcherism to its benefits for specific firms and branches of the British economy as reflected in their declared rates of profit. He does not specify the precise mechanisms through which this correlation is realized. But he implies that it is through the dominance of these interests in the counsels of the Conservative Party and/or through the spontaneous, *post hoc* gratitude of specific interests to the Party which has advanced their profits. Even in the latter terms, reductions in monetary contributions might simply have reflected lower profits rather than a principled rejection of Thatcherism and all its works. More generally this is a crudely instrumentalist view which ignores the relative autonomy of the state and the complexities of political struggle.[11] Moreover, whilst some traditional supporters have reduced or halted contributions, other sectors have begun or increased contributions. The latter might have benefited from the Thatcher regime but, if we consider specific firms rather than broad sectors, another factor seems significant. For, as Overbeek has remarked, the most notable correlation with these contributions is the gift of peerages and honours to contributors.[12] Thus the sale of titles rather than the boost to profits (let alone specific sectoral benefits) might explain what's happening.

More generally, in emphasizing the *continuity* of policy throughout the period of Conservative hegemony, it does not really explain the shift in economic strategy in Britain from Keynesianism to monetarism. Nor does it capture the political significance of this strategic shift – whether in terms of its political background or in terms of its political repercussions. This is not to deny the evidence which Ross gathered (or similar studies by the Labour Research Department have continued to gather). It is to argue for putting them in a broader context of the kind recommended below.

The City Rules, OK?

A less simplistic explanation can be found in analyses which try to show how Thatcherism serves the interests of one or more specific fractions of capital which are dominant (or even hegemonic) in Britain's system of political economy. This approach either focuses on the relative dominance of specific groups of capital within the national and/or international economy and the capacities this gives them to wield power; or on the position of political, intellectual and moral leadership which these fractions have supposedly won in this system. Thus specific financial contributions to the Conservative Party would be relatively insignificant sources of influence as compared to the overall dominance of specific fractions.

Sometimes this approach is justified by nothing more than an elision between (a) monetarism as an emphasis on sound money and (b) money capital as the source of revenue controlled by banking or financial interests. Bhaduri and Steindl provide one of the better argued examples of this approach. They are not so much concerned with Thatcherism or Reaganism as a whole as with the rise and fall of monetarism as a social doctrine. They claim that restrictive monetary and fiscal policy has always been supported by banks and financiers (the City, Wall Street) and explain this in terms of *cui bono?* They argue that monetarism 'serves as an antidote against Keynesian ideology which assigns to the banks the role of instruments of the government's full employment policy'.[13] The high interest rates entailed in the pursuit of monetarist policies also benefit the banks and their rentier allies. Thus the rise of monetarism from a local sect to a global eminence was preceded by a shift in power from industry to banks: this occurred through the rise of the Euromarkets and other forms of banking business. They also explain the demise of monetarism in terms of the adverse effects of tight money on the banks' customers (in industrial as well as less developed countries) so that banks began pressing for more liquidity to ease the plight of industry and third world debtors.[14]

Such an approach is unsatisfactory to the extent that it reduces Thatcherism to its monetarist moment and, even if this were sensible in the early years of the Conservative government, it would prove irrelevant once monetarism was abandoned by the government after just three years in office. Bhaduri and Steindl avoid these problems precisely because their analysis is confined to monetarism. But for those who equate Thatcherism and monetarism, these problems are very real. By broadening the analysis of Thatcherism, however, one might be able to rescue this fractionalist approach.

A broader and more defensible approach would consider Thatcherism's economic strategy in more general terms. Thus some studies suggest that Thatcherism is re-asserting the hegemony of financial capital and/ or capital with an overseas orientation in the British system. This was necessary either because there had been a period of unstable hegemony in which industrial interests (especially industry whose major market was domestic) tended to predominate or, indeed, because there had been a total crisis of hegemony. What Thatcherism represents, according to this sort of analysis, is a strategy for capital accumulation which prioritizes the interests of financial and/or international capital over those of the domestic industrial sector. This requires a general reorganization and reorientation of the social and political order as well as the economy.

Thus Tom Nairn has argued that Thatcher's 'experiment' is no more than an attempt to use the recession to hasten and complete the dominance of finance capital and the multinational sector. Indeed he claims that this dominance has never been 'more confidently and blatantly exercised than under Mrs Thatcher's administration'.[15] Thus, far from de-industrialization somehow representing an economically irrational consequence of Thatcherite 'freedom', it is actually the apotheosis of this 'freedom'. For it represents 'Southern hegemony permanently liberated from the archaic burden of the Industrial Revolution's relics, the subsidies that prop them up, and the trade unions that agitate for them'.[16]

Nairn suggests that this financial dominance is linked to the accelerating internationalization of the British economy. Thus 'the metropolitan heartland complex will become ever more of a service-zone to international capital – the conveniently offshore location for investment or reinvestment, insurance and speculation, guaranteed by both public and private institutions underwritten by a famous social stability.'[17] This strategy fits well with the limited technocratic capacities of the British state and the strength of the bourgeois hegemony rooted in civil society and parliamentarism: for these would be far less appropriate to a more dirigiste or corporatist strategy. A further material basis for this strategy were the rents from North Sea oil: these enabled City interests to consolidate themselves *without* frontally attacking the working class. Moreover, since the old sunset industries cannot be revived and the Thatcherites are not much interested in helping the unemployed, they are relying on market forces to promote recovery by turning the North directly over to foreign capital.[18]

Similar analyses have been proposed by other theorists, economists and political commentators. Just two more examples must suffice. Thus John Foster has argued that monetarist doctrines are 'based on the political interests of the City and are an attempt to strengthen the position of financial capital relative to other income and wealth categories in the economy'.[19] Likewise Fiona Atkins has tied the rise of Thatcherism to the reorganization of capital active in Britain in the last fifteen years rather than to the growing appeal of authoritarian populism to the working class. She suggests that Thatcherism favours international capital, with its interests in the free movement of capital and high interest rates, against domestic capital; and adds that its authoritarianism is due to the inability to maintain the old social democratic class compromise organised around national Fordism (see below pp. 127–33) once the internationalization of the economy has become disarticulated from the old nation-state system. She concludes that authoritarian populism may not be an 'exceptional and temporary form' responding to simple domestic economic crisis or crisis of domestic postwar settlement in decaying post-imperial Britain: it may represent a technique of legitimation, more akin to the bureaucratic authoritarian regimes normal in Latin America, and associated with the growing gap between national politics and an internationalized economy.[20]

In general these theorists argue that the hegemonic fraction includes not only financial capital but also internationally competitive and/or multinational industrial capital. In both cases it is clearly implied that domestic industrial capital as a whole and medium and small capital in particular suffer from Thatcherism. In addition the strength of these fractional interests is related not simply to their position within the Tory Party but also, and more fundamentally, to the institutional structure of the state as a system of 'structural selectivity'.[21]

A different fractional classification is offered by Overbeek from the viewpoint of the Amsterdam regulation school.[22] The latter distinguishes two main fractions (productive capital rooted in the labour process and circulating capital involved in banking and commercial activities) and suggests that each fraction has distinctive interests and attitudes towards economic and political regulation (or 'control'): the former being more inclined towards class compromise and state intervention, the latter towards liberalism and laissez-faire.[23] Overbeek suggests that the Thatcherite neo-liberal accumulation strategy corresponds to a comprehensive concept of control serving the interests of circulating capital and concerned to remake Britain into a global service economy. But, against any simple instrumentalist reading of these links, he notes that the typical Thatcherite MP or minister does not directly represent international capital, which in the late 1970s still leaned towards corporate liberalism. Instead the background of the first Thatcher government reflected the ideological peculiarities of neo-liberalism, with its appeal to small capital, self-made businessmen, and the petty bourgeoisie.[24] It is the match between this ideology and the monetary concept of control which, according to Overbeek, explains how Thatcherism managed to express the interests of circulating capital which had regained dominance in the late 1970s. This was expressed both in the growing dominance of banks over industry and in the conjunctural 'monetization' of industrial capital, that is, its strategic orientation to profits rather than to sheer sales volume. This economic shift was matched by the growth of neo-liberal concepts, the active recomposition of a petty bourgeois social basis, the creation or promotion of organizations (for example the Institute of Directors) to represent the newly dominant sectors, and the erosion of the corporate liberals' power base among the 'wets' in the Conservative Party.[25]

Indeed Overbeek suggests that:

> The Thatcher government isolates itself from practically all representative organisations of domestic capital, and is even unresponsive to the reservations that certain sections of the City have voiced over its monetary policies or the liberalisation of the City itself, which exposes all City firms to enormously intensified international competition even on their home markets. This extreme liberal strategy could – somewhat boldly – be characterised as a comprador-strategy. Since 1979 British capital is increasingly being 'de-nationalised', and this process of de-nationalisation finds expression in the fact that the network of interlocking directorships among the largest British industrial and financial firms has become less tightly knit, thus breaking with the trend of the years prior to the Thatcher reign.[26]

Overbeek approaches Thatcherism not so much from the particular interests which it (may) have benefited as from the general accumulation strategy it is pursuing. But, if we accept his terms of analysis, they imply a crucial contradiction in Thatcherism. The political and ideological context of Thatcherism is the revolt of the petty bourgeoisie and small and medium capital against the economic and social impact of the Keynesian welfare state. For the rhetoric of Thatcherism is not restricted to sound money or fighting inflation. It also emphasizes the virtues of individual entrepreneurial spirits, small business as the source of job creation, the growth of the service sector (which is largely domestic in orientation), and other themes which might seem to contradict the thesis of financial and international industrial hegemony. Thus, whilst Thatcherism may be opposed to the organized labour movement, it need not follow that it is pro-capitalist.[27] Overbeek deals with this contradiction by asserting a functional correspondence between petty bourgeois and capitalist ideology.

But this is less than satisfactory. If the social basis of Thatcherism lies in the petty bourgeoisie and small capital, this could well require the Tories to make compromises and concessions with their own social basis as a precondition of continued tenure in office. Leys alludes to this problem in one of his comments on Thatcherism. He writes that:

> the contradiction between neo-liberalism and the government's attachment to privilege was revealed in its lack of interest in a radical reform of the state and 'civil society' – the private social and economic framework of British life. The notorious inefficiencies of British life, from the secretive and ineffectual system of state economic policy-making to the archaic

systems of taxation, banking, and law, the insanely slow and costly system of real-estate conveyance, and an educational system as spectacularly inadequate in its day as it had been in 1900 – such spheres were not objects of Mrs Thatcher's concern. She distrusted the civil service, the universities and the BBC for their past attachment to the social democratic consensus, but her 'populism' stopped short of a radical assault on the structures on which the establishment's power rested, perhaps because she and *the middle class were too attached to them.*[28]

Even when this distinctive context is recognized, it seems to be dismissed as insignificant and inessential. Thus Nairn regards the rhetoric of petty bourgeois resentment as the 'perfect doctrinal disguise' for the actual thrust of Thatcher's strategy and thereby reduces its impact to that of an ideological cover for the patrician governing clique of City and multinational interests. It has no effect on the real dynamic of Thatcher's policies or their likely tensions and contradictions. Thus, in seeking to establish too close a fit between the interests of specific fractions and the politics of Thatcherism, fractionalist approaches run the risk of ignoring its economic, political and ideological dilemmas and contradictions as the Thatcherite forces seek to win support, neutralize opposition and advance their long-term strategic objectives.

The Logic of Capital

Finally we find some analysts who treat Thatcherism as reflecting a more general logic of capital in the context of an economic conjuncture characterized by continued de-industrialization in Britain and a worsening of the international economic crisis. They reject the idea that Thatcherism is the simple tool of particular interests and note that the sort of policies it is pursuing are too widespread around the advanced capitalist world to be explicable in terms which are specific to Britain or its particular economic and political institutions and class configuration. Instead the policies with which it is associated are deemed to serve the more general interests of capital – even if their specific national form derives from the peculiarities of individual social formations.

Clarke provides a good example of this approach in his analysis of monetarism. He notes that

> Marxists are unanimous in their belief that 'monetarism' is in some sense a class doctrine and a class politics, expressing an aggressive capitalist response to the deepening crisis, rolling back the working class advances of the post-war decades, and restructuring capitalist social relations in order to secure the restoration of favourable conditions for renewed capital accumulation. The term 'monetarism' indicates the central thrust of this politics: all things must be answerable to money. And, of course, the power and values embodied in money are the power and values of

capital, which dominates the circulation of money and of which money is the most abstract and most general form.[29]

Clarke also emphasizes that the practice of monetarism should not be confused with its petty bourgeois ideological expression nor with its political base in petty bourgeois resentment against organized labour and big capital. For not only has the practice of monetarism contradicted many of its initial ideological justifications but it also pre-dated the development of the political base which brought explicitly monetarist parties to power. Thus Clarke correctly notes that attempts to regulate money supply proved relatively ineffective under the last Labour government as well as under the present Thatcher administration. But these attempts are nonetheless crucial because they represent a kind of ritual whereby governments continually reaffirm their subordination to capital through the financial markets. This explains why, even after the Thatcher regime abandoned monetary targets, it substituted Public Sector Borrowing Requirement (PSBR) targets which served the same purpose.[30]

Clarke concludes that the rise of monetarism cannot be seen as a political triumph for a specific fraction of capital nor for a radically new form of state intervention. Instead it represents the culmination of a lengthy process of restructuring of both capital and the state in response to an acute recession rather than to mere shifts in political dogma. It is the severity of the recession which explains the greater commitment to monetarism in Britain and not the conversion of the Conservatives to monetarist doctrines. The resort to monetarism was imposed on all governments through the combination of financial crisis and working-class defensive power. Firstly, as financial crises occurred ever more quickly and with ever more severity, the state found its room for manoeuvre more and more restricted. Although these crises assume a monetary form (reflected in foreign exchange markets and/or domestic money markets and/or in soaring inflation), they actually express the crisis of capital in general. For money capital is the most abstract form of capital – which also includes industrial and commercial capital. These crises necessarily involve the state since it is directly integrated into the circuit of money capital through its roles as central banker, taxer and spender. Moreover, since the organized working class has retained sufficient defensive strength to block the state's ability to restructure capital in its own name, the state has been obliged to pass the restructuring process back to capital through the impact of bankruptcies, fiscal incentives, subsidies etc. In this sense monetarism acts as a substitute for active and direct state intervention in reorganizing the capitalist economy.[31]

Such an approach avoids the problems involved in instrumentalist and fractionalist analyses. It also provides a useful critique of one-sided political or ideological accounts of monetarism and reveals the fundamental background to the rise of monetarist regimes. But it can provide no account of how the political and ideological struggle modifies the timing of restructuring and also limits its effectiveness. Monetarism was a plank in the Heath government's 'Selsdon Park' strategy and it became an important element in the closing years of the last Labour government. Only under Thatcherism was it tested to destruction. There is a danger that, by invoking the forces of 'capital in general', such an account not only reduces Thatcherism to monetarism but also attributes a singular and unique logic to capital. This would leave unexplained the relative success or failure of such restructuring processes in different societies. And it would also fail to explain the different forms which economic and political restructuring takes in different countries. In Britain we find a particularly stark example of the neo-liberal strategy but relatively clear-cut neo-corporatist patterns can be found in Sweden or West Germany (even under a Christian-Liberal regime) and more neo-statist strategies in Japan or France. There is no single logic of capital and it cannot therefore be used to explain the specific forms of restructuring in different societies. This does not mean there are no generic capitalist tendencies (we will be referring to some later) but it does mean that their realization will always be modified and overdetermined by other factors.

Putting Politics Back in Command

A second broad approach to Thatcherism examines it in terms of its political preconditions and its repercussions on the British state. In terms of the currently popular (if seriously misleading) dichotomy between society-centred and state-centred approaches, these studies can be classed as essentially 'state-centred'. There are two main types of approach: those which focus on the structural or institutional problems to which Thatcherism might be a political response and those which examine the *sui generis* political forces which have created the space for Thatcherism. Our own work has operated with these sorts of approach in the past,[32] but here we will review some other examples.

The Overloaded Crown

One state-centred approach focuses on the institutional crises within the state system which undermine its capacities to manage political problems or to secure political support for its crisis-management solutions. In this context the rise of Thatcherism has been explained in terms of its anti-statist project and its consolidation in terms of its actual capacities to reduce overload by reducing the state's role and/or refusing to negotiate with vested interests which previously enjoyed privileged access to government.

The work of the Conservative activist and political scientist Jim Bulpitt is particularly interesting here. In clear opposition to the sorts of analysis reviewed above, Bulpitt argues that monetarism is not so much an economic strategy as an attempt to return to the traditional political practice of Conservatism. It was adopted by Thatcherism mainly to deal with the general *political* problems of the United Kingdom and the specific political problems of the Tories in the 1970s. In this sense, it is not an economic theory in search of politics: it is statecraft in search of a convenient economic theory to serve political ends.[33]

Indeed monetarism promised to resolve both the crisis of the Tory Party and the emerging crisis of political authority at the centre through one and the same piece of statecraft. According to Bulpitt the conditions needed for a party to practice statecraft effectively are: successful party management, a winning electoral strategy, hegemony over the political agenda, and the competence to govern once in office. Monetarism was an essential plank in the Party's electoral strategy and also helped to set the political agenda. In this way it promised to help the Conservatives to extend their electoral base beyond southern England and to break out of seemingly permanent and ineffective opposition. At the same time monetarism promised to make governance easier by by-passing the twin problems of an overloaded central power and an underdeveloped corporatism. Monetarism would free central government to manage the economy through instruments and policies it controlled and enable it to choose which interests should be consulted, for monetarist techniques rely on manipulating the money supply, public spending and interest rates. These all fall within the legitimate and traditional sphere of central government control and can be managed without needing to negotiate far and wide with groups over which the state has but limited influence. Moreover, to the extent that the state must take account of and/or consult outside forces in developing a monetarist strategy, these represent interests acceptable to the Conservatives: domestic finance capital and international monetary forces rather than trade unions or specific industrial sectors. Thus, simply through the adoption of a monetarist economic approach, the Conservatives could hope to solve problems which might otherwise destroy them.

Since gaining office, of course, monetarism has somewhat dashed such expectations. For, although it offered the Conservatives autonomy in *economic* management, it did not help to resolve the *political* problems facing central government in its relation to the periphery. Thus Thatcherism in office has become more interventionist and authoritarian towards the periphery. It has not proved sufficient to insulate the centre from the periphery but the government has also been forced to take steps to control the latter more directly. This represents a much more decisive break with traditional Conservative statecraft than the adoption of monetarism. The latter was simply an alternative to the Keynesian means of insulating the centre from direct interventionist pressures: but the continuing efforts to centralize power clearly break with the tradition of delegating wide powers of self-government to local authorities and other peripheral interests.[34]

A similar view has been proposed by Kenneth Minogue. Drawing on the idea of institutional sclerosis, he claims that, 'the reason Britain's first woman Prime Minister has been so smartly promoted to the status of an "ism" is that she so precisely mirrors – even down to its limitations – the beliefs needed to begin reversing a century of British economic decline'.[35] Her intransigence was needed because a tangle of special groups had arisen, each seeking to protect itself against the costs of economic decline and depending on a subservient state to aid them. By the mid-1970s the government had been reduced to just one special interest among others and became integrated into an emergent corporate state. In this context the key question was who would prove inflexible: government or society. Thatcher has been inflexible in order to make society more flexible and to reduce the scope of action of the overextended state. Thus she is the apostle of small, strong governments in the interests of flexible and dynamic economies.

To redress the political balance in this section, we now consider Joel Krieger's analysis of the 'hypercapitalist' regimes led by Mrs Thatcher and President Reagan. Krieger considers them atypical because they are abnormally strongly ideological in motivation for modern British or American governments and also highly statist in approach. Both regimes emerged when electoral opportunities coincided with a far-reaching erosion of the principles, practices and institutions of the Keynesian welfare state. They are pursuing what Krieger terms a 'de-integrative' strategy which is resulting in the creation of a 'divided and amoral political community'.[36] He claims that both regimes are trying to fragment opposition, withdraw from corporatist arrangements and deploy a crude power politics to secure for themselves extensive discretion inside the state system and in its interaction with class and elite interests. In particular Krieger emphasizes the de-integrative character of Thatcherism, for it is currently disenfranchizing groups outside the mainstream (for example, blacks) who were only recently integrated into national politics. It is also making it far more difficult for women, ethnic minorities, gay people, the unemployed and even those in non-union jobs to engage in meaningful participation. This goes hand in hand with a clear rejection of the universalist and redistributive ethos of the welfare state, repudiation of the pursuit of full employment goals through state intervention, and divisive appeals to specific sectional interests. In this context it is interesting to note that Krieger emphasizes a different type of AP from Stuart Hall: whilst Hall emphasizes *authoritarian populism*,

Krieger notes the role of *arithmetical particularism*. This relies more on making various sectional appeals (on issues such as housing, race, entrepreneurial values, or anti-Labour and anti-union sentiments) than on a general populist mobilization around a unified electoral programme similar to that embodied in the Butskellite programme of the postwar settlement.[37]

Both the above-mentioned conservative analyses explain monetarism and Thatcherism in terms of institutional and political crises rather than just economic crises. The former are clearly connected to economic decline but it is the political repercussions of decline which receive more attention. In addition both stress the independent contribution of specifically political factors to the crisis and the search for a solution. What is particularly interesting in Bulpitt's analysis is his emphasis on the role of political parties in defining statecraft: for success in this field depends on effectively linking strategies to win electoral and party support with strategies which can secure a balanced state with the capacities to govern the economy and maintain an unstable compromise in civil society. This provides one way into the complex problems of political leadership in society as well as questions about the cohesion of the state system. Where these analyses are less convincing is in their analysis of economic crisis. Here they refer mainly to the symptoms of the crisis and do not (legitimately, given their concerns) explain why a crisis emerged or took the form it did. At best Minogue's notion of institutional sclerosis points to some important possible sources of crisis but his analysis of this problem is largely gestural. Nonetheless we will return to both issues later in our analysis.

Free Market, Strong State

Andrew Gamble, writing from the left, has focused on the social market economy and the strong state. He locates Thatcherism in the context of a global recession and continued relative decline of the British economy and the disappearance of the material bases for the postwar social democratic settlement, but he also stresses its specifically political character. The Conservative Party was worried about the weakening of state authority in four areas: the representation of interests, economic management, public finance, and social order. If its social market strategy were to work, the Conservatives would have to restructure civil society as well as to liberate markets. The Tory Party would have to become a bourgeois modernizing party and tackle Britain's anti-industrial culture at its heart – the political, intellectual and business establishment centred on the public schools, the universities, the professions, the civil service and the City. At the same time the state must be strong enough to oversee and police the unemployed and the poor, industrial threats and terrorism. Nonetheless Gamble suggests that the state will not develop the real capacities needed to ensure economic modernization.[38]

The Battle for Hearts and Minds

A third broad approach to Thatcherism considers how Thatcherite discourse serves to situate subjects, make sense of their experiences, mobilize support behind particular projects and establish the basis for political, intellectual and moral leadership. This focus was prompted in part by dissatisfaction with the poverty of economistic analyses and in part by independent developments in the analysis of ideology. Since we consider the work of Stuart Hall in the second part of our book, the present account of ideologically oriented work will focus on its basic theoretical framework and assumptions. We will also consider two other applications: those of Alan O'Shea and Raymond Williams. The principal difference between the sort of analyses of Thatcher's ideas, the contribution of the New Right, or the values and beliefs of Thatcherism considered above and the analyses considered here lies in the extent to which the latter penetrate beneath the surface of identities, common sense beliefs, political loyalties, and hegemonic projects to establish the causal mechanisms which have produced them. They ask the key question: 'How does Thatcherism work?'.[39] They find the answer in its ability to penetrate and represent popular experience and explain this in turn in terms of the discursive strategies adopted by Thatcher.

The Genesis of Authoritarian Populism

Stuart Hall's work on 'authoritarian populism' is probably the best-known account of Thatcherism. His analysis of authoritarian populism and its associated hegemonic project of the new Conservative politics which it served reached a wide audience through its regular and timely appearance in *Marxism Today* and *New Socialist*. Indeed, the intuitive appeal of Hall's interpretation, combined with a general dissatisfaction with the economistic thinking common on the left, resulted in Hall's theses winning a certain local hegemony, especially in the Eurocommunist wing of the Communist Party, which, by the early 1980s, had gained control over *Marxism Today*, the Party's monthly theoretical journal. Nonetheless the prehistory of Hall's interest in authoritarian populism and Thatcherism dates back to his research at the Centre for Contemporary Cultural Studies at Birmingham in the mid-1970s. Beside other work this produced the important collaborative study on *Policing the Crisis* with its analysis of how increasing coercion (broadly interpreted) compensated for a crisis of consent and generated an authoritarian populism as its complement.[40] We refer to this study in Part II of our book.

In practical terms Hall has indicated that experiencing 'Thatcherism' might be the price the left must pay for real advance in Marxist theory.[41] For, as he has long argued, Thatcherism's success shows how hegemonic projects must contest, disarticulate and displace pre-existing ideological formations and develop an alternative common-sense and societal vision. The elements comprising the ideological matrix of Thatcherism are, in purely logical terms, contradictory. But this holds for all successful ideologies. More important is how these elements are unified through the play of connotations and the construction of chains of equivalence which connect different elements, focus them around particular identities and draw specific conclusions about the behaviour appropriate to people with such identities. Attempts to absorb individuals into the Thatcherite hegemonic project succeed in so far as the hegemonic discourse plays upon and resonates with elements of the identities, daily experience and beliefs which people already have. And it can do this because subjects do not have fully fixed loyalties and beliefs nor internally unified and coherent ideologies. Instead their identities are fractured, multiple and contradictory so that space exists for ideological struggle. In undertaking this work the Thatcherites have been able to build on their capture of the Conservative Party leadership. For this provided an organizational base around which other ideological currents could coalesce.

In theoretical terms, Hall suggests that Thatcherism is a valuable case study for recent theories of ideology. He himself draws upon a wide range of positions in order to produce a rich and complex account of the ideological instance. One source is Althusser's work on ideology considered as a distinctive practice rather than species of (false) consciousness. Althusser argued that ideology involves more than ideas in people's heads: it is embedded in and reproduced through specific social practices and institutions (or 'ideological apparatuses') and has material effects by endowing subjects with practical identities. Whilst accepting these arguments, Hall distances himself both from Althusser's class reductionist and functionalist claim that ideology gives subjects the identities appropriate to their place in capitalist society and from his somewhat tautological claim that the key ideological apparatuses are part of the state. Instead, invoking Gramsci, Hall argues that hegemony is fought for and won on the terrain of civil society. A second source has been the reinterpretation of Freud's work by linguistic psychoanalysts such as Lacan to provide an account of the fragmented nature of the individual subject and its search for identity as the basis for the effectivity of ideology. Here too Hall takes some elements without adopting the whole position. A third source is Foucault's later work on the interrelations between power, knowledge and subjectivity, and their association with specific forms of discourse and institutions. But Hall criticizes both Foucault's unresolved ambiguities about the exact status of the 'discursive' (a general problem in discourse-theoretical analysis) and his neglect of how diverse micro-power relations are condensed into larger complexes in and through the state and hegemonic projects.[42]

Above all, however, it is the Gramscian example which inspires Hall. He describes his work on AP as an 'attempt to characterize certain strategic shifts in the politico-ideological conjuncture. Essentially it refers to changes in the "balance of forces". It refers directly to the modalities of political and ideological relationships between the ruling bloc, the state and the dominated classes. It attempts to expand on and to begin to periodize the internal composition of hegemonic strategies in the politics of class democracies. Theoretically it is part of a wider project to develop and expand on the rich but too condensed concept of hegemony. It is a sort of footnote to Gramsci's *Modern Prince* and *State and Civil Society*.'[43]

While sympathetic to the general thrust of Hall's work and aspects of his various conjunctural analyses, our initial critique argued that there were serious shortcomings in his account of Thatcherism in terms of authoritarian populism. Hall's reply clarifies some points concerning the purpose and scope of 'authoritarian populism' but does not answer our real objections. We tried to present these more precisely in our reply to Hall. In essence, we remained unclear as to exactly what was being described under the label of 'authoritarian populism': was it (a) a new form of state; (b) the ideological complement to a more directly disciplinary form of state; or (c) the specific conjunctures of class struggle in a given country?

In retrospect authoritarian populism has been all three of these things (and more) at various times. Although the conjunctural changes in the state identified in *Policing the Crisis* do not really amount to a new form of state, consolidated Thatcherism is quite clearly reconstructing the state system. As an ideological complement AP has a continuing vitality. And it is particularly active in some conjunctures of struggle. Nonetheless, in contrast to Hall's approach, our account assumes that Thatcherism's success (if any) as a hegemonic project cannot be analysed solely in ideological terms. It must also be related to the emergent accumulation strategy and to a particular state strategy which seeks to institutionalize this project.

Thatcher's Subjects

As with so many other students of Thatcherism O'Shea is as keen to tell us what Thatcherism is not (or not just) as he is to offer us his own account. We have already seen this stratagem at work in other approaches and we will certainly be making similar points about our own account. Thus O'Shea argues that Thatcherism is not just a set of policies but also involves a set of politically effective discursive strategies. This does not mean that Thatcherism should be reduced to a cult of the personality or studied purely as a rhetorical style as if its linguistic forms were no more than the vehicle for transmitting an already defined ideology. Instead he emphasizes that discursive forms actually help to construct the terms and the boundaries of the way we can think about a particular topic. It is certainly true that many elements of Thatcherism already existed in various forms of popular common sense. But they were inchoate and had yet to be integrated into a popular, chauvinistic and morally righteous discourse with a definite set of referents and clear political implications. This work was achieved through Thatcher's own pronouncements and self-image.[44]

We agree with this analysis and have already made similar points in chapter 1 on the problems involved in reducing Thatcherism to the personality and/or personal beliefs of Margaret Thatcher. O'Shea also claims that the decisively new element in Thatcherism is its populism. As with other ideologies Thatcherism combines various elements into a relatively unified philosophy and a more or less coherent set of identities. What is distinctive is the way in which this is achieved through a subtle combination of two forms of populism: firstly, an antagonistic discourse mobilizing the British people against the social democratic state and, secondly, a more neutral concept of a consensual, non-antagonistic people which submerges their identities and antagonisms.[45] Crucial to the success of this discursive strategy is the highly condensed and complex 'national-popular' identity which it invokes and the way in which complex economic considerations are subsumed under simple moral ideas.[46] Considered as a populist discourse Thatcherism is concerned to identify and mobilize a new Thatcherite subject ('the ordinary individual protecting his sphere of freedom') as well as to construct a distinctive historical identity for Thatcher.

More than many theorists working within this approach O'Shea has emphasized that the re-articulation of different ideological elements has certain limits. Each element has its own history and cannot be redeployed at will.[47] Thus the identities, subject positions, ideological elements and other building blocks of ideological struggles are not just passive resources which can be articulated and re-articulated in any combination. Nor do they merely provide the ideological form or cover in and through which a pre-constituted set of policies can be presented and legitimated. They are not incidental forms but enter in crucial ways into the very construction of hegemonic projects.[48]

There is much with which we agree in the general approach to ideology deployed by O'Shea and in its application to Thatcherism as a hegemonic project. Nonetheless we would also like to identify four problems which affect not only his account but others using the same basic approach. These questions concern: the unity of Thatcherism, its continuity, the issue of discursive consumption, and the problem of evidence.

Firstly this sort of approach runs the risk of imposing a spurious unity, however subtle, on Thatcherism. It is far better to treat Thatcherism as an *ensemble* of discursive strategies which can be deployed for specific purposes, dropped for others, recombined, etc., than to suggest that it constitutes a relatively unified system formed through subtle combinations of contradictory elements. There is no reason to believe that either Thatcherite discourse or its more general strategy is not selective, not influenced by shifts in opinion polls, not influenced by the need to counter alternative discourses, not influenced by shifting priorities or little local difficulties. We shall give just a few examples. We have recently seen an attempt to moralize and give Biblical justification to the politics of greed exemplified in the 1988 budget. Previously there had been a resort to authoritarian populist wars of manoeuvre to disguise economic crisis and political drift in the summers of 1981 and 1982 or the miners' strike in 1984–5. It would be quite wrong to suggest that these shifts are all part of a seamless web or that they were all pre-planned as part of a long-term project. In this sense it might be wise to emphasize the functions of relative *incoherence* in any effective discourse.

Secondly, O'Shea's analysis sometimes suggests that there has been no real break in Thatcherism since 1979. He argues that the principal discursive work had already been completed between 1968 and 1979, as if the history of Thatcherism ended in 1979. Thus he claims that Thatcherism was already a unified philosophy by 1979; that monetarism had been successfully normalized and moralized between 1977 and 1978 by suggesting that it was the only alternative solution and made sense by analogy with family budgeting; that Thatcher's agenda was gradually constructed between 1968 and 1979 out of old traditional right elements and free market monetarism; and that the connotations of national identity had already been thoroughly reworked by 1979.[49] Stopping the clock on the development of Thatcherism in this way does not help us to analyse how it conducts ideological wars of manoeuvre or calls some elements into play in some contexts but not others. It also implies that, once Thatcher came into office, not much changed ideologically. There is little reason to accept this.

A third problem with this general approach to identifying and describing mechanisms of discursive production is that it does not tell us about discursive consumption. Ideologies must not only be transmitted; they must also be received, understood and acted upon. Why, using O'Shea's examples, was monetarism harder to naturalize than other elements of Thatcherism? Why couldn't Thatcher's populist discourse be applied to community control of the police as well as to rank-and-file control of militant trade union leaders? Why, indeed, was Thatcherism proving so unpopular in the winter of 1981/2? Answering these questions requires one to address two different issues, only one of which is raised by O'Shea himself. Firstly, why do some elements become relatively fixed and prove so recalcitrant to re-articulation? And, secondly, how do underlying institutional structures and social networks organize social relations and thereby make different individuals and forces more or less available for ideological appeals and political mobilization – exposing them to different combinations of appeal and different types of structural constraint in supporting or contesting a particular hegemonic project. Only when these sorts of question are addressed can we understand not only the discursive appeal of Thatcherism but also the structural roots which it has managed to sink.

Fourthly, there is a problem of evidence. O'Shea claims that one cannot assess the impact of Thatcherism through statistical research into public opinion because its real influence is at the level of the political agenda which defines the questions posed in opinion polls rather than the balance of opinion expressed on any issue.[50] Whilst this is a valid criticism to some degree, it should not lead us to discount the growing evidence that Thatcherism has not yet struck strong roots in the public mind. Much of the mobilization around Thatcher's agenda was conjunctural and support has fluctuated with feelings of economic prosperity, shifts in unemployment and many other material factors. Moreover, if Thatcherism had already refined its project and struck deep popular roots by 1979 (or 1982, or 1987), why was it necessary to mount yet another war of manoeuvre/position in 1988?

Mobile Privatization

Raymond Williams' discussion of 'mobile privatization' was not originally developed to account for the apparent success of Thatcherism but he did subsequently apply his analysis to Thatcherism's ability to recruit support across the classes.[51] Williams coined the term mobile privatization – in the course of an analysis of the development of radio and television[52] – as an attempt to characterize the form and content of cultural identities associated with a range of social and technological developments in industrial capitalism. Specifically, he argued that the breakdown and dissolution of older and smaller kinds of settlement and productive labour had resulted in both an increasing potential mobility for many members of society and a retreat from extended kinship and community networks towards a more privatized style of family unit. The material basis of this lay in the increasing diffusion of mass-produced consumer durables for home-centred consumption by the bulk of the population. Further, the augmentation and centralization of publicly funded forms of welfare provision have also undermined the need for locality-based forms of communal provision and self-activity. (This observation in itself has been something of an orthodoxy within sociology since the early studies of the Institute of Community Studies.)

What was original in Williams' discussion was his focus on the form of cultural identities associated with these societal changes. Thus mobile privatization is the condition where 'at most active social levels people are increasingly living as private small-family units, or, disrupting even that, as private and deliberately self-enclosed individuals, while at the same time there is a quite unprecedented mobility of such restricted privacies'.[53] This form of identity is then dependent on certain external conditions: cheap and easy credit to buy the consumer durables; the welfare state to look after educational and health requirements, etc.; and crucially, the availability of full employment for an expansive version of this mobile privatization to embrace most of the population. However, the consciousness developed inside such conditions was never deeply formed by the preconditions for its own realization. Moreover, whatever the depth of capitalist crisis, the numbers of those recruitable to the continuing pursuit of such an apolitical lifestyle will always be likely to constitute a majority over those unable to do so.

With respect to the rise of the New Right in Britain, the USA, and to a lesser extent elsewhere in north-western Europe, Therborn has stated this position very clearly.

> Welfare state capitalism . . . harbours and fosters a political anti-body of considerable importance: *right-wing liberalism* . . . This new right is a product of the boom, the changing mode of accumulation, and the cultural transformations that issued in welfare state capitalism. It is a force of mobile, secular managerialism and privatisation, little attached to traditional properties and symbols of authority, and therefore also attractive to sectors of the working class and the middle strata cut loose from their communal neighbourhoods and their cultural and political traditions.[54]

In developing this sort of approach one would achieve a rather different understanding of Thatcherism from that implied in analyses of authoritarian populism or Thatcherite discourse. In a sense what this approach does is identify some of the material bases for the appeal of Thatcherism, that is, to provide a partial explanation for the reception of Thatcherite discourse. Stuart Hall's work has often stressed the need to explore the material connections between discourse, lived experience and fundamental social transformations. By elaborating the analysis of mobile privatization and extending the same sort of enquiry into other fields we could deepen and enrich the ideological approach to Thatcherism.[55]

Feminist Analyses of Thatcherism

We now turn briefly to feminist analyses of Thatcherism. Despite widespread agreement that Thatcherism has seriously damaged women's interests in Britain, there is little consensus among feminists on its nature or the most appropriate response to adopt towards it. The initial reactions to Thatcherism took the form of vocal resistance to the cuts which were adding new injury to the traditional insults of discrimination and marginalization. The cuts affected women more than men because of their more marginal position in the private sector, their predominance in public sector employment and the ways in which reductions in the state's caring role displaced the burden on to women in the family sector. However, in parallel with the more common gender-blind analyses of Thatcherism, once the initial shock of the cuts had been absorbed, attention turned towards more qualitative judgements of Thatcherism. For feminists this has meant reassessing the patriarchal implications of Thatcherism.

She may be a Woman, but She's not a Sister

During the 1979 election campaign some women argued that voting Tory would advance women's interests because it would secure the election of Britain's first female prime minister. This claim simply inverted the feeling among many men that, wherever woman's place might be, it was certainly not in Number 10. As other feminists were quick to note, however, Margaret Thatcher may be a woman, but she is not a sister. There was no reason to expect that, once elected, Thatcher would pursue the interests of women rather than those of her class and/or party. This belief is mirrored in the oft-quoted comments of Cabinet ministers and commentators that Thatcher is the best, if not the only, *man* in the Cabinet. All of this is summed up in Bea Campbell's observation that 'uniquely among politicians, in the public mind she belongs to one sex but could be either'.[56]

That she was no sister soon became apparent from the impact of the cuts associated with Thatcher's economic experiment. Many of the government's measures hit women disproportionately and seemed to confirm the old ideas that women worked only for pin money or should stay at home and care for their husbands, children and sick or elderly relatives. Whether this was deliberate or an unintended by-product of the general economic and political strategy might be considered secondary but it has nonetheless proved controversial among some feminists.[57]

Against those who interpret Thatcherism primarily as anti-feminism, Elizabeth Wilson has argued that the Thatcherite project is class specific rather than opposed to all women. It has launched a direct class attack to raise productivity, increase profits and weaken unions; this has certainly widened the gap between women (especially at the expense of black and ethnic minority women) but this often stems from more general shifts and an anarchic restructuring that affect the whole working class. In this sense reducing protection for women *at work* is an essential part of the Thatcherite economic project rather than part of a plan to send women *back home* where they supposedly belong. This can be seen both in their increasing incorporation into the paid labour force *on the worst possible terms* and in the absence of both a strong family policy and curbs on sexual exploitation.[58] In developing this view Wilson not only implies that patriarchal analyses are misleading but also claims that the AP approach is particularly off-target when dealing with the relations between Thatcherism and women because of the unvoiced and incoherent nature of its policies in this area.

Such analyses have shown the limitations of focusing primarily on the adverse distributional impact of Thatcherism. Whilst there may be widespread consensus on the actual costs of Thatcherism to women (to the extent that the Conservatives have never attempted to massage the figures as they have those for unemployment – instead they keep mum), such facts do not speak for themselves. This is the same problem, of course, that we encountered with other surface accounts. One must look behind the figures to assess how far these changes are due to Thatcherism as such (as opposed to the economic crisis or general capitalist restructuring), to establish exactly what policies have been adopted towards women by the Thatcher governments and how coherent they might be, and to explain why they have had such clearly contradictory and confusing effects. On these questions there is little agreement.

Going beyond a consideration of unequal distribution, some feminists have argued that Thatcherism is an expression of unchecked patriarchy and thus belongs to the same group of phenomena as fascism. In this sense Thatcherism is the quintessential enemy of feminism.[59] Whilst criticizing such essentialism, Tessa ten Tusscher has rightly argued that, in failing to make gender relations central to the analysis, 'an essential element of the package which constitutes the New Right or Thatcherism has been systematically either ignored or marginalized'.[60] Most discussion runs in a treadmill of male-defined analyses offering male answers to male questions and therefore produces a partial account of the New Right which fails to explain (and indeed lacks the analytical tools to explain) the moral, traditional and familial aspects of the Thatcher administration's ideology and practice. Although these aspects are crucial for an understanding of Thatcherism and the New Right, leftwing analyses either ignore them or simply subsume them under the notion of populism.

Ten Tusscher herself explains them in terms of the combination of two crises; that of patriarchal domination (which emerged in the 1960s) and the global crisis of capitalism (which emerged in the 1970s). Before the latter crisis emerged the tendential emancipation of woman through the entry of women into the labour force and their progress towards sexual liberation served the interests of capital by providing cheap labour and opening new fields for mass consumption. With the open outbreak of capitalist crisis, however, the New Right gained the necessary space to attack women's gains by reuniting the interests of capital and patriarchy. Thus the New Right aimed both to restore class forces in favour of capital and gender relations in favour of men.[61]

Nonetheless, although its intentions are anti-feminist, Thatcherism need not be so explicitly anti-feminist as the Moral Majority in the USA. This is explained through the fact that women's rights are not entrenched by legislation in Britain so that Thatcherism can simply uphold traditional family values and restrict women's access to scarce resources.[62]

The Discourse of Thatcherism

In *Iron Ladies* Bea Campbell analyses 'how Thatcher gives back to women an image of woman, how that image is deployed in Thatcherite ideology, and explores the limits of Thatcherite woman in the Tory Party's "longer trajectory"'.[63] In some respects her analysis is reminiscent of Stuart Hall's more general work on authoritarian populism and the discursive strategies of Thatcherism but, in applying this sort of method, she reveals the limited impact of AP in the case of Thatcherite attempts at political mobilization around women's issues and identities.[64] She argues that Thatcher's gender was crucial in developing Thatcherism as a populist ideology and supports this by considering: (a) the role of the 'housewife' as a populist ideological construct to popularize monetarism, to emphasize women's domestic duties and to draw a contrast with the masculine world of unionism; and (b) the ways in which Thatcher presents and manipulates her image as both woman and warrior. That these discourses involve ideological work is shown by the fact that Thatcher only includes women in them as housewives and even then ignores how their lived experience contradicts their idealized image.

Bea Campbell suggests that Thatcher's politics are patriarchal but that she herself conforms to neither traditional femininity nor feminism: instead she embodies a female power which unites patriarchal and feminine discourses. She has not so much feminized politics as offered feminine endorsements to patriarchal power and principles.[65] Campbell also notes how the triumph of Thatcherism was that of traditional Tory women (with their moral authoritarianism and familial ideology) and alienated Tory women attracted to nineteenth-century liberalism and its free market commitment to free choice. But even the traditionalist agenda could gain ascendancy only through its articulation to racism, anti-statism and monetarism. In this sense Thatcherism came too late: feminism had already established an alternative agenda, so that ordinary party members could not be contained by the moral right. The availability of competing ideologies and identities blocked any essentialist reduction of women's roles to the domestic and reproductive.[66] Overall this means that the elements of Thatcherism are diverse and contradictory and must co-exist with a Conservative feminism rooted in liberalism. This has limited any direct emphasis on traditional familialism and encouraged instead an emphasis on the family as the anchor of anti-statism and economic liberalism and as a moral bulwark against all manner of evils.

This can be seen in the failure of Thatcherism's articulation of moralism and monetarism to produce a moral crusade and counter-revolution against the gains women had made from the postwar settlement and women's liberation. It produced at best a tactical realignment in party. This can be seen in the widespread opposition inside the government and establishment to Victoria Gillick's campaign to deny contraceptive advice to minors.[67] Similar points are made by other feminist theorists. Thus Wilson notes that the Festival of Light failed to get a moral majority off the ground in the 1970s and that no coherent consensus has since developed for an authoritarian populist response to feminism, permissiveness or the patriarchal crisis. Likewise Jean Gardiner notes that the Tory position on women is less explicit and united than on issues such as unions or labour local authorities.[68]

General Comments on Feminist Analyses

Apart from their particular concern with gender issues, there is little theoretically distinctive about most feminist analyses of Thatcherism. Thus Campbell's interesting work combines historical and journalistic approaches with an account of ideologies which draws on Stuart Hall's influential work; Wilson and Gardiner adopt a Marxist-feminist analysis which emphasizes capital and class as the primary motive force behind Thatcherism; many other studies adopt a largely descriptive and distributional focus. Alone among the studies reviewed here ten Tusscher does provide a distinctive explanation, however, and this can be strongly recommended as bringing something new and distinctively feminist to the analysis of Thatcherism.

Theoretical Reflections

We have now sketched various accounts of Thatcherism from different theoretical and political positions. It is impossible to say which of them provides the most incisive or valid analysis because there is only limited agreement among them about the nature of Thatcherism itself. Indeed, if there really are many Thatcherisms, many valid descriptions and explanations could presumably be given. This should not be taken to imply that all accounts are equally valid or equally useful. It merely means that validity must first be assessed in terms of the particular definition of Thatcherism to which an account is linked and to the precise problem which is being posed about Thatcherism in this context. To give just a few contrasts: approaching Thatcherism in terms of economic experiments and in terms of an anti-feminist project are clearly different exercises; so are treating Thatcherism as a personal philosophy and as an emergent strategic line. This also means that arguments and evidence which might be relevant for testing one interpretation of Thatcherism (for example, as statecraft) may be quite irrelevant for testing ideas located in another context (for example, personal philosophy). And, even when we isolate a number of descriptions and explanations which appear valid within specific approaches, this tells us nothing about their practical or theoretical relevance. If we were interested in fine-tuning Thatcherism's neo-liberal accumulation strategy we would focus on quite different issues from those of interest to forces trying to mobilize political resistance around a future Labour government. Finally, if Thatcherism itself is a dynamic and changing phenomenon, then descriptions or explanations valid for one period may be irrelevant or misleading for others.

Many Thatcherisms, Many Theories?

In this context it is interesting to note how often the proponents of the various approaches reviewed above seek to distinguish their particular approach from others without condemning them entirely. Thus commentators often present their approach as a simple alternative, as a useful supplement or as equally significant. Particularly telling here is the frequent use of the 'not just' or 'and also' approach: for Thatcherism, we are variously told, is 'not just' this or that – it is also that or this. No one, to our knowledge, has yet claimed that his/her account alone provides the truth, the whole truth and nothing but the truth. Those who come close to so doing usually fall into reductionist accounts. Thus Ross tells us that only someone who is naive or deliberately wishes to conceal the truth would treat Thatcherism as primarily political or ideological. Likewise Glyn and Sutcliffe inform us that it is not an outmoded nineteenth-century ideology but 'a coherent set of policies aimed at enabling market forces to restore adequate conditions for producing surplus-value'. But much more common are arguments like that of Bulpitt, informing us that Thatcherism is a political practice with an economic doctrine; or O'Shea, that it is not just personality or

policies, but also a specific type of populist discourse; or Clarke, that it
involves not just ideology or economic doctrine but also the underlying
logic of capital; or ourselves, that it is not just authoritarian populism,
but also a two-nations hegemonic project, etc. Even Minogue seems to
relent and concede that 'Thatcherism' is 'not just' a term invented by
leftwing critics to concentrate their venom on Thatcher and all her
works: elsewhere he has written that Thatcherism is also a particular
style of politics conforming to Britain's needs as a country beset with
institutional sclerosis. What these various attempts to bend the stick in
the other direction indicate is the perception that Thatcherism is a
complex phenomenon which cannot be properly explicated in a one-
sided manner. Different commentators may focus on specific aspects in
the light of their own professional and/or political interests and skills,
but few would claim that they alone discerned the essential truth of
Thatcherism. And those who do are unlikely to be right.

This pluralism is worth emphasizing because it corresponds so well
with the basic methodological requirements for a rounded account of
complex historical phenomena. These are best analysed as a complex
resultant of multiple determinations rather than as the simple product
of a single causal mechanism. In this sense not only depth but also
breadth of analysis are needed. Thus a full account should combine
different moments (economic, political, ideological, patriarchal and so
on) to show how they interact to produce the phenomenon at issue.
This in turn requires both that the approaches to the different dimensions
are complementary and that they have similar degrees of depth. As Hall
notes in response to a comment that he had neglected the economic
dimension, it would seem odd to combine naive economic analysis with
a highly sophisticated ideological one. Whether this really justifies
sticking with one-sided analyses or demands that somehow or other we
develop strengths in several fields must, for the time being, remain an
open question.

These remarks explain in any case why our review has not been
concerned to identify the one true account of Thatcherism. Instead it
has tried to explore the problems (both methodological and substantive)
involved in a range of different approaches. Even those accounts we
reject on methodological, substantive or political grounds often generate
interesting 'facts', anomalies or paradoxes which cast new light on
Thatcherism and/or need to be re-examined to see how they might fit
with accounts which we prefer. In general we are inclined to recommend
studies which offer both depth and breadth of analysis, but one or other
is still better than neither. Nonetheless, since we adopt the resolute
approach in denying that Thatcherism can be understood as a unitary
phenomenon with unambiguous and unchanging identity and purpose,
it would be absurd to single out just one of the approaches reviewed
above as the best. They are all one-sided in their different ways and

each has its own strengths and weaknesses. Combining the best of them would be a far better strategy than prioritizing just one. In later chapters we attempt to bring different perspectives to bear in the manner of triangulation to provide a better 'fix' on Thatcherism.

Uneven Theoretical Development

In this respect today's theorists are better placed than earlier commentators, for the rise of Thatcherism coincided with one of the recurrent crises in Marxism. In making this observation we are not trying to suggest a relation of cause and effect – in either or both directions. Instead we want to highlight the problems this posed for Marxist analyses of the nature of Thatcherism and the most appropriate strategies to be adopted towards it. Among other responses this crisis led many of the leading contempotary Marxist theorists to reject both economism and class reductionism and to stress the relative autonomy or independent logics of the political and ideological domains. This was reflected in tendencies toward equally one-sided 'politicist' and 'ideologist' accounts of Thatcherism. This posed several problems for Marxist theorizing and the development of political strategies.

The first problem has been one of uneven theoretical development. In rejecting economic determinism some Marxist commentators were led to neglect economic categories and to underplay the significance of class interests. At the same time there was an upsurge of interest among Marxists in the political region, evident from their many attempts to theorize the state system and to stress the specificities of political class struggle in liberal democratic societies. In addition to the famous Miliband–Poulantzas debate and the less well received and understood 'state derivation' approach, there was also a major Gramsci boom, with enormous interest in questions of hegemony. In parallel (and sometimes closely interwoven) with these interests in politics and the state, there was also growing interest in the ideological domain and in discourse more generally. Gramsci's work was also significant here but many other theoretical currents fed into the floodtide of research.

One effect of this crisis in Marxism and the associated unevenness in theoretical development was to encourage left theorists to use political and/or ideological categories when analysing Thatcherism. There were certainly interpretations of Thatcherism couched in terms of capitalist crisis or the class struggle but these often involved little more than ritual incantation of the basic tenets of Marxist fundamentalism and the specific claim that Thatcherism was capital's inevitable response. The fashionable prejudice against economism combined with the relative poverty of these economistic analyses led other left theorists to venture explanations drawing on political and ideological categories. One such analysis was that offered by Stuart Hall in terms of 'authoritarian populism' (see below) but many other analyses were also offered along these lines. We have already drawn attention to some of the problems of one-sided political or ideological analyses in earlier parts of this chapter and will return to them below.

Analyses of Thatcherism have since been rounded out because there have been further developments in Marxist theorizing across a broad front. This can be seen in the economic, political and ideological domains and, as these advances have penetrated into more general left analyses, earlier interpretations have been reworked.

Firstly, the global economic recession and social restructuring since the mid-1970s has led to renewed interest in long cycles or long waves of economic growth. Secondly, related to these concerns, there has been growing interest in Fordism, neo-Fordism and post-Fordism as forms of labour process and forms of social and political organization. Together these provide a more general framework to interpret recent changes in British political economy. Thirdly, in challenging orthodox Marxist analyses of capitalist reproduction, the regulation approach has developed a complex set of concepts for analysing capital accumulation. It provides a rich and detailed account of the capitalist economy in particular conjunctures and also provides a series of links to the political and ideological domains. Particularly significant in this regard is the regulationist analysis of regimes of accumulation and their corresponding modes of regulation. Fourthly, there have been major theoretical advances in analysing the 'politics of production', its articulation to the mental/manual division of labour, the forms of technical and social organization in the enterprise etc. These have also contributed to a more nuanced and sophisticated analysis of the labour process and its implications for class relations. Overall, then, we have a complex set of economic categories and concepts with which to rethink the current conjuncture and the role of Thatcherism in re-shaping the British economy.

At the same time political analysis has broken out of the sterile instrumentalist vs. structuralist debate and moved on to develop a rich and detailed account of state forms in terms of their impact on class forces and their role in institutionalizing different types of class compromise. The analyses of corporatism so much in vogue in the late seventies and even in the early eighties, when, in Britain at least, corporatism was under attack, had a central transitional role here. They highlighted the complexity and mediations of the state both in its own terms and in relation to civil society and the economy.

Likewise we now have analyses of the ideological which pay attention to the forms of discourse. These have advanced our understanding of the specific mechanisms which influence the political and ideological appeal of Thatcherism. We must pay equal attention to issues of meaning, reference and interpretation in order to grasp the limits of Thatcherism's appeal and influence.

A key aspect of these theoretical developments is their introduction of ontological depth into social analysis. Hitherto Marxist analyses of the political and ideological had tended to concentrate on the surface of social relations and events or to short-circuit their analysis by invoking abstract theoretical concepts and laws as adequate to describe and explain concrete conjunctures. Thus politics tended to be analysed mainly in terms of the changing balance of political forces and strategies and description of the circumstances in which this occurred. Ideology was analysed in terms of values and beliefs, consensus, etc. In contrast the economic level has been analysed in depth – moving from the fundamental laws of motion of capitalism through tendencies and counter-tendencies to the actual economic outcomes. Recent work has begun to analyse the underlying structures of political organization and action, as well as the mechanisms of ideological production, the varied means of ideological transmission and the differing conditions for its reception. This enables us to work towards a more equal weighting for economic, political and ideological dimensions.

Concluding Remarks

The effect of the theoretical developments occurring since Thatcher came to power some ten years ago has been to promote the analysis of Thatcherism in more sophisticated terms. The more one-sided analyses have faded somewhat and a new consensus seems to be emerging on the nature of Thatcherism. We deal with this below: here we merely want to signal the importance of looking both at the changing character of Thatcherism (including its movement from one stage to another) and the changing character of the theories available to left theorists in their efforts to analyse Thatcherism. Whether these developments are related remains to be seen. For the moment we will turn to one debate on the nature of Thatcherism which shows some of the problems generated through the uneven theoretical development within Marxism as well as through the uneven development of the Thatcherite phenomenon itself.

PART II

Critique and Counter-Critique

3

Introduction to Part II

The following three chapters reproduce articles from *New Left Review*. In the first of these we criticized Stuart Hall's analysis of Thatcherism in terms of authoritarian populism and offered an alternative account more oriented to its political dynamic. In the second article Hall offers a reply which serves both to clarify his aims and methods in analysing Thatcherism in these terms and to make a number of more general points about left theorizing and strategy. The third article presents our reply to this counter-critique and attempts to bring our analysis of Thatcherism up to 1985. Since there is little point here in detailing the various arguments at stake, this introduction will simply try to put all three articles in their historical context. Accordingly we will return to the periodization of Thatcherism offered in chapter 1 above. There we suggested that there have so far been three main periods of Thatcherism: (1) the rise of Thatcherism as a social movement, 1968–79; (2) the period when Thatcherism was consolidated, 1979–82; and (3) consolidated Thatcherism, 1982 onwards. Here we will amplify our remarks by considering the various sub-stages of each period and their political and theoretical significance for any understanding of Thatcherism.

The Rise of Thatcherism

This period was significant because Thatcherism acquired the potential to become a regime-in-the-process-of-formation. It slowly developed an appropriate politics of support able to mobilize an adequate popular base and to develop links with an establishment visibly in a state of shock. It had also begun work on an embryonic politics of power for the time when it might hold office: its economic strategy was largely based on monetarism and an assault on the economic and political gains of the labour movement and it had a limited hegemonic project based on the concepts of social market economy and strong state. Finally it had a strategy for resolving the dual crisis of the state: it would retreat from corporatist entanglements, abandon attempts at dirigisme and develop a laissez-faire role more in keeping with the liberal traditions of the British state. This period can be divided into three stages:

Avant la Lettre

Obviously Thatcherism did not emerge *ex nihilo*. It built on the failures of Powellism and Heathism – the two preceding Conservative reactions to the crises of the postwar settlement (hereafter PWS) and Keynesian welfare state (hereafter KWS). Powellism emerged in the late 1960s and survived until 1974. It mobilized significant support among the working class and petty bourgeoisie as a populist, authoritarian and liberal political ideology. But it actually enjoyed only limited penetrative and transformative capacities because its populism was racist and 'little Englandist', its authoritarianism was largely constitutionalist (emphasizing the sovereign rights of Parliament and the substantive rule of law), and its liberalism was Manchesterian (stressing the need for tax reductions, sound money and perfect competition). Together these features cut Powell off from a broader base of popular support (neither his racism nor his constitutionalism had a general resonance) as well as from support from modernizing and/or pro-European elements in the Establishment (worried about his perfect market fantasies and hostility to Europe). Edward Heath tried to pursue a Fordist modernizing programme based on *neo*-liberal rhetoric and Keynesian practice but his attempt foundered when his programme produced 1 million unemployed and a law-and-order crisis. Heath still operated within the postwar social democratic consensus and lacked any real alternative popular base (technocratic managerialism having but limited appeal), so that these problems provoked his U-turn first to an abortive corporatism and then to dirigiste controls. His failures brought Labour to power with the promise of a Social Contract with the unions and also provided an object lesson in political errors for the Thatcherites.

Despite the marginalization of Powellism and the self-destruction of Heathism, the early and mid-1970s saw a variety of social, moral and political reactions to the burgeoning crisis of the KWS. But these remained fragmented despite significant individual pockets of support. Among these reactions we can mention the moral campaigns of the early 1970s, such as the Festival of Light or the National Viewers' and Listeners' Association; the rise in 1974 and 1975 of various economic-

cum-political associations, such as the National Federation of the Self-
Employed, the Association of Self-Employed People, the Independent
Business Persons' Association and the National Association of the Self-
Employed.[1] Together with older associations (for example, the Union
of Independent Companies or the Association of Independent Businesses,
'these new associations gave voice to the grievances of non-corporate
business in Britain'.[2] The breadth of discontent could also be seen in
the formation of vigilante groups (such as, GB75 and Civil Assistance),
the Middle Class Association (to defend petty bourgeois values and
interests) and, more significantly, The National Association of Freedom
(1975—). The latter was not only an ideological organ for the radical
right but also advocated litigation to confront the government and
unions.[3] Finally we should note the growth of research and policy
formation centres oriented to the New Right – the Institute of Economic
Affairs, the Centre for Policy Studies and the Adam Smith Institute.
These were significant because they show how much economic, political
and ideological ferment there was to capitalize upon once Thatcherism
emerged to give these movements and their supporters a firm lead.

Thatcherism as a Social Movement, 1975–1978/9

Margaret Thatcher won the Conservative Party leadership in an election
contest against Edward Heath in 1975. She proceeded to shape and
organize a diffuse social movement against the crisis of the PWS, its
creeping socialism and the labour movement which supported it.
Thatcherism managed to overcome the complementary weaknesses of
Powellism and Heathism alike. Firstly, in contrast to Powellism, it
mobilized both popular and electoral support around key material issues
(free collective bargaining, tax cuts, anti-inflation, council house sales)
as well as an authoritarian *populist* stand on moral and political issues;
and it won crucial support from the Establishment with its doctrines of
the social market economy and strong state rather than those of the free
market economy and the nightwatchman state. Its promises to stop the
socialist and trade union rot appealed to both popular and Establishment
interests. Secondly, in contrast to the Heath experiment, it rejected the
U-turn inducing commitments to the PWS and instead mobilized
popular support against the settlement and all its works. In this sense
it was less concerned simply to shift the balance between capital and
labour within the crumbling framework of the PWS than to abandon
the whole project in favour of a new edifice more favourable to capital.
    The key to Thatcherism's success as a social movement lies in three
crucial political breakthroughs. Firstly, it managed to link the long-
standing but hitherto diffuse, unvoiced petty bourgeois resentment
against the PWS with emergent working class discontent over the forms
and results of the economic and political crisis-management practised

under both Tory and Labour governments in the 1960s and 1970s. And, secondly, it mobilized this popular support behind an electoral strategy and a political programme. Thatcher was the leader of a major party and this gave her a credibility which Powell had lacked. Thirdly, owing to the crisis of the incumbent Labour Government and its corporatist strategy, she also won growing support from the Establishment as it realized that neither Labour nor a Butskellite Conservative Party could manage the economy or resolve the crisis of authority. This *rassemblement* around the Thatcherite banner was reinforced by the growing polarization between the main political parties so that the typical Establishment solution of a government of national unity was not really on the political agenda.

The Point of No Return, February 1979

The public sector strikes in the 'Winter of Discontent' meant Labour could not win the next election (which had to occur by October 1979). For these strikes crystallized the contradictions in the government's economic and political strategy and revealed the weakness in its social basis. From the outbreak of the strikes in February 1979, the real political initiative passed to the Conservatives. This did not mean that their electoral success would in itself determine the subsequent career of Thatcherism. Indeed, although Thatcher had won popular support, she was still in the minority within the Conservative Party in Parliament and in her own Cabinet. The first period ended with the election.

Consolidating Power, 1979–1982

At the start of the second period Thatcher's main political concern was how to consolidate her power base, and her main economic concern was how to cut inflation and prepare for economic recovery. There were three stages in this period: (a) the stage from the election to the 1981 budget was marked above all by the dilemmas and contradictions involved in trying simultaneously to consolidate support and fight the good fight against inflation; (b) the defiant 1981 monetarist budget accorded priority to the economic experiment and was followed by four seasons of discontent until the spring of 1982 without prompting any significant U-turn; and (c) the third stage is centred on the Falklands war and witnessed the provisional consolidation of Thatcherism on three main fronts: Cabinet, Party and people.

Winning Support or Beating Inflation?

The first Thatcher government embarked on its neo-liberal monetarist programme but was also concerned to consolidate political support from the electorate, the Conservative Party, and the Establishment. These concerns were not fully compatible. Indeed the first budget was not just risky but also contradictory: in seeking to reward supporters and implement manifesto commitments it involved measures which undermined the battle against inflation. The problems involved in pursuing a consistent line were complicated by the fact that Thatcher had not yet consolidated her power within the Cabinet and faced opposition from key elements in the Bank–Treasury axis as well as leading spokesmen for the business community.[4] Ignoring criticism and using her prime ministerial powers, she managed to establish her dominance within Cabinet by late 1980 and then opted for a hard-line monetarist budget in 1981. Since the labour movement was divided, disorganized, defensive and defeatist throughout this stage, the most important opposition came from inside the Establishment.

Four Seasons of Discontent

The industrial crisis intensified under the impact of the 1981 budget and the de-industrialization process and unemployment accelerated. The crisis of government authority also deteriorated and the opposition to Thatcherism mounted. By mid-1981 it was threatened on all fronts: the Cabinet, the Conservative Party in Parliament and the country, the Lords, most sectors of commerce and industry, the City, the newly formed Social Democratic Party, the electorate, the streets.[5] And in many quarters the U-turn was confidently expected. It never came. Effective opposition failed to crystallize in either Parliament or the system of corporatist representation: the Labour Party was divided and conceded political terrain even whilst criticizing the economic consequences of Thatcher, the unions were disorganized through unemployment and legislation, the Institute of Directors emerged as a counterweight to the CBI in media debates, and the Thatcherite press, whilst lukewarm, still operated in terms of Thatcherite common sense. Thus Thatcher battled on, relying on political dominance and coercion where necessary and looking for the light at the end of the tunnel.

The Falklands Episode

In the spring of 1982 Thatcherism was apparently rescued by the Argentinian invasion of the Falkland Islands. Without wishing to deny the boost this gave to the Conservatives' popular support we would also note that the government had already embarked on the long retreat from monetarism before the invasion and that an economic recovery had begun. In combination these enabled Thatcher to establish her control over the Cabinet, the Party, the Establishment and the country. The wets were finally defeated in the Cabinet and the Party and the main axis of conflict became consolidation vs. radicalism; the Establishment was pleased to see the retreat from monetarism; and the electorate was pacified through the Falklands war, the reflationary budget in 1982, and the cyclical upswing after the 1980–1 recession. Thus the stage was set for the second election victory.

Consolidated Thatcherism

The second period had been largely concerned with the control of inflation and political consolidation. The third period was marked by initial uncertainty about how to move beyond austerity and what to do after the political defeat of the wets. It witnessed the gradual development of a more positive accumulation strategy, a relatively coherent state project and a new hegemonic project. It can be divided into three stages: first, from the Falklands to the 1983 election, marked by further consolidation; second, a period of relative stabilization (equilibrium of compromise) in the new conflict between consolidators and radicals; and third, the period since the 1986 party conference, marked by the victory of the radicals and the emergence of a third line of conflict, between neo-liberal and neo-statist currents within the Thatcherite camp.

Further Consolidation   In the first stage the necessary organizational work for the next election was undertaken but its opportunistic timing, divisions among the opposing parties and the unpopularity of Labour meant that little work on the manifesto was possible or necessary. The party policy study groups had been chaired by backbenchers rather than ministers and the manifesto itself was frankly consolidationist. Few new pledges were made, apart from that to abolish the GLC and metropolitan counties.

Relative Stabilization   On the surface this stage was one of drift: Thatcherism seemed to have lost its radical drive. There were conflicts between the consolidators and the radicals on many issues with no clear once-and-for-all victory and the most spectacular events (abolition of the GLC and metropolitan counties, rate-capping, the year-long miners' strike) seemed little more than wars of manoeuvre whose implications for the consolidator vs. radical split were ambiguous. Beneath the surface the structural bases of economic and political power were being transformed so that the underlying balance of power was slowly shifting in favour of radical Thatcherism. But the main outlines of the period are clear even if the details are still fuzzy. The basic strategy was to consolidate past gains, press ahead cautiously on a broad front, launch more radical attacks on selected targets and move carefully beyond legal and monetary restraint towards a broader-based neo-liberal strategy. This requires us to examine not only the public face of Thatcherism but also its less public, piecemeal measures to put economic strategy on neo-liberal, supply-side lines as the retreat from technical monetarism accelerated. The new accumulation strategy was announced in 1984 (in Lawson's Mais lecture) and the definition of a new hegemonic project. In place of 'jobs for all' and 'social democracy' Thatcherism would offer the 'entrepreneurial society' and 'popular capitalism'.

Radical Thatcherism   Fear of drift led the Thatcherites to insist on a radical party conference in 1986 and a radical manifesto for the next election. Key initiatives were to be undertaken in education, training, health, the local authorities and inner cities. This radical stage has now been in progress for two years and there seems little let-up in the combined war of position and manoeuvre on all fronts.

The Debate in Context

Having briefly presented our periodization, we can now locate the debate represented in the following three chapters. It is clear that the initial analyses offered by Stuart Hall dealt with the period when Thatcherism had not yet gained office. They had three main concerns: (a) a critique of economistic and 'class politics' readings of Thatcherism; (b) development of an alternative account of Thatcherism in terms of its authoritarian populist appeal in a period of economic, political and ideological crisis crystallized around the crisis of the postwar social democratic settlement with its commitments to the Keynesian welfare state; and (c) recommendations about the appropriate left strategy to neutralize Thatcherism's appeal and to develop an alternative left hegemonic strategy. As comments on the first period of Thatcherism they revealed much about it and clearly established the role of authoritarian populism in sustaining the rise of Thatcherism as a social movement.

Our first critique was written in a quite different conjuncture: some five years after Thatcherism had first gained office. It criticized methodological and substantive aspects of Stuart Hall's general account of AP and its relevance to analysing Thatcherism; and it proposed an alternative account in terms of the dual crisis of the British state. Having criticized Hall's account of the *rise* of Thatcherism, this critique then looked mainly at Thatcherism's ability to stay in power despite initial policy inconsistencies and electoral unpopularity. In this context it emphasized above all the crises of party political and corporatist representation and the inability of forces opposed to Thatcherism to unify around a shared alternative economic and political strategy. Clearly this critique was particularly influenced by the second stage of the second period, that is, the four seasons of discontent, when the most pertinent question was: how is Margaret Thatcher getting away with it? Our analyses of the dual crisis of the state were particularly relevant here in explaining the room for political manoeuvre enjoyed by Thatcher and the more Bonapartist features of her statecraft.

Stuart Hall replied to this critique both directly in *New Left Review* and indirectly in various incidental remarks in other papers. The main points in his reply were: re-affirming the importance of the ideological dimension and of authoritarian populism, re-affirming the importance for left strategy of developing an alternative common sense and getting involved in popular politics, and adding new elements to his analysis related to contemporary economic and political developments. He did not directly challenge the account of the dual crisis of the state.

Finally, in replying to this response, we shifted our ground in two ways. We located the debate over Thatcherism in a more general theoretical account of the contemporary state and we also examined the evolving economic strategy of Thatcherism in terms of a neo-liberal transition from Fordism to post-Fordism. In this way we brought the analysis forward to the current conjuncture and made it more directly concerned with the issues in political economy relevant to the second stage of consolidated Thatcherism.

In subsequent work both Hall and ourselves have discussed the economic and political strategies of Thatcherism and the left as well as commenting on the outcome of the 1987 election. What is remarkable in these later contributions is the extent to which we both converge in our analysis of the current conjuncture – whatever our disagreements may have been over the interpretation of Thatcherism in the past. There are still clear differences of approach and emphasis in our work (for example, on the significance of the North–South split in the 1987 election) but there is also a clear agreement about the significance of Thatcherism for the restructuring of the British economy and British state along more flexible 'post-Fordist' lines.

Putting the debate in context in this way suggests two methodological conclusions which were less clear at the time the debate was conducted. Firstly, the successive rounds in the debate over Thatcherism were strongly, if unconsciously, conditioned by the successive stages of Thatcherism. Hall's early work dealt with the rise of Thatcherism, when issues of ideology and popular mobilization were crucial in shaping the reaction to the crisis of the postwar settlement. Our critique was influenced by the experience of the consolidation stage – especially the question of 'how on earth Thatcher's government could get away with it'. Moreover, in claiming that AP could not explain important features of the Thatcher government's first years in power, we tended to draw the illegitimate conclusion that it was also irrelevant to the rise of Thatcherism. In subsequent work we have examined the emerging economic and political strategy of Thatcherism as it has moved from a critique of the postwar settlement and an essentially negative strategy of monetarist austerity and authoritarian populism to a more positive strategy of flexible accumulation and popular capitalism. In this sense the most appropriate concepts and tools of analysis for understanding Thatcherism have changed as Thatcherism itself has changed: only with hindsight has it become clear how far different conjunctures shaped the reactions and responses to Thatcherism.

A second methodological point, stressed by Hall in his reply to our first critique, is that his work focused mainly on the ideological dimension of Thatcherism and did not intend to provide an overall interpretation. This raises the problem of how one analyses real, concrete phenomena: what exactly is involved in the method of articulation needed to study concrete, complex phenomena and what is the most appropriate way to develop concepts relevant only to one dimension or aspect of such phenomena. The contrast between Hall's early work and our first critique reflects the contrast between Hall's one-sided emphasis on the ideological and popular in the rise of Thatcherism and our one-sided emphasis on the political conditions for the consolidation of Thatcherism. The convergence in later work reflects our common concern with the emerging economic and political strategy of the Thatcher government. There are still differences between our respective analyses which must be explored but they are less marked than first readings of the debate would suggest.

There are also political lessons to be drawn. The nature of the debate has been widely misunderstood. Political and academic commentators alike have tended to polarize positions in the debate – encouraging others to take sides when the extent of disagreement (especially in retrospect) is marginal when compared with the obvious gulf between (a) Hall and ourselves and (b) the economic or class reductionist analyses put forward elsewhere on the left or, again, (c) the social democratic reformism of the centre or right of the labour movement. By locating the debate over Thatcherism in both methodological and conjunctural terms, these similarities can be brought out and a common front established against other positions. This is particularly important politically but could also have important intellectual lessons.

4

Authoritarian Populism, 'Two Nations' and Thatcherism

Faced with the devastating electoral and political successes of Thatcherism in the past five years, the British left responded in various ways. Some activists anticipated the imminent collapse of Thatcherism due to a sudden upsurge of union militancy, popular disturbances or urban riots; or due to a Conservative U-turn prompted by rising unemployment and political unrest. Others called for the Labour Party to adopt more radical economic and political policies and to restructure itself as a vehicle for the eventual implementation of a socialist alternative economic strategy. They hoped that this would undermine Thatcherism by refuting its claim that there is no alternative; or that it would at least give the left the initiative when Thatcherism collapsed for other reasons. Yet others concentrated on the ideology of Thatcherism and called for a similarly ideological strategy from the left. They attributed Thatcherism's success to the initiatives of the New Right in constructing a new hegemonic project and mobilizing popular support for a rightwing solution to the economic and political crisis. Complementing this apparent celebration of Thatcherism is the charge that the left has failed to adopt a 'national-popular' approach of its own to ideological and political struggle and has fallen back on economistic or voluntaristic analysis of the growing crisis of social democracy and the left in Britain.

This last approach is represented above all in the work of Stuart Hall, but it has since been adopted quite widely on the left. The guiding thread of Hall's work is the argument that Thatcherism rests on 'authoritarian populism'. He argues that 'authoritarian populism' (hereafter AP) successfully condenses a wide range of popular discontents with the postwar economic and political order and mobilizes them around an authoritarian, rightwing solution to the current economic and political crisis in Britain. This success is regarded with grudging admiration because Thatcherism took the ideological struggle more seriously than the left and has reaped the reward of popular support. Some conclude that the left must articulate Thatcherite themes into its own discourse, but others, such as Hall, insist that Thatcherism can best be defeated by developing an alternative vision of the future, a socialist morality, and a socialist common sense. Thus the apparent ideological celebration of Thatcherism is complemented by an emphasis on ideological struggle in the socialist response. This approach has been much acclaimed on the left even if it has not yet become the dominant approach to Thatcherism.

The Ideological Celebration of Thatcherism

We criticize some implications of this approach in the present section and will consider alternatives below. Firstly, we argue that the precise meaning of 'authoritarian populism' is unclear and that this can lead to incoherent or inconsistent explanations. This derives in turn from an uncritical use of Gramsci's rather descriptive accounts of hegemony and/or from an over-extension of AP to very different fields and levels of social, political and ideological analysis. In particular these studies generalize too readily from changes in the ideological field to other areas of British society. This tends to obscure the real sources of support for Thatcherism because they are subsumed indiscriminately under the rubric of AP. This problem is compounded since the politics of electoral support is often conflated with the politics of governmental power. Thus the AP approach ignores some potential sources of contradiction and tension within Thatcherism and overstates its general strength and resilience.

In later sections we consider the economic and political background of Thatcherism and the specific characteristics of its economic and political strategy. Our account is not totally at odds with Hall's approach and it often accepts or expands themes found in *Policing the Crisis*[1] and *The Politics of Thatcherism*.[2] But we do wish to reject the 'ideologism' of the AP approach. Thus we also consider the political and institutional context in which Thatcherism developed, as well as the crisis of hegemony to which it represents one response. In particular we focus on the 'dual crisis of the state' as a neglected aspect of the crisis of the British state and on the 'two nations' character and effects of Thatcherism as a neglected aspect of its politics of power. We also argue that a one-sided emphasis on AP can produce mistaken conclusions about the most appropriate leftwing strategy to counter Thatcherism.

The Background to 'Authoritarian Populism'

The intellectual background to the AP approach is found in the work of Stuart Hall and his former associates at the Centre for Contemporary Cultural Studies.[3] Their work is directly concerned with historically specific, 'conjunctural' phenomena in the cultural and political fields and is strongly influenced by Gramsci's *Prison Notebooks*. The most significant source of the AP approach is the Centre's work on the 'moral panic' over mugging which occurred in Britain in 1972–3 and its wider political and ideological context. This study of *Policing the Crisis* charted the rise of an exceptional form of representative state in Britain and also alluded to the development of 'authoritarian populism'.[4] But it was other work by Stuart Hall himself which really sparked the debate on 'authoritarian populism' on the British left. An influential article on the rightward drift of British politics and culture appeared in January 1979,[5] and there has since been a spate of articles by Hall and others on AP and its implications for Thatcherism. *The Politics of Thatcherism* presents some of these contributions but there are many others.

Hall's use of the term 'authoritarian populism' is most directly concerned with the emergence and success of Thatcherism. But it also refers to a wider political transformation – aspects of which were first charted in *Policing the Crisis*. This described the general shift in the seventies towards the coercive, disciplinary pole of state power at the expense of the consensual, hegemonic pole. This is ascribed to the decay of the postwar settlement under Conservative hegemony in the fifties and the subsequent failure of a labourist, corporatist alternative. Thus the crisis worsened and class struggle intensified. By 1966 the social democratic alternative was so exhausted that crisis-management through whatever means became more urgent than reconstituting consensus. The shift towards open repression and the 'law-and-order' society gathered pace. However, faced with a massive political defeat at the hands of the miners in 1972, Heath returned to the corporatist strategy. The new Labour government in 1974 retreated further from the 'law-and-order' society but retained key elements of a more repressive mode of mass integration. There was also growing ideological polarization, a coordinated swing towards tougher social discipline on the right, and, most significantly, the capture of the leadership of the Conservative Party by the radical right represented by Margaret Thatcher.[6]

In his more recent work Hall describes the 1974–9 Labour government as 'pragmatic and creeping authoritarianism' but does not consider that the Labour Party itself presided over the constitution of 'authoritarian populism'. This must await the emergence of Thatcherism, which marks a qualitatively new stage in postwar British politics.

It is in this context that the contributions to *The Politics of Thatcherism* must be located. The general line in these essays is that 'Thatcherism' appeared at a historic conjuncture where three trends converged: first, the long-term structural decline of the British economy synchronized with the deepening into recession of the world capitalist economy; second, the collapse of the third postwar Labour government and the disintegration of the whole social democratic consensus which had provided the framework of British politics since 1945; third, the resumption of the 'new Cold War'.[7] Its contributors then deal with different aspects of Thatcherism, its policies and their impact. Among many issues discussed are the economy, trade unions, the welfare state and health service, women, law and order, and the party system.

However, although many contributions to *The Politics of Thatcherism* recognize the complex conjuncture to which Thatcherism corresponds, it is the notion of 'authoritarian populism' which has fired the imagination of many on the left. This is particularly clear in the specific strategic conclusions which have been drawn concerning the best response to Thatcherism. But we must first consider the problems involved.

The Ambiguities of 'Authoritarian Populism'

The notion of 'authoritarian populism' has a certain intuitive appeal to those on the left seeking to explain the apparently irrational support which Thatcherism has won for its attacks on working people. For it links with a respectable theoretical tradition concerned with hegemony and also attributes an authoritarian and recidivist character to the Thatcherite project. But behind this intuitive appeal lurk some significant inconsistencies and ambiguities. Indeed, the very phrase 'authoritarian populism' indicates these difficulties by coupling the notions of 'authority' and 'people'. Sometimes its authoritarian, disciplinary, coercive pole is emphasized, sometimes its populist, popular and consensual pole. This can be seen in several areas.

Hall notes that AP implies a convergence between the demands of those in authority and the pleas of the populace for the imposition of a solution to the current crisis. But at various times he has interpreted this as involving the rise of an exceptional form of the capitalist state, the routinization of coercion as the mode in which consent is secured, or simply the articulation of a new type of political project with popular support.[8]

Hall also relates AP to 'passive revolution'. Gramsci introduced the latter concept to describe a social transformation which occurs without mass mobilization – because it results from a gradual accumulation of small-scale, 'molecular' changes and/or because it is organized from above. When emphasizing its populist, popular, consensual aspects, Hall sees AP as a passive revolution from below; when emphasizing its authoritarian, disciplinary and coercive aspects, he regards it as a passive revolution from above.[9]

There is also some ambiguity concerning the relationship between the people and the power bloc. Sometimes Hall sees it as a *populist unity* between the people and the power bloc, so that organic links are constructed between the dominant and dominated classes; sometimes as a *populist rupture* in which the people are collectively mobilized against the power bloc; sometimes as a species of *populist ventriloquism* in which the power bloc speaks in the name of the people and dissimulates its own ideas as those of the people.[10]

More generally 'authoritarian' and 'populism' often have very different connotations. At various times AP is 'authoritarian' because it calls for a strong state and social discipline, is transformist in effecting a passive revolution from above, articulates authoritarian themes, or is hostile to popular-democratic ideas, movements and institutions. Likewise AP is 'populist' because it addresses a set of popular issues, stresses nationalist over sectional interests, redefines the nature of the British people, or simply appeals to the people. In short, it seems that the AP approach appeals to the left because it condenses a large number of interpretative schemes and can be stretched in different ways according to circumstances.

These ambiguities are not restricted to the analysis of Thatcherism but also influence accounts of other political phenomena. Thus Hall offers three different views on the rise of the Social Democratic Party: in terms of the general rightward drift which brought Thatcherism to power, in terms of the survival of the postwar social democratic consensus in the face of Thatcherism's 'damaging raids', and in terms of 'Social Caesarism' due to a catastrophic political vacuum.[11] These explanations could, of course, capture different aspects of the SDP. But this is never clarified and the ambiguities remain.

Indeed the very elasticity of the concept of AP is a source of inconsistencies and difficulties. This is why we argue that it mystifies the real sources of support for Thatcherism. But this does not mean all reference to 'authoritarian populism' must be expunged – merely that the term be used carefully. This might suggest that we could clarify its meaning and then proceed to analyse Thatcherism. But, insofar as the AP approach deals one-sidedly with the ideological dimension of Thatcherism, this would still involve real theoretical and political problems.

The Ideologism of 'Authoritarian Populism'

This ideological bias has three main sources. It is grounded in the intellectual origins of the AP approach, its preferred methodology and its substantive research focus. Firstly, with its deep foundations in

Gramsci's analyses of hegemony and its initial articulation with the Althusserian Marxist thematic of relative autonomy, there was already a danger that the AP approach would move in a politicist or ideologist direction. Hall subsequently moved away from Althusserian Marxism to a more 'discourse-theoretical' approach. Whereas the former involved a formal insistence on economic determination in the last instance, the latter tends to treat the effectivity of language and discourse as *sui generis* and autonomous. This reinforces the danger of ideologism – especially when it is coupled with a vehement opposition to 'economism' and 'class reductionism'.

Secondly, as his analysis of 'authoritarian populism' has developed, Hall has drawn increasingly on discourse theory. He examines hegemony in terms of the formation of social subjects and considers how Thatcherism articulates the relations between people and state. Thus 'authoritarian populism' is seen as an attempt radically to deconstruct the social democratic hegemonic framework involved in the postwar settlement and to construct a new 'common sense' and a new 'hegemonic project'. Hall now sees Thatcherism in terms of its mobilization of popular support through a chain of equivalences of the kind: market = free choice = freedom and liberty = anti-statism = put an end to creeping collectivism.[12] In emphasizing the specific discursive strategies involved in Thatcherism, AP risks ignoring other elements. In particular, it could neglect the structural underpinnings of Thatcherism in the economic and state systems and its specific economic and political bases of support among both people and power bloc.

Thirdly, in focusing on one area of social life (the media and politics as centres of ideological struggle), the AP approach treats it as a paradigm for other spheres of society. This generates an excessive concern with the mass media and ideological production at the expense of political and economic organization and the concrete reception of political ideologies within determinant conditions. There is barely any reference to the material rewards accruing to those sections of society, within and without the power bloc, who have supported the Thatcherite camp.

Thatcherism as Monstrous Monolith

Although Hall and others have raised the question of the audience's reception of ideologies, the danger remains of assuming that the 'message' as emitted is identical to the message as received and understood. The AP approach correctly notes that the Tories provided appealing explanations for the failure of Keynesianism, offered a means to express resistance to the defects of bureaucratic welfarism, legitimated the individuating experience of work in modern capitalism, etc. But it does not establish which of these messages, if any, were accepted and by whom. Thus the AP approach tends to homogenize the impact and universalize the appeal of Thatcherism.

The AP approach focuses on the ideological message of Thatcherism and thereby endows it with an excessively unified image. It sometimes implies that all sections of society support Thatcherism for the same (ideologically induced) reasons. This neglects possible internal cleavages within the social basis of Thatcherism. One wonders whether the 24 per cent of the unemployed and the 55 per cent of professional middle-class men who voted Conservative in 1983 really did so for the same reasons.

If we are to begin such an analysis, we must consider the appeal of Thatcher to individuals across a broad spectrum of social locations. Which aspects, if any, of the Thatcherite project appeal to small business owners, middle-aged workers, black people, the long-term unemployed and full-time housewives? Is the impact of authoritarian populism, as mediated through a national press, nationwide radio and network television, uniform across the country? Or are there marked regional differences between North and South, between England and the Celtic fringes? If the impact is not uniform, what accounts for this? How do we explain the marked volatility of support for Conservatives, Labour and Alliance between 1979 and 1983? Why was there a massive haemorrhage of skilled working-class votes from Conservative to Labour, then from Labour to SDP, then from SDP back to the Conservatives in the wake of the Falklands, and finally (but for how long?) a lesser swing back to Labour since the election of Kinnock to the leadership. What does it mean for Conservative support that the tax burden has risen for all but the top bracket of taxpayers, that unemployment has increased, and that there is still widespread support for the Beveridge system of social security and the NHS? Are anti-statist themes as resonant in the Conservative assault on the health service as in the attack on nationalized industries? In short, if we deconstruct Thatcherism, what follows for its popular impact? And, equally, what follows for socialist strategy?

Thatcherism must be seen less as a monolithic monstrosity and more as an alliance of disparate forces around a self-contradictory programme. We need to analyse the specific mechanisms by which specific groups were mobilized behind the general campaigning themes of 'resolute government', the 'national interest', patriotism, union bashing etc., rather than concentrate on those empty (or over-full?) phrases themselves. This would indicate the potential ruptures in the Thatcherite alliance. It would also reveal potential strengths in the Thatcherite project where support for Thatcherism might be widened and deepened as a result of Tory policies.

The Political Economy of Thatcherism

The AP approach concentrates on ideological outputs and thereby fails to challenge the New Right's account of the current situation. Thus it tends to accept Thatcher's rewriting of postwar history, in which 1979 marks a decisive break. This is implied in its confused account of the historical background to Thatcherism as the crisis of the postwar, social democratic settlement, and in its ambiguities concerning whether there is a new, popular consensus around authoritarian populism. Both implications must be challenged.

The Postwar Settlement

Firstly, the AP approach exaggerates the unity of the Keynesian Welfare State (hereafter KWS) and its social democratic character. It thereby tends to explain the failures of the KWS, the drift into a 'law-and-order society', and the eventual rise of 'authoritarian populism' in terms of the self-contradictory character of the Labour Party as the principal vehicle of the KWS. It chiefly focuses on the organizational and ideological repercussions of the contradiction between Labour's role as the *party* of the working *class* and its role as a *government* presiding over the *nation*. It is only in this context that the 'great moving right show' gets on the road and exploits the popular resentments against the social democratic and statist KWS system.[13] This approach connects neatly with a critique of the Labour Party for labourism, parliamentarism etc., but it also neglects other problems with the KWS. In particular it ignores the initial lack of socialist hegemony in the KWS, the self-contradictory character of the KWS system as established in Britain, and the absence of favourable economic and political conditions for the subsequent pursuit of a social democratic KWS. Thus, in privileging social democratic responsibility for the current crisis, the AP concedes too much to the Thatcherite critique of the postwar settlement as a manifestation of 'creeping socialism' and overweening statism.

It can certainly be accepted that the commitments to full employment and the creation and expansion of the welfare state were major elements in the postwar settlement. But these co-existed with support for the international reserve and transaction roles of sterling and for a military establishment and defence tasks which were incompatible with an effective KWS system.[14] In turn this reveals the hybrid and contradictory character of the postwar settlement and the limits of social democratic hegemony therein. There is an obvious genetic fallacy in arguing that, because Labour presided over the establishment of the welfare state and the commitment to full employment, these must have been socialist in political and ideological character. This argument not only ignores the prehistory of the 'road to 1945' (especially the role of Liberals and 'One Nation Tories' and the general character of the wartime coalition government) but also neglects the significance of 'Butskellism' and 'MacWilsonism' in the 1950s and 1960s.

Anthony Barnett has recently suggested that the distinctive cross-class and inter-party consensus that emerged from the coalition government (which he terms 'Churchillism') inhibited both the development of a vigorous, rightwing bourgeois party such as the Gaullist movement and the development of a nationally hegemonic Brandt/Schmidt type of social democracy.[15] This underlines the weakness of social democracy in Britain. Castles has likewise emphasized that the dynamic of the KWS under working-class hegemony in Scandinavia stands in marked contrast with the dynamic of the KWS in countries where bourgeois parties and/or the bourgeois class have retained political and ideological hegemony.[16] Similarly Ian Gilmour, in rejecting rightwing Conservative charges that his own Tory Party had been marching in a socialist direction since the Labour landslide in 1945, comments that the postwar consensus was 'founded upon making capitalism work . . . [and] was rather more of a Tory than a Socialist consensus'.[17]

The postwar consensus around the KWS was limited by the postwar consensus on Atlanticist foreign policy and City financial policy and was conducted not under the *hegemony* of the Labour Party and/or the working class, nor even of the industrial bourgeoisie, but under the *dominance* of financial capital. This must qualify any argument that there has been a radical break between a social democratic era and the present Thatcherite ascendancy. This holds in two senses. Firstly, there are some significant areas of continuity in such areas as foreign and diplomatic policy, subordination to US policy, policies on law and order, 'home affairs' more generally, Treasury dominance etc. And, secondly, crucial ruptures associated with Thatcherism were actually initiated during the period of so-called social democratic consensus: abandonment of full employment, public expenditure cuts and privileging the fight against inflation.[18] This suggests that Thatcherism has simply provided an ideological gloss to these tendencies and thereby reinforced them.

If the AP approach is right to argue that there can be no return to the Keynesian Welfare State *status quo ante*, this is not simply because Thatcherism has redefined the terrain of struggle and the political agenda. It is also because the KWS itself was fatally flawed *ab initio* for two reasons. It was articulated into a conservative rather than social-democratic political and ideological consensus; and pursued under constraints imposed by the economic dominance of City and international capitalist interests.

The Postwar Settlement in Crisis

The KWS became increasingly crisis-prone as the long wave of global capital accumulation was exhausted in the seventies and Britain's structural weaknesses became more severe. The contradictory framework of the KWS means that there has always been a political cycle in its development. This is seen in the politically mediated 'stop–go' cycle and a succession of liberal and corporatist political strategies. But this dynamic became more marked in the seventies. The growing crisis of the KWS witnessed a trade unionist and corporatist *offensive* by the labour movement (from the 1972 miners' strike through the 1974 elections and the early days of the Social Contract to the referendum on continued membership of the EC in 1975). This produced significant economic-corporate gains but no fundamental reorganization of capital, the state system or the power bloc to the long-term advantage of labour. Beneath the conjunctural fluctuations of economic and political power, the political and ideological hegemony of capital was only temporarily threatened and its economic dominance (especially that of the City and international capital) was not checked. After the exhaustion of the labour movement's offensive, there came a period of *relative stabilization*. The Labour government presided over this, but the real action occurred in civil society. Class forces were not so much in a state of paralysis as regrouping for the next round of struggle. Thus, whereas the Labour movement outside Parliament was going on the retreat and moving even further into an economistic and defensive war of manoeuvre (symbolized, *par excellence*, in the 'Winter of Discontent'), the right was preparing for an offensive in which a political and ideological war of position was given priority and the roll-back of the earlier economic-corporate gains of the labour movement was also placed on the political agenda.

Thatcherism is significant here because it provided the focal point around which the counter-offensive mobilized. This was all the more urgent because the international recession and the death-throes of the already flawed KWS made it impossible to return to the KWS *status quo ante* and demanded forward movement merely to stabilize the political system. This was also recognized on the left; but only the right engaged in the necessary war of political and ideological position.

In this sense Thatcherism does represent a break with the postwar settlement. But this must be carefully specified. It has neither produced a new, national-popular consensus nor created a new, organic power bloc. To establish these claims we consider first the popular appeal and impact of Thatcherism and then the initial backing it received from sections of the old power bloc.

Rupture or Continuity?

The AP approach sometimes implies that Thatcherism has hegemonized the people with a new and unified programme. Yet it is also recognized that many elements of Thatcherism have a long history in the electoral ideologies and perspectives of the Tory Party;[19] and that, 'though Thatcherism has proved to be an effective, populist force, it continues to be a minority one'.[20] This leaves serious ambiguities as to the real nature of the rupture produced by Thatcherism even on the ideological level. Our own view is that, if there is a novelty in Thatcherism, it lies in two areas. Firstly, Thatcherism has closed the gap between the AP and 'neo-liberal' electoral ideologies of grassroots Tories and the political perspectives of the Tory leadership – dislodging the old 'one nation' and 'right-progressive' Tories from control.[21] And, secondly, in linking 'authoritarian populism' and 'neo-liberalism' to a new *productivist* ideology, Thatcherism justifies an implicit 'Two Nations' strategy. But even here Thatcher has not yet articulated a full-blooded neo-liberal approach to the welfare state – instead she advocates a *social* market economy and has moved cautiously in tackling key elements in the welfare state.

It would be quite wrong to underestimate the pragmatism of Thatcher's strategy simply because she proclaims herself a conviction politician and appears to be ideologically motivated. From the moment she stood against Heath for the party leadership, the vehemence of the *oppositional* elements in her electoral perspectives has not been matched by an equally clear-cut programme of action for government. Style should not be confused with substance. Thatcherism changes continually in the light of circumstances. The AP approach demonstrates how Thatcherism has attempted to establish a chain of equivalences among themes such as monetarism, the strong state, law and order, the family etc. But it also tends to reify these linkages and to ignore their changing emphases and contexts.

The AP approach also seems to imply that working-class Conservatism is motivated by authoritarian populism as a new national-popular project. Yet Engels complained to Marx over a century ago that 'once again, the proletariat has discredited itself terribly',[22] and there has always been a sizeable working-class Conservative vote. This reflects the dual appeal of the Conservative Party as it mobilized two kinds of working-class support – deferential voters inspired by the 'traditional emotions' and secular, self-seeking voters.[23] This suggests that the support for Thatcherism should not be reduced to 'authoritarian populism' (which largely continues the appeal to the 'traditional emotions' in changed circumstances) but should also be related to more pragmatic interests in lower direct taxation, council house sales, rising living standards for those still in private sector employment, lower inflation, and so forth.[24]

Continuity rather than rupture is also seen in the Conservatives' failure to organize the working class politically (as opposed to receiving its votes). They made several attempts to do so after 1867 and failed – recruiting few activists and party officials (let alone MPs) among manual workers and having at best a marginal conservative trade union movement etc. This problem is still significant today. Thatcherite organizations are largely confined to the ideological sphere (Institute of Economic Affairs, National Viewers' and Listeners' Association, Festival of Light, Society for the Protection of the Unborn Child, etc.) and are only loosely connected with the Conservative Party. Moreover, even if there is considerable popular support for Thatcherism, it is not reflected in the economic and/or political organizations of the working class or the new middle class. This confirms that Thatcherism involves a passive revolution rather than mass mobilization – let alone a fascist mass mobilization.[25] Where are the Thatcherite 'new model' unions, the Tebbitt Labour Front, the Thatcherite Youth, the women's movement, Thatcherite sports leagues, rambling clubs, etc., which might consolidate and fix a mobilized working class? They do not exist and this highlights a certain vulnerability for the Thatcherite project.

We are clearly not arguing that Thatcherism could only survive if all its support from the working class (and other social forces) was motivated by 'authoritarian populism' and/or if the working class (and other social forces) were mobilized in Thatcherite organizations. We are merely pointing out that there is no single ideological or organizational basis of Thatcherism and that its success depends on other factors – including luck. It has certainly been fortunate in the disintegration of the Labour Party over issues such as industrial relations, the EEC, incomes policy, defence policy, etc., the formation of the SDP and the electoral impact of the SDP–Liberal Alliance.[26] Three areas of struggle will prove crucial in future. Firstly, the Thatcherite definition of the political agenda must be imposed and a Thatcherite common sense consolidated. Secondly, there must be continued success in the war of manoeuvre to *dis*organize the opposition to Thatcherism. And, thirdly, the Thatcher government must continue to deliver material concessions to at least some significant groups of electors.

The Economic Interests Behind Thatcherism

'Authoritarian populist' themes certainly appealed to grassroots Tories and others among the electorate. But this does not mean that AP directly influenced the economic policies pursued by Thatcherism and/or motivated their support among different class forces. The interesting question is how rhetoric for the Party faithful was translated into substantive programmes and policies. Popular support for AP arguments does not explain how powerful interests came to accept such stale nostrums. The answer must be sought in three areas: firstly, in the sphere of economic power; secondly, in the sphere of state structures and the dual crisis of the state; and, thirdly, in the circumstances of 'relative stabilization' and rightwing offensive surrounding Thatcher's election to the party leadership.

The economic interests behind Thatcherism cannot be reduced to those of the City and the multinationals. Rather Thatcherism is based upon an uneasy and potentially unstable alliance of interests. Firstly, the large increase in the size and mobility of market funds during the 1970s made it increasingly difficult for the authorities to use open market operations to control interest and exchange rates. The government was therefore faced with the alternatives of tighter controls or the promotion of laissez-faire in the financial markets to allow them to determine interest and exchange rates. The City was strongly opposed to the former but could happily support the latter insofar as control of the money supply was achieved by a deflationary fiscal policy. These City interests received political and ideological expression through Sir Keith Joseph's 'conversion' to monetarism and anti-statism and through the role of leading City commentators and financial journalists as the organic intellectuals of a new economic strategy.[27]

Secondly, the moves towards monetarist targeting in the US Federal Reserve Bank and the IMF stimulated changes in the Bank of England's view (and in the City more generally) and this contributed to the Callaghan–Healey administration's adoption of 'technical monetarism' under pressure from the IMF. Thirdly, although the Treasury was sceptical about the mechanism and costs of monetarism *per se*, it welcomed this ideological shift as helpful to its traditional campaign to limit public expenditure and tame the fiscal crisis.

Fourthly, on the industrial front, few anticipated the depth of the coming recession, and the CBI welcomed the promises of lower inflation and tax cuts for businessmen. There was also a widespread desire to use the recession to 'reimpose managerial authority'. Furthermore, the City and neo-liberal Conservatives hoped the recession would force the industrial restructuring which corporatism had failed to deliver. Finally, the unions were to be excluded from the policy making process, and this also appealed to the City and key industrial sectors (see below).

The Dual Crisis of the British State

This coalition of interests provided the Thatcher government with the initial economic authority to implement radically new policies just as its electoral mandate provided political authority and AP provided ideological

legitimacy. But these relatively conjunctural factors were reinforced by
the 'dual crisis' of parliamentarism and corporatism in the postwar
British state. For there are simultaneous, albeit unevenly developed,
crises in the spheres of parliamentary representation and corporatist (or
functional) representation. The development of the KWS and other
forms of intervention in postwar Britain has undermined the role of
parliamentarism, but no effective alternative (such as corporatism) has
been evolved. Yet, without suitable forms of 'democratic' consultation
and/or regulation corresponding to different spheres and forms of state
intervention, the effectiveness of state policies is undermined and their
legitimacy is questioned. This was increasingly true of Britain in the
sixties and seventies.

The combination of parliamentary and corporatist modes of interest
intermediation, and their specialization in different political and economic
tasks, are supposed to enhance the adaptive capacities of the political
system.[28] But in Britain neither mode of political representation can
function in the appropriate manner. Each is subject to a complex crisis
affecting its institutional form, its representational ties, and its economic
and political rationality.[29] In turn this is overdetermined by the dynamic
of class (and non-class) relations and the economic and political strategies
pursued by different social forces. The combination of these crises
intensifies the effects of each. This aggravates the problems of the
British state in securing its operational unity, economic and political
efficacy, and overall legitimacy.

This is reflected in the increased *decisional autonomy* of the state elite.
But is also associated with the declining economic and political *efficacy*
of state intervention through rational-legal administration of measures
in accord with the substantive rule of law *and/or* through corporatist
means. These crises created the opening for the enhanced decisional
autonomy of the Thatcher government to pursue its programme in the
face of a crisis-prone party system and an unstable and ineffective
corporatism.[30]

In particular the trade union movement and business associations
remain so decentralized and fragmented that they cannot play any
efficient (as opposed to 'dignified') long-term role in the formulation,
coordination and implementation of an effective incomes policy or an
active structural policy. This is reinforced in the British case by the
separation of the industrial and political wings of the Labour movement
and the dominance of the City and multinational corporate interests
within the Conservative Party. In both cases this has complicated the
problem of coordinating functional representation and parliamentary
representation.

Given the continuing structural crisis of the British economy and the
failure of Keynesianism and post-Keynesian techniques, it is not really
surprising that monetarism found increasing favour in some quarters,

for it allegedly cut through the knotty problem of how to regenerate the British economy when tripartism and state intervention had failed. In future it would be unnecessary to consult trade unions and to make them concessions in return for non-binding and undeliverable sacrifices. It would also be unnecessary to establish elaborate bureaucracies for discriminatory state intervention, whose attempts to use taxpayers' money and *ad hoc* rules to promote economic growth were throwing good money after bad and destroying business confidence in the stability of its decision-making environment. At the same time monetarism could be sold to the electorate in terms of its purported tax cuts, reduced inflation, increased incentives etc., and its homely connotations of sound housekeeping and restored responsibilities for the family at the expense of the 'governess state'.

To the crisis of corporatism must be added the crisis of the parliamentary and party systems. Three aspects are particularly important here. The growing difficulties facing KWS economic strategy are reflected in the breakdown of the inter-party consensus on accumulation (leading to divergent economic strategies) and the exacerbation of intra-party conflicts (notably within the Labour Party but also between an emergent 'New Right' and the disorganized 'right progressive' or 'One Nation' tendency in the Conservative Party). The third aspect is the conjoint impact of the crisis of the KWS and inter- and intra-party conflicts upon the social bases of the political party system and its capacities to integrate diverse social and economic groups into the capitalist order. This is reflected in the growing volatility of electoral support for the established parties (and, judging by recent evidence, the Liberal–SDP Alliance) and the development of significant marginal groups whose interests and/or demands find no channels of representation within the established parliamentary and party systems. Together these three aspects call into question the capacities of the prevailing system to perform their integrative, legitimatory and accumulation functions.

Given the crisis of the Conservative Party, there was a space for the resurgence of petty bourgeois *ressentiment* and its increasing influence in the counsels of the Conservative Party.[31] At the same time the crisis of representation within the Labour Party and the more general process of partisan *de-alignment* meant that there was an increasing mass of potentially floating voters. This encouraged a growing resort to *populism*, that is, direct appeals to the 'people' over the heads of their representatives in competing parties and Parliament. This 'populism' is of a quite specific kind. It is not concerned with an active populist mobilization – which would be threatening to the decisional autonomy of Thatcherism. Instead it is concerned to outflank organized opposition from government backbenchers (especially the so-called wets) as well as from the labour movement. For, if Thatcher represents the people directly, opposition can be presented as undemocratic. In this sense Thatcherite populism is indeed predominantly plebiscitary and ventriloquist in character: Thatcher speaks in the name of the people against all sectional interests, including those in her own party.[32]

Thus we disagree with Keith Middlemas, who argued shortly after the 1983 general election that Margaret Thatcher had restored the primacy of party over the system of corporate bias in British politics.[33] Whilst Thatcherism has systematically demoted the role of functional representation in political and economic crisis-management, it has not presided over a reassertion of parliamentary control mediated through the political party system. The Conservatives certainly won a landslide victory in 1983, which enhances their capacities to control the Commons; but this control is very much one that is orchestrated *from above*, by a small prime ministerial clique within (but not necessarily of) the Cabinet together with Thatcher's official and irregular advisers. In the last five years the concentration and centralization of power in the state administration has accelerated at the expense of Parliament and parties. Britain is moving towards a presidential system: government legitimacy is dependent upon the popular prestige of the Prime Minister and her ability to appeal directly to the people. Moreover, alongside the resort to populism, there is an increasing appeal to *raison d'état* to justify decisions. Populism and prerogative powers further enhance the decisional autonomy of government. But, as the series of policy errors and political embarrassments – the so-called banana skins – since the general election indicates, decisional autonomy does not guarantee good government. In this respect the crisis of parliamentarism and the party system continues and the formulation and implementation of policy (including economic strategy) lacks the necessary democratic regulation from the party system as well as from functional representation.

This affects monetarism as well as other areas of government policy. Although monetarism appears to offer a way out of the impasse of economic policy created by the dual crisis of the state, it does so only by divorcing economic policy making from any effective anchorage in *formal* political and economic representation. This has certainly enhanced Thatcherism's room for manoeuvre in pursuing its monetarist strategy in the face of rising unemployment, continued de-industrialization, rising levels of taxation, increasing proportions of state spending in GDP, deterioration in the non-oil balance of trade, and so forth. It remains to be seen whether this has also made the strategy more coherent and capitalistically rational through the increased *relative autonomy* which it offers Britain's 'Bonaparte in petticoats'.

Economic Failure, Political Success

The formation and implementation of Thatcherite policy and its implications for hegemony are less concerned with popular mobilization than with the complex relations among the dominant classes and the structural crisis in the state. Even Thatcher's populism must be located in relation to these aspects of the power bloc and the state. 'Authoritarian populism' explains little here, compared with its power in explaining how policies are legitimated and accepted. For Thatcherism does offer justifications for public expenditure cuts and the loading of costs on to the weakest or the unionized – something Labour could never do. But many fundamental shifts in common sense, such as the priority to reduce inflation and the need to weaken the unions, do not derive directly from authoritarian populism. Thatcherism has certainly diminished the credibility of alternative economic approaches and has also convinced many people that future benefits will follow from present suffering. Dissatisfaction with present policies has been contained within manageable bounds. These bounds could burst open, however, if the benefits are too long coming. It is here that the weakest link in Thatcher's hegemonic chain of office can be found.

Indeed, once we examine her political programme, we discover significant sources of opposition as well as possible bases of support. Whilst there are some policies and programmes which might seem to deliver material concessions and/or disorganize the forces opposed to Thatcherism, there are others which would seem to threaten Thatcherism's social bases of support and to provide a basis for unified resistance. Moreover, if the policies do not succeed, Thatcherite common sense would also be undermined.

Thatcher's Economic Experiment

If monetarism means that the rate of growth of the money supply is closely controlled in order to affect the price level, then Thatcher has failed to be monetarist. Instead inflation has dropped as a result of lower commodity prices in the world recession, massive unemployment, capital's inability to raise prices as competition intensified, and the huge collapse in economic activity as Britain was hastened into recession at least a year ahead of other nations. Anti-inflation policy remains central but it has been achieved through generalized deflation rather than effective control of the money supply. This has obvious strategic implications as workers' power is devastated and the senile areas of British industry suffer involuntary euthanasia. But there is a basic contradiction at the heart of this strategy – there is no real means of ensuring productive restructuring, investment and innovation to secure sustained recovery and growth. Meanwhile the strong state acts to sort out the unions and liberate the entrepreneurs. This involves a leap of faith: there is little evidence that, once unions have been shackled and entrepreneurs liberated, markets will autonomously generate domestic expansion without any substantial governmental direction or coordination. Diminishing the state's economic role and abolishing inflation are supposed to create the climate for recovery. Yet the means to that end is a constant dampening of economic activity through the Medium Term Financial Strategy and panic cuts to sustain both the MTFS and the confidence of financial markets. All the while the life blood of productive investment haemorrhages abroad and public capital spending collapses at home.

Thus stagflation is replaced by simple stagnation as disinflation and reduced budget deficits displace direct efforts to secure profitable accumulation. Piecemeal facilitative subsidy and intervention still thrive, but there is no semblance of an industrial policy and little acknowledgement of the need for a propitious combination of a strong domestic market (not overwhelmed by import penetration) and government purchasing to allow even 'sunrise' industries to flourish. There is no guarantee that the slump wipes out only the backward and dying firms. A role is also played by contingent factors such as debt ratios, dependence on public works, sensitivity to exchange rates and import penetration. Open markets, sound money and free capital movements may well be a recipe for City profits (and perhaps for the multinationals as well), but they also store up a long-term crisis for expansion and employment. So, having preached a combination of monetarism and laissez-faire, unified by the dominance of disinflationary policy, the government has nowhere to go and nothing to do once inflation falls and stagnation continues.

This outlook entails that the fiscal crisis generated by the recession policies will be met by increased pressure on 'current account' costs in social security and unemployment benefit. It is these costs, together with youth 'training', nuclear 'defence', and 'policing the crisis', which generate fiscal pressures – not the allegedly excessive demands imposed by rampant pressure-group democracy. Capital investment has been sacrificed to such costs since 1974. Even where cuts have involved restructuring or privatization, these have not been coordinated for a rational pursuit of efficiency or service. The cuts have a direct public impact and their supposed benefits recede even further.

The Declining Tory Vote

We now turn to the political impact of the Thatcherite project. This must be considered on three levels: the politics of support, the recasting of the institutional forms of political domination, and the recomposition of the power bloc. One of the most significant areas of the politics of support is the partisan alignment of the electorate. Here the picture is very mixed.

The Tory vote has been in decline since 1931, the Labour vote has been eroded steadily since 1951 and the Liberals have been gaining more votes for the last three decades; the big cities have been moving against the Tories from 1959, the South-East against Labour since 1966; the North–South divide has been deepening since 1945. Together these trends mean that, in the North, Labour was largely fighting the Conservatives in 1983 and, in the South, the Tories were largely fighting the Alliance. The Tories have also been losing support in the 'Celtic fringes' since the mid-fifties and have already lost their Unionist base in Northern Ireland. In addition the Conservatives' traditional relative advantage among the professional middle class and among white-collar workers has been steadily eroded. Likewise women and black voters have increasingly moved away from the Tories.[34]

The need to reconstitute the electoral base of the Conservative Party was clear after the Heath administration's failures between 1970 and 1974. Thatcher promised to break with 'One Nation' consensus politics and to develop a new appeal. Indeed, despite its rhetoric of the common good and of healing the division in society, Thatcherism is clearly engendering new cleavages and polarizing society. The 'traditional emotions' are significant here but so is the pragmatic appeal to those linked to the productive sectors of the economy. The promise of greater material rewards and lower taxes played a key role in the recomposition of the Conservative vote. Thus 'the fact that the Tory Party actually increased its vote among skilled manual workers means that the relative Conservative unpopularity here had almost disappeared by 1983. Thatcher's unique success with skilled workers enabled her to arrest – even to reverse in the short-term – the structural decline in Tory support'.[35] At the same time it is the skilled working-class vote which has proved most volatile, and as a result the Conservative Party remains vulnerable. In this sense we agree with Hall and Jacques when they write that 'Thatcherism's strength reflects the labour movement's weaknesses'.[36]

Recasting the State

When she was first elected to office, Thatcher was obliged to engage in various compromises and concessions to consolidate political support. This helps to explain the inconsistencies in Thatcherite policies during her first phase in power. But the Falklands crisis was a fundamental factor in entrenching her personal position and the policies with which she is identified. She has also proceeded apace with restructuring the state, so that the impact of these policies is reinforced and institutionalized. In turn this would make it more difficult to reverse Thatcherism should

Labour return to power. In particular the state has been Thatcherized through civil service reorganization and politically motivated promotion to key official posts; through the enhancement of Treasury control over all areas of government; through a much reinforced policing apparatus and redefinition of 'subversion'; through the radical centralization of government power and the assault on local government; through a programme of denationalization and competition which would be difficult to reverse; through privatization in the welfare state – thereby constructing new interests around private provision both among clients and within the professions and supply industries; through the radical restructuring of education and the expansion of the Manpower Services Commission (MSC); and so forth. The extent to which these new forms, areas, and patterns of state activity are reversible varies; but each constitutes at least a short-term obstacle to an alternative economic and political strategy. This has important implications for the development of the political struggle.

Margaret Thatcher's 'Two Nations'

Government policies are having a complex and uneven impact on such societal cleavages as productive/parasitic, rich/poor, North/South, employed/unemployed, etc. This impact is often unintended or, at least, goes unarticulated. The Tory contributions to the 1984 budget debate, for example, rarely spoke of – let alone to – the unemployed. The nature of these cleavages has changed as Thatcherism has shifted its battle ground from opposition to the old consensus to construction of the new order. Increasingly Tory populism is taking the form of unification of a privileged nation of 'good citizens' and 'hard workers' against a contained and subordinate nation which extends beyond the inner cities and their ethnic minorities to include much of the non-skilled working class outside the South-East. In this sense we believe that Thatcherism can fruitfully be seen as a 'two nations' project. We would highlight the following factors:

1   Thatcherism has broken with the Conservative 'one nation' approach to the KWS. In both its social democratic and Tory 'one nation' versions the KWS was presented as an attempt to integrate the poor, deprived and underprivileged into membership of the community through economic growth, full employment and, increasingly, universal welfare benefits. This concern was heavily qualified, of course, by incompatible financial and military commitments (see above). Moreover, the KWS commitments were more honoured in the breach than in their successful fulfilment – a fact which became increasingly evident as private experiences became public knowledge in the sixties and seventies. But Thatcherism explicitly rejects these commitments: it is more concerned with managing the political

repercussions of an 'underclass' whose existence is taken for granted rather than seen as a rebuke to society's conscience. Indeed it is happy to expand this underclass of the unemployed and new waged poor to stimulate the purgative effects of economic crisis. It also intends to cut an allegedly overgrown welfare state and to construct a minimal, selective, 'social security' state akin to that in the United States.

2   The KWS rested on an image of social divisions in terms of *multiple, horizontal* strata with more or less access to desired values. Sometimes these strata were identified in class terms, but no fundamental antagonism between the different classes was implied. All were actual or potential members of the 'one nation'. In contrast Thatcherism presents an image of social divisions based on a *single, vertical* cleavage stretching from top to bottom of society which opposes the productive to the parasitic. This opposition between 'two nations' is seen as inherently antagonistic and cannot be transcended through the collectivism of the KWS. In general the productive sector is held to comprise those who produce goods and services that can be profitably marketed without the need for state subsidies. The parasitic include not only the various pauper classes (the unemployed, pensioners, the disabled etc.) but also those whose economic activities in the public or private sectors are unprofitable in terms of capitalist forms of accounting. Only those state employees are excluded whose activities are essential to the minimal nightwatchman role of the state – the police, armed forces, tax gatherers etc. This is not to suggest that Thatcherism reduces all social antagonisms to the 'productive/parasitic' cleavage in some sort of discourse of equivalence. Other dichotomies are also deployed in Thatcherism, for example individual freedom vs. state coercion, East vs. West etc. But the 'productive/parasitic' distinction does provide a most useful insight into the dynamic of Thatcherism.

3   In terms of the politics of support, the 'two nations' approach requires that the productive be rewarded *through the market* for their contribution to production (or at least to the provision of profitable marketed goods and services); conversely the parasitic must suffer for their failure to contribute adequately (if at all) to the market (with little regard to the question of whether they are 'deserving' or otherwise). In this way Thatcherism hopes to recompose the conservative working class in a secular, instrumentalist, privatized direction, to bring about a more productivist orientation in the trade union movement, and to encourage greater investment and risk-taking etc. At the same time the declining revenues and deteriorating conditions affecting the parasitic will eventually force them back into the market or, at least, minimize their burden on the taxpayer and productive elements in society.

4   In terms of the politics of power, the 'two nations' approach requires both administrative re-commodification and further state intervention to create the conditions favourable to greater production. And, insofar as this hurts marginal or marginalizable groups, it also requires increased repression and police measures. There is an authoritarian element in the Thatcherite programme. But it is much better interpreted in terms of the problems of

economic and political *crisis-management*, in a context of re-commodification and retrenchment, than in terms of a generalized authoritarian populism.

The Limits of 'Two Nations'

The further pursuit of this emergent 'two nations' strategy could powerfully consolidate Thatcherism and leave Labour to defend the weak and marginal sections of society. Thus the fundamental political choice could become one between a new, 'two nation' Toryism and a 'one nation' rightwing social democracy from the Alliance. Fortunately there are some powerful counter-tendencies to this:

1   Popular support for the welfare state, and especially the health service, remained strong during the election and the Tories were obliged to commit themselves to a 'no cuts' policy. This support is reinforced by the opposition of public sector unions to further reductions in this area. Despite the fact that in the short term Lawson has forced through the public spending cuts required by the MTFS, the dilemma between raising taxes or cutting public services – given expanding commitments to defence and law and order – cannot be avoided in the medium term (1985/6).[37]

2   At present the 'second nation' is highly fragmented but there are multiple sites of resistance – especially at the local level. There is increasing evidence of politicization and a broadening of perspectives within the new social movements (especially the feminist movement and CND) and at the level of local trades councils and local government. It may yet prove possible to move 'beyond the fragments' if the Labour Party only plays a more constructive role here on the national level.

3   The government's strategy towards local government, and the metropolitan councils in particular, has already produced considerable opposition going well beyond Labour Party circles. Indeed, it has already generated major conflicts in the Conservative Party in Parliament and the country at large.

4   The combined effects of Conservative legislation and mass unemployment have not yet tamed the unions. The precise outcome of the 1984–5 miners' strike will have major implications for both government and unions. Should the miners inflict a defeat on the government, this will force a new 'realism' upon it; while if not, the interrupted movement towards a new 'realism' within the unions may regain strength.

5   The law-and-order issue is highly complex. Recent policies have provoked civil libertarian and professional opposition, as well as working-class resistance to new forms of 'policing' the economic crisis, ranging from the 1981 riots to the miners' strike itself.

It is clear from this brief survey that Tory hegemony is by no means consolidated. The Labour movement is still deeply divided over its response to Thatcherism but remains defensively strong. Moreover, although the middle classes are unlikely to form the hard core of a future socialist movement (as opposed to its Alliance opposition), some sections are hostile to Thatcherism and could open cleavages advantageous to the left. Two further weaknesses should be noted. Firstly, since the main redistributional effects of state services are across the life-cycle, many of the privileged 'good citizens' will feel the direct consequences of any cuts during child-rearing and retirement – this represents a major obstacle to the 'two nations' strategy. Secondly, insofar as rapid inflation has been the basis for the creation of an inchoate populist category of 'consumers', whose interests in the moderation of inflation have been mobilized to justify public spending cuts, then the reduction of inflation may undermine the argument for further cuts – and most people prefer better public services to further tax cuts.

A Thatcherite Power Bloc?

We now consider the politics of power and Thatcherism's support within the dominant classes. Unfortunately the AP approach diverts attention from the power bloc in Britain and the shifting relations within this so-called Establishment. There are also weaknesses in Thatcher's project here.

The coalition of interests whereby Thatcher achieved a 'warrant of autonomy' for her policies – a 'mandate to impose transitional costs' – has already been described. To what extent does this 'warrant' continue? And has Thatcher consolidated a power bloc? The role of the state in organizing a power bloc has long been recognized, and there can be little doubt that Thatcherism has already had major repercussions on the state. But the state does not constitute the power bloc simply through some act of will or through some automatic political mechanism. Currently the reorganization of the power bloc seems limited by Thatcher's distaste for the concessions involved in building a power bloc and by the contradictions in the sources of support for Thatcherism. In turn these must be related to the more general structural contradictions in the nature and location of British capital. But to complement our analysis of the popular support for Thatcherism, we still need to consider the prospects for a new power bloc in Britain.

1   The City was pleased with the move to laissez-faire in the financial markets, but a powerful current also bemoaned the ensuing volatility in the exchange and interest rates. This current favoured a stabilization policy by the government – the conflict between the government and the City was reflected in the sacking of the Governor of the Central Bank. The City would undoubtedly like to see further public spending cuts to contain the PSBR, but we should not forget that the City can continue to prosper on the basis of an upturn in the global economy – hence its concern with high US

interest rates – even if the relative decline of the UK economy continues apace.

2　Industry in general has welcomed the reduction in inflation and the opportunity to 'reimpose managerial authority'. But neither of these gains could be guaranteed during a prolonged recovery. The reported increase in productivity appears to have been largely the result of a one-off shake-out of labour and an epidemic of bankruptcies. Meanwhile industry is still unhappy with high interest rates, the level of the national insurance surcharge, the failure to reduce taxation, the level of local property taxes (rates), and the worsening imbalance between public expenditure on the capital and current accounts. In addition some industrialists regret the absence of a concerted industrial policy.

3　Most crucially the perennial problem of restructuring remains. As John Ross has demonstrated, 'essentially, the experience of British capital under Thatcher breaks down into three categories. First, certain economic sectors underwent rapid growth almost throughout the recession . . . oil. agriculture, communications, finance and electrical engineering . . . Second, a series of sectors of the economy underwent no major decrease in output at all . . . food, drink, and tobacco manufacturing, mining, and retailing. Third, the sectors which underwent massive decline under Thatcher were general manufacturing and construction'.[38] In a period of rapid structural change, profits are not necessarily made by the firms which want new plant and machinery. Thus financial intermediaries become crucial. But the commercial nature and overseas orientation of the City mean that – in the absence of a concerted industrial policy by the state – the key role will devolve to the clearing banks. This hardly augurs well for industrial regeneration.

4　The current policy of privatization could serve several purposes here. It could create new sources of support for a Thatcherite power bloc and also bail out the PSBR, thereby sustaining Thatcherite economic strategy. Whatever the long-term economic rationale behind these policies, their short-term impact on the power bloc should not be ignored.

5　The unions, notwithstanding the NEDC, the MSC, etc., remain excluded from the policy-making process and are in a weak position vis-à-vis capital. They have been forced into taking a largely reactive role with respect to government policy. Nor has there been any resolution of the crisis of Labour Party–union relations.

6　Finally we would note Thatcherism has done little to solve the dual crisis of representation as an essential preliminary to a political reconstitution of the power bloc. It is precisely because the crisis of the state persists that Thatcherism retains its warrant of autonomy. During the first Thatcher government the maintenance of political domination depended on a series of short-term tactical shifts rather than a coherent long-term policy. However, the Falklands war marked the end of the first phase of Thatcherism and the beginnings of its stabilization. Following the election victory of 1983 and the budget of 1984 there appears to be a more coherent, long-term strategy at work. This is more directly concerned with the needs of economic regeneration and political reconstruction for the next long wave of capitalist expansion. Whether it succeeds in reconstituting the power bloc remains to be seen.

In conclusion, Thatcher's warrant persists with general support from the City, mixed blessings from industry, and divided opposition from organized labour. The City can continue to prosper independently of the fortunes of the domestic economy; but with respect to industry, the problem remains. Nevertheless the traditional weakness of the CBI as a peak organization of capital, the power of the small business ideology of economic liberalism, the European connections of the multinationals, and the absence of an alternative (they could hardly support the left's alternative economic strategy!), mean that industry still goes largely unrepresented and remains passive. Can Thatcher consolidate a 'two nations' strategy based on the 'sunrise industries' and the South-East while the rest of British capital, especially manufacturing industry, experiences continued decline? There are many obstacles to such a strategy, some of which we have already described, but other factors seem more propitious.

Concluding Remarks

Above all, Thatcher's room for manoeuvre will depend on the left's capacity to develop a coherent and unified response. Even in relation to Thatcher's economic strategy, this response involves more than the labour movement and should be extended to other social forces. When we consider the more general social restructuring which Thatcherism is attempting, the role of new social movements would become even more significant in fracturing Thatcher's populist appeal. In turn this must obviously be linked with tactics to intensify divisions in the Thatcherite coalition and to develop an 'alternative vision of the future'. In the meantime her enhanced decisional autonomy continues to rest upon an uneasy coalition of interests – she lacks both the active support of the whole of British capital and any support from organized labour.

The Proper Scope of 'Authoritarian Populism' as an Interpretation

In reviewing interpretations of Thatcherism as 'authoritarian populism', we have argued that they are incoherent, mystifying, celebratory, homogenizing and so forth. Does this mean that the notion of AP should be rejected out of hand? We would argue that there is a rational kernel in these interpretations and that it is important to safeguard it. The problem with AP is that the concept has been overused in discussing Thatcherism. In the following remarks we summarize our own view of the proper scope for this interpretation.

Common Sense   AP could refer to a new common-sense, practical morality, philosophy, and ethic. Insofar as it is a new common sense (or a rearticulation of older common-sensical themes), it would have no necessary class or partisan belonging but would inform the attitudes, activities and loyalties of people from various classes and partisan constituencies. AP is suggestive here and could be further explored.

Political Agenda   AP could refer to a new political agenda, that is, to new issues and political priorities. Thus, just as the KWS settlement placed full employment and social welfare on the political agenda (alongside the commitment to sterling and a defence role East of Suez), greater economic freedom and individual responsibility together with the strengthening of the state apparatus in its new, more restricted role could have been placed on the agenda through the rise of AP. But the shifts in the political agenda are by no means exhausted by AP, nor are they equally shared by all parties.

Hegemonic Project   AP could also refer to a definite hegemonic project which articulates an alternative vision of the national-popular interest with the specific policies necessary to secure its realization. These projects may well vary across parties even though the background assumptions of common sense and political agenda remain the same; or the same party could formulate successive hegemonic projects to meet changing circumstances within the same framework. Despite some consensus on an AP agenda, the major parties are far from sharing the same vision of the national-popular interest. Likewise the Conservative party itself has not always given the same weight to AP elements in its own national-popular project.

Accumulation Strategy   AP could refer to a specific strategy for economic regeneration and expansion. This is most unlikely. Perhaps this is why many critics have defined Thatcherism as 'neo-liberalism' plus 'authoritarian populism' or as 'a social market economy' plus 'the strong state' – that is, as an accumulation strategy articulated with an AP orientation. Although an anti-statist rhetoric of freedom and responsibility has been deployed in defence of Thatcher's accumulation strategy, the notion of AP is particularly unhelpful in grasping its specificities.

Electoral Ideologies   AP could refer to the electoral ideology of a political party, the themes that are articulated among party activists and its committed voters. AP provides a useful insight into the electoral ideology of Tory supporters, especially in the constituency organizations; but there is nothing particularly novel here, because some form of AP has long been a major element in conservatism. Whether AP now figures in other parties' electoral ideologies is debatable.

Electoral Perspectives   We agree with Andrew Gamble in distinguishing electoral perspectives from electoral ideologies.[39] Perspectives refer to the way in which party leaders reconcile the electoral ideologies of rank-and-file activists and the views of the mass electorate as a precondition of winning office. There was certainly a significant shift in the Tory Party from the Butskellite period (but also a return to the themes stressed in the Edwardian and inter-war periods) insofar as the Conservatives placed much greater stress on AP in their mass electoral appeal under Thatcher. This was particularly clear in the 'realigning election' of 1979 but less obvious in 1983. In both cases, however, AP elements were articulated with other themes, such as neo-liberalism, egoism, nationalism etc.

Government Programmes   AP might also refer to the specific 'politics of power' pursued by the Conservative government. Policies such as privatization, industrial relations reform, public spending cuts, higher defence spending, support for information technology, the activities of the MSC, the attack on local government autonomy, etc., may sometimes receive an AP justification for presentational purposes. But their real motive force is often located elsewhere – including short-term expediency, political miscalculation, neo-liberal commitments, the 'special relationship' with the USA, directives from the EEC, etc. Governmental programmes cannot just be read off from electoral ideologies and/or perspectives.

Electoral Recomposition   AP has sometimes been invoked to explain the recomposition of the electorate along party lines. But there has always been a strong AP element in the electorate, which went unvoiced in the electoral perspectives and appeals of the Butskellite era (the so-called 'silent majority'); equally, the swing to the Conservatives could have as much to do with instrumental calculation, secular concerns more generally, electoral volatility, negative voting etc., as with AP.

Power Bloc Decomposition   Significant shifts in the domain of the power bloc do seem to have occurred – although a new, organic bloc has not yet emerged. It is important to analyse the internal decomposition of the power bloc in terms other than those of AP – although it might have encouraged this decomposition through the development of a populist rupture. We are also unconvinced that AP is the key element enabling the crisis-torn power bloc to win a partial, provisional and unstable hegemony over the people.

Reorganization of the State   The restructuring of the state under Thatcherism can be illuminated by AP. The emphasis on law and order, the strengthening of the state apparatus, the concentration and centralization of power, the increased central state influence over education, youth training, welfare etc., do seem to be linked to AP and problems of crisis-management. But it is still necessary to distinguish between the structural problems and/or ideological crisis that have provoked such reorganization and the justifications offered for it.

Changes in the Ideological Field   The concept of AP is particularly useful in understanding the changing role of the mass media, especially the popular press, in the ideological struggle. But we should not over-generalize from the media to other sites of ideological contestation.

From Ideologism to Politicism?

So far we have concentrated on a critique of the AP approach to Thatcherism but retained crucial elements from it; and we have presented our own, more political and institutional analysis. Thus we would seem open to the recent criticism that

> it is not serious to suggest, as is sometimes done, that the relation of companies to the Conservative Party, or a phenomenon such as Thatcherism, is simply based on 'ideology' or 'purely political' consider-ations . . . there is also a very clear economic dimension. Certain sections of the capitalist class have gained enormously from the Conservative Party in general and Thatcherism in particular and continue to finance the Tory Party to a high degree. Other economic sectors have ceased to gain as much as before and are withdrawing their level of funding.[40]

Since we have ourselves dwelt on political and ideological motivations, does this mean that our analysis is not serious?

Firstly, Ross does not deny that ideology and politics are important but he does want to emphasize the direct economic motivations involved in business support for Thatcherism. We also discuss the economic dimensions of Thatcherism and the economic interests mobilized behind it. Moreover, whilst taking 'ideology' and 'politics' seriously, we deny that AP is directly relevant to the origins of Tory economic policies or the motives of those economic interests which initially backed Thatcherism. Indeed we find Ross's statistics impressive.

But we cannot agree with an analysis which virtually reduces Thatcherism to its benefits to specific branches of the British economy, as reflected in their declared rates of profit. For Ross does not specify the precise mechanisms through which this correlation is realized. Instead he implies that it is through the dominance of these interests in the counsels of the Conservative Party and/or through the spontaneous, *post hoc* gratitude of specific interests to the Party which has advanced their profits. This is a crudely instrumentalist view which ignores the relative autonomy of the state and the complexities of political struggle. It gives no real explanation of the shift in economic strategy in Britain from Keynesianism to monetarism since it emphasizes the *continuity* of policy throughout the period of Conservative hegemony. Nor does it capture the political significance of the shift in strategy – in terms either of its political background or of its political repercussions. Thus we would argue for a more complex analysis of the political conjuncture and the discursive strategies whose effect is to benefit some companies more than others.

Ross also fails to address another crucial problem. The political and ideological context of Thatcherism is the revolt of the petty bourgeoisie, small and medium capital, and even sections of the working class against the economic and social impact of the Keynesian welfare state. It also operates in the context of the 'dual crisis'. Both factors mean that the policies of Thatcherism are far from unambiguously favourable to the City, international capital, and those sectors concerned with the working-class market. The social basis of Thatcherism in the petty bourgeoisie and small capital means the Tories must make compromises and concessions to these groups; and the logic of electoral competition requires concessions to significant sections of the working class. An overemphasis on economic funding could involve dismissing this distinctive political and ideological context as insignificant and inessential. It could lead to a denial that politics and ideology affect the real dynamic of Thatcher's policies or their likely tensions and contradictions. And this would lead to as many mistakes in strategy as a purely ideologist approach.

Strategic Conclusions

The main danger of the AP approach is that it generates inadequate strategic conclusions. At the level of left strategy such an appraisal leads to deep pessimism ('battening down the hatches') or to calls for a long-term construction of an 'alternative vision'. Both responses leave the way open to purely defensive, short-term and uncoordinated resistance to Thatcherism at the expense of any coherent, positive, medium-term economic and political strategy. Let us grant, for the moment, that some elements of a Thatcherite hegemony have been consolidated and that this constitutes a danger for the left. This would not alter the fact that there is, as Raymond Williams has reminded us, 'at least an equal danger from acquiescence by the Left in an interpretation which, as it were, would blame the majority of the British people for not accepting a socialist analysis'.[41] In sum, insofar as it focuses on the electoral ideology of Thatcherite politics, the AP approach commits two errors. It misrecognizes the fluidity of the current political situation, ignores the opportunities thereby created, and therefore produces inadequate strategic recommendations.

Although AP is fruitful in certain areas of analysis, it misses important contradictions and tensions in Thatcherism. It focuses mainly on the politics of electoral support (its mobilization, its mediation through the press, the electoral impact of AP etc.) and thereby ignores the politics of governmental power and the recomposition of the power bloc. In contrast the concept of 'two nations' allows us to examine the links between the politics of electoral support and the politics of power and to consider the contradictions and tensions between them. By focusing on the productive/parasitic distinction, we can relate Thatcherite discourse to the nature and limits of her economic strategy. For this approach suggests that future support depends on the effectiveness of the government's accumulation strategy and political programme. In turn this points us toward the international constraints on Thatcherism and qualifies the tendency for an AP approach to focus exclusively on the domestic ideological struggle. The ability to predict certain crucial ruptures or breakpoints in the economic development of Thatcherism will help the left in formulating an adequate response.

Indeed, only by examining the government's programme as well as its rhetoric can we formulate an appropriate strategy. One problem with the AP approach is that it homogenizes Thatcherism not merely across different dimensions of social reality but also across time. It is important not to treat the Thatcherism of the last half of the 1980s as identical to that preceding the 1979 election. The election in 1983 was different from that in 1979: 1979 was a realigning election, 1983 consolidated the Thatcherite mould. The 1987 election will be different again and the left must recognize this. The Tories are already conducting a new war of position to justify an attack on the welfare state, and the left should itself be seeking to go on the offensive with its own medium-term strategy by 1985/6.

A return to the KWS *status quo ante*, as proposed by Hobsbawm,[42] is neither desirable nor, indeed, possible. For this would be to return to an incoherent and contradictory project and to affirm the hegemony of non-socialist forces. This means that we must develop an alternative strategic view. It requires both a reassessment of the left's immediate defensive priorities and the formulation of new offensive objectives. This should involve attention to the following areas: (a) The politics of support – what policies are open to the left to recast an electoral majority? (b) The politics of power – what governmental programme is necessary/feasible to achieve such policies? (c) The restructuring of the state – given the dual crisis already referred to, what forms of representation/intervention can be constructed to aid the formation/implementation of a domestically oriented socialist growth strategy?

Notwithstanding our suggested criticisms of Stuart Hall in preceding pages, it is most important to pay tribute to his recent interventions. These have been a powerful force in rethinking traditional conceptions of the relations between economy and polity, class and party, structures and strategies. He has also been a central figure in bringing the importance of the political and ideological struggle for hegemony to the attention of the left in Britain. In this way Hall raises the burning issue of how to respond to the erosion of the traditional working-class basis of British Labourism. Nevertheless, while Hall constantly proclaims the need for the left to develop an 'alternative vision' and a new hegemonic strategy, we feel that his emphasis on the political and ideological level itself alone inhibits constructive strategic thinking. Thus, whilst the AP approach has been able to suggest certain *necessary* conditions for rethinking left strategy in Britain, it is far from establishing the *sufficient* conditions for a successful alternative strategy. We hope that our account of the dual crisis and of the 'two nations' strategy of Thatcherism will complement Hall's own work on 'authoritarian populism' and thereby contribute to further discussion of the pressing strategic issues.

[*As published in autumn 1984*]

5

Authoritarian Populism:
A Reply by Stuart Hall

In 1984 Jessop, Bonnett, Bromley and Ling contributed a long and important article 'Authoritarian Populism, "Two Nations" and Thatcherism'. This article took issue with 'authoritarian populism' (hereafter, alas, AP) and the use of that concept in my work on Thatcherism; and proposed some wide-ranging alternative theses. I should like myself to take issue with some aspects of their argument, not so much to defend my work as, through mutual discussion and debate, to advance our understanding of the phenomenon of Thatcherism.

My view, briefly, is that in their genuine desire to produce a *general* and definitive account of Thatcherism as a global phenomenon, Jessop et al. have been led to mistake my own, more delimited project for their own, more ambitious one. In so doing, they obscure or misread many of my arguments. They produce, in the end, a rather confused tangle of important arguments and spurious debating points. Let me say categorically that 'authoritarian populism' (AP) has never been intended to, could not possibly have been intended and – I would claim – has never been used in my work, to produce a *general* explanation of Thatcherism. It addresses, directly, the question of the forms of hegemonic politics. In doing so, it deliberately and self-consciously *foregrounds* the political–ideological dimension. Thatcherism, however, is a multi-faceted historical phenomenon, which it would be ludicrous to assume could be 'explained' along one dimension of analysis only. In that basic sense, I believe the Jessop et al. critique to have been fundamentally misdirected. The misunderstanding begins, so far as I can see, with their partial and inadequate account of the genealogy of the concept.

AP first emerged, as they acknowledged, from the analysis of the political conjuncture, mid-1960s/mid-1970s, advanced by myself and others in *Policing the Crisis*.[1] That analysis accurately forecast the rise of Thatcherism, though it was researched in the mid-seventies and published in 1978. It pointed, *inter alia*, to a shift taking place in the 'balance of social and political forces' (or what Gramsci calls the 'relations of force'), pinpointed in the disintegration of the social democratic consensus under Callaghan and the rise of the radical right under Thatcherite auspices. It argued that the corporatist consensus – the form of politics in which Labour had attempted to stabilize the crisis – was breaking up under internal and external pressures. However, the balance in the relations of force was moving – in that 'unstable equilibrium' between coercion and consent which characterizes *all* democratic class politics – decisively towards the 'authoritarian' pole. We were approaching, it argued, a moment of 'closure' in which the state played an increasingly central 'educative' role. We noted, however, the degree to which this shift 'from above' was pioneered by, harnessed to, and to some extent legitimated by a populist groundswell below. The *form* of this populist enlistment – we suggested – in the 1960s and 1970s often took the shape of a sequence of 'moral panics', around such apparently non-political issues as race, law-and-order, permissiveness and social anarchy. These served to win for the authoritarian closure the gloss of populist consent.[2]

Development of the Concept

The actual term 'authoritarian populism', however, only emerged in 1978 after I read the concluding section to Nicos Poulantzas's courageous and original book, *State, Power, Socialism*, which was also – tragically – his last political statement. There, Poulantzas attempted to characterize a new 'moment' in the conjuncture of the class democracies, formed by 'intensive state control over every sphere of socio-economic life, combined with radical decline of the institutions of political democracy and with draconian and multiform curtailment of so-called "formal" liberties, whose reality is being discovered now that they are going overboard'.[3] (I especially relished that final phrase, since it put me in mind of how often the fundamentalist left is scornful of civil liberties until they find themselves badly in need of some.) More seriously, I thought I recognized in this account, and in my brief conversations with Poulantzas at the time, many similarities between his characterization and those I had been struggling to formulate in *Policing the Crisis*, 'Drifting into a Law-and-Order Society' and so on.

Poulantzas called this the moment of 'authoritarian statism' (AS). He added, *inter alia*, that it was linked with 'the periodization of capitalism into distinct stages and phases'; that it existed 'in the form of regimes that vary according to the conjuncture of the country concerned'; that it covered, specifically, *both* 'the political crisis and the crisis of the state'; that it was intended to help us periodize 'the relationship between the state and the political crisis'. He insisted that it was *neither* the birth pangs of fascism nor an 'exceptional form of the capitalist state' nor even 'the fulfilment of the totalitarian buds inherent in every capitalist state'. Indeed, the importance of AS was that it represented a new combination of coercion/consent, tilted towards the coercive end of the spectrum, while maintaining the outer forms of democratic class rule intact. It did, he argued, relate to 'considerable shifts in class relations' (not, devotees of *Class Politics* please note, to the so-called 'disappearance of class or the class struggle', whatever that entirely fictional construction of theirs might mean). But also, that it coincided with the generalization of class conflict and other social struggles to 'new fronts'. It thus represented a fundamental shift in the modalities through which ruling blocs attempt to construct hegemony in capitalist class democracies. That was its explicit field of reference. There is little need to elaborate on AS further, if only because Bob Jessop must be thoroughly familiar with it since he is one of Poulantzas's most meticulous and accomplished commentators and critics, as his forthcoming study will show.

Poulantzas's concept seemed to me extremely useful – but weak in two major respects. It misread the emerging strategy, since one of the fundamental things which seemed to me to be shifting was precisely the abandonment of the 'corporatist' strategy central to Labourism, and its replacement by an 'anti-statist' strategy of the 'New Right'. (An 'anti-statist' strategy, incidentally, is not one which refuses to operate through the state; it is one which conceives a more limited state role, and which advances through the attempt, ideologically, to *represent itself* as anti-statist, for the purposes of populist mobilization.) I assumed that this highly contradictory strategy – which we have in fact seen in operation under Thatcherism: simultaneously dismantling the welfare state, 'anti-statist' in its ideological self-representation *and* highly state-centralist and dirigiste in many of its strategic operations – would inflect politics in new ways and have real political effects.

Secondly, I believed that Poulantzas had neglected the one dimension which, above all others, has defeated the left, politically, and Marxist analysis theoretically, in every advanced capitalist democracy since the First World War: namely, the ways in which popular consent can be so constructed, by a historical bloc seeking hegemony, as to harness to its support some popular discontents, neutralize the opposing forces, disaggregate the opposition and really incorporate *some* strategic elements of popular opinion into its own hegemonic project.

These two arguments led me to build on Poulantzas's insights, but to shift the characterization of the conjuncture from 'authoritarian statism' to 'authoritarian populism'. I hoped by adopting this deliberately contradictory term precisely to encapsulate the contradictory features of the emerging conjuncture: a movement towards a dominative and 'authoritarian' form of democratic class politics – paradoxically, apparently rooted in the 'transformism' (Gramsci's term) of populist discontents. This was further elaborated in my article 'Popular-Democratic versus Authoritarian Populism', where I drew on the seminal work of Laclau, and his notion of 'populist rupture'. But I distanced my more delimited use of the term 'populism' from his more inclusive one, attempting thereby to distinguish the genuine mobilization of popular demands and discontents from a 'populist' mobilization which, at a certain point in its trajectory, flips over or is recuperated into a statist-led political leadership.

Levels of Abstraction

I grant that this genealogy is nowhere fully laid out, though I would claim that it is plain enough from the context and sequence of my work. I also grant that there was too little rigorous or logical 'construction of concepts' here. The concepts, I am afraid, were generated in the heat of conjunctural analysis – I was trying to comprehend the shift towards Thatcherism as it was taking place. So, admittedly, the theorization is a bit rough and ready. I explored the idea of 'passive revolution', for example; and I still believe it has something to contribute to our understanding of populist (as opposed to popular) strategies. But I could not at the time bring off the link and have not been able to do so since. Like many of Gramsci's most fruitful concepts, AP remains 'over-descriptive'. Perhaps I have caught his disease. I suspect that a more fundamental disagreement divides my position from that of Jessop et al. here. I do not believe that all concepts operate at the same level of abstraction – indeed, I think one of the principal things which separates me from the fundamentalist Marxist revival is precisely that they believe that the concepts which Marx advanced at the highest level of abstraction (the mode of production, capitalist epoch) can be transferred directly into the analysis of concrete historical conjunctures. My own view is that concepts like that of 'hegemony' (the family or level of abstraction to which AP also belongs) are of necessity somewhat 'descriptive', historically more specific, time-bound, concrete in their reference – because they attempt to conceptualize what Marx himself said of 'the concrete': that it is the 'product of many determinations'. So I have to confess that it was not an error or oversight which determined the level of concreteness at which AP operates. It was quite deliberately and self-consciously *not* pitched at that level of 'pure' theoretical-analytic operation at which Jessop et al. seem to assume *all* concepts must be produced. The costs of operating at this level of abstraction are clear. But to me – in the wake of the academicizing of Marxism and the theoreticist deluge of the 1970s – so are the gains.

I would argue, therefore, that I have only used AP at the level of abstraction and with the range of reference outlined above. I have never claimed for it the general explanatory sweep which Jessop et al. attempt to graft on to it. I am therefore not at all surprised to find that AP is only a partial explanation of Thatcherism. What else *could* it be? It was an attempt to characterize certain strategic shifts in the political–ideological conjuncture. Essentially, it refers to changes in the 'balance of forces'. It refers directly to the modalities of political and ideological relationships between the ruling bloc, the state and the dominated classes. It attempts to expand on and to begin to periodize the internal composition of hegemonic strategies in the politics of class democracies. Theoretically – if anyone is interested – it is part of a wider project to develop and expand on the rich but too condensed concept of hegemony. It is a sort of footnote to Gramsci's 'Modern Prince' and 'State and Civil Society'. It references, but could neither characterize nor explain, changes in the more structural aspects of capitalist social formations. I do not understand how, even grammatically, AP could have been misunderstood as a concept operating at the latter level. 'In this field, the struggle can and must be carried on by developing the concept of hegemony,' Gramsci observed, in *The Prison Notebooks*. AP is a response to that fateful injunction.

Jessop et al. are certainly in need of no further instruction from me about the concept of hegemony. However, I cannot resist pointing out, at this stage in the argument, that I have *never* advanced the proposition that Thatcherism has achieved 'hegemony'. The idea, to my mind, is preposterous. What I have said is that, in sharp contrast to the political strategy of *both* the Labourist and the fundamentalist left, Thatcherite politics are 'hegemonic' in their conception and project: the *aim* is to struggle on several fronts at once, not on the economic-corporate one alone; and this is based on the knowledge that, in order really to dominate and restructure a social formation, political, moral and intellectual leadership must be coupled to economic dominance. The Thatcherites know they must 'win' in civil society as well as in the state. They understand, as the left generally does not, the consequences of the generalization of the class struggle to new arenas and the need to have a strategy for them too. They mean, if possible, to reconstruct the terrain of what is 'taken for granted' in social and political thought – and so to form a new common sense. If one watches how, in the face of a teeth-gritting opposition, they have steadily *used* the unpopularity of some aspects of trade union practice with their own members to inflict massive wounds on the whole labour movement, or how they have steadily not only pursued the 'privatization' of the public sector but installed 'value for money' at the heart of the calculations of *every*

Labour council and every other social institution – health service, school meals, universities, street cleaning, unemployment benefit offices, social services – one will take this politico-ideological level of struggle somewhat more seriously than the left currently does. That is the *project* of Thatcherism – from which, I am sufficiently in apostasy to believe, the left has something to learn as to the conduct of political struggle. But I do *not* believe and have nowhere advanced the claim that the project has been delivered.

Indeed, I have several times pointed out the yawning discrepancy between Thatcherism's ideological advances and its economic failures. I have consistently argued against the view that Thatcherite neo-monetarism could provide solutions to Britain's structural economic crisis. As the authoritarian face of Thatcherism has become – in line with my analysis – more and more pronounced, it seems to me self-evident that Thatcherism remains *dominant* but *not* hegemonic. It must impose – because it cannot lead. But I have also tried quite carefully to define what we might mean by its 'success'. In 'Thatcherism – A New Stage?' I said *inter alia*: 'It is beset by internal contradictions and subject to real limits. It won a measure of electoral support . . . It cannot deliver on them all . . . It is not touching the structural economic problems at home . . . and it is powerless to ward off the savage effects of a global capitalist recession.'[4] But I also warned that Thatcherism had won power on '*a long leash*' and would not be blown off course 'by an immediate crisis of electoral support'. I added that it would be perfectly possible for Thatcherism to 'fail' in delivering a solution to Britain's economic crisis, and yet to 'succeed' 'in its long-term mission to shift the balance of class forces to the right'. Big capital, I suggested, has supported Thatcherism because it sees in it 'the only political force capable of altering the relations of forces in a manner favourable to the imposition of capitalist solutions'. In that sense, I argued, 'the long-term political mission of the radical right could "succeed" even if this particular Government had to give way to one of another electoral complexion.' To that extent, I concluded, 'Thatcherism has irrevocably undermined the old solutions and positions.' That analysis was offered in 1980, but I believe it to have been fundamentally correct and to have been confirmed by subsequent developments. In the face of that, it is ludicrous to suggest that I have argued that Thatcherism has already achieved hegemony.

'Ideologism'?

This brings us to the charges advanced by Jessop et al. of 'ideologism'. This is so impacted that it is hard to disentangle. First of all I think they are themselves at fault in eliding the levels of political and ideological struggle, and in suppressing what they must know well – the need for concepts which define their specificity. They may be right in saying that AP does not sufficiently distinguish between these two dimensions of struggle. However, I do hold to the position that, in my own work, I have consistently struggled *against* any definition of hegemony which identifies it as exclusively an ideological phenomenon. On the contrary, I have repeated *ad nauseam* Gramsci's argument about hegemony being impossible to conceptualize or achieve without 'the decisive nucleus of economic activity'. It is therefore particularly galling to be accused of advancing an explanation of Thatcherism as exclusively an ideological phenomenon, simply because I have drawn attention to features of its ideological strategy which are specific and important.

It seems well-nigh impossible on the left to affirm the importance and specificity of a particular level of analysis or arena of struggle without immediately being misunderstood as saying that, because it is important, it is the *only* one. I have tried in my own work not to make that easy slide. I work on the political/ideological dimension (a) because I happen to have some competence in that area, and (b) because it is often either neglected or reductively treated by the left generally and by some Marxists. But the idea that, because one works at that level, one therefore assumes economic questions to be residual or unimportant is absurd. I think the ideological dimension of Thatcherism to be critical. I am certain the left neither understands it nor knows how to conduct this level of struggle – and is constantly misled by misreading its importance. Hence I was determined to bring out this level of analysis – and AP in part served to do just that. But since AP was never advanced as a general or global explanation, it entailed no prescriptions whatsoever as to the other levels of analysis. The fact is that until these other dimensions are in place *alongside* the concept of AP, the analysis of Thatcherism remains partial and incomplete. But the 'foregrounding' involved in AP was quite deliberate. 'Bending the twig' towards the most neglected dimension, against the drift of current discussion, Althusser once called it. Jessop et al. have, I think, missed my tactical purpose; they have thereby robbed themselves of insights from which their own analysis might have profited.

When they do turn to the question of ideological foregrounding, I think they misrepresent the work done with AP. Even on the ideological front, Thatcherism has adopted other strategies – like the construction of an intellectual leadership, the formation of a new stratum of 'organic' intellectuals, the level of the organization of theoretical ideas in certain strategic academic, research and other intellectual sites – to which I have also drawn attention, but which have nothing whatsoever to do with the AP strategy and the construction of the popular consent to power. Thatcherism also has a distinct political strategy for the internal recomposition of the power bloc and the state machine which is not 'purely' ideological – whatever that means – and has little to do with AP. It is true that, when I turn to describing the ideological *mechanisms*, I use the insights of 'discourse theory'. That is because I believe that discourse theory has much to tell us about how Thatcherism accomplishes the condensation of different discourses into its contradictory formation, and how it 'works' so as to recruit people to its different, often contradictory, subject positions: even though it has only had partial success in its project to construct a new kind of political 'subject'. But I have long ago definitively dissociated myself from the discourse-theoretical approach to the analysis of whole social formations, or even from the idea that the production of new subjectivities provides, in itself, an adequate theory of ideology (as opposed to a critical aspect of its functioning).[5] I have characterized that as a species – long familiar to the tradition of 'Western Marxism' – of neo-Kantianism. In doing so, I have also tried carefully to demarcate the immensely fruitful things which I learnt from Ernesto Laclau's *Politics and Ideology in Marxist Theory* from the dissolution of everything into discourse which, I believe, mars the later volume, *Hegemony and Socialist Strategy*, despite its many insights.[6] These distinctions were widely debated in the so-called Hegemony Group in 1980–3, in which Jessop himself took a leading role, so I find it difficult to be now mis-identified by Jessop et al. with the latter position.

I believe from what I have already said that it is also quite difficult to sustain the charge that I treat Thatcherism as an 'uncontradictory monolith'. The entire thrust of my work on the ideology of Thatcherism has been to try to show how Thatcherism has managed to stitch up or 'unify' the contradictory strands in its discourse – 'the resonant themes of organic Toryism – nation, family, duty, authority, standards, traditionalism, patriarchalism – with the aggressive themes of a revived neo-liberalism – self-interest, competitive individualism, anti-statism', as I put it in 'The Great Moving Right Show'.[7] In the same piece, I pointed to the highly contradictory subject-positions which Thatcherism was attempting to condense. I deliberately adopted Gamble's brief but telling paradox – 'free market, strong state'. How all this could be described as representing Thatcherism as an uncontradictory ideological monolith beats me. Nor do Jessop et al. score points by showing that many of these elements in Thatcherism are not new. 'Some of these,' I said in the very next sentence, 'had been secured in earlier times through the grand themes of one-Nation popular Conservatism: the means by which Toryism circumnavigated democracy.' I thought this of particular importance in giving substance to Gramsci's argument that, often, ideological shifts take place, not by substituting one, whole, new conception of the world for another, but by presenting a novel combination of old and new elements – 'a process of distinction and of change in the relative weight possessed by the elements of the old ideology'. I don't see how all that could conceivably be construed as endowing Thatcherism with an 'excessively unified image'.

The Keynesian Welfare State

For the reasons I have already advanced, there are many things which Jessop et al. argue in the succeeding sections of their article with which I wholeheartedly agree. Their analysis and mine are only, I am afraid, in competition with one another in the rather spurious atmosphere of polemical contestation which they quite unnecessarily generated. Nevertheless, I believe that the failures they show in understanding how AP works carry over into their own substantive analysis. Thus they repeat the now-familiar lefter-than-thou argument that the break-up of the postwar consensus could not be of much political significance because the 'Keynesian Welfare State' (KWS) was never 'socialist'. This is supposed to inflict further damage on the concept of AP. However, I am perfectly well aware that the KWS was not socialist. In *Policing the Crisis* I spent a great deal of space analysing the limits of the KWS and spelling out the contradiction of Labour in power, wh ch I quite specifically characterized as 'social democratic' not socialist in political content. The argument has, so far as I know, *never* been that the KWS was 'socialist' and that we should therefore now go back to it. That is a figment of the fundamentalist left imagination. What I have argued and do argue is that the KWS was a contradictory structure, a 'historic compromise', which both achieved something in a reformist direction for the working class *and* became an instrument in disciplining it. Why else should anyone on the left be now campaigning for the restoration of the cuts in the welfare state if it did *nothing* for the working class? I have also argued that, if we cannot mobilize a full-scale popular agitation around the limited demands of maintaining and expanding 'welfare state reformism', on what grounds could we conceivably conceptualize the political conjuncture as one likely to lead to an 'irreversible shift of power' towards immediate working-class power? I keep not getting an answer to this conundrum, and must presume this is because the symbolics of who can swear loudest at the reformism of Labour governments is more important on the left than hard analysis. It seems to be convenient to answer, not the question I pose but another, fictional one because the latter usefully demonstrates the degree of my apostasy! I am surprised to find Jessop et al. allowing themselves to drift into that vulgar exercise.

I have other problems with the analysis they advance, though on these I can be briefer. I do not find the 'two nations' hypothesis at all convincing. 'Good citizen' and 'hard worker' seem to me poor characterizations of the critical points of reference in the Thatcherite strategy. Thatcherism deliberately – and from its viewpoint, correctly – eschews *all* reference to the concept of *citizenship*. 'Worker' is also a difficult one for it to negotiate, and it constantly prefers 'wealth creator'. Jessop et al. pose the 'hard' question of the relation of Thatcherism to specific class interests. But they fail to provide the non-class-reductionist articulation to class positions they call for. 'An uneasy and unstable alliance of interests'? Amen – but we all got as far as that long ago. I also think that Jessop et al. are still too mesmerized by a problem which has long ago disappeared, in the sociological form in which it was carefully tended in the 1970s, into oblivion. That is the question of 'corporatism'. The problems to which 'corporatism' was a response in the 1970s remain. The corporatist strategy is in abeyance – one of Thatcherism's accomplishments: though a healthy dose of Kinnockism will undoubtedly revive its deeply undemocratic features and endow it with a life-after-death.

On many other aspects of the Jessop et al. analysis, I do not substantially differ. But on the central thrust of the argument, I think their article sophisticated but mistaken. They have badly skewed their own analysis and our general understanding of the Thatcherism phenomenon by entering into a misconceived confrontation with my work and with the concept of AP. They have profoundly mis-read the entire Gramscian terrain in which, from beginning to end, the whole AP discussion has been rooted. I am afraid they have sometimes had their eye cocked more towards scoring points than deconstructing Thatcherism. Nevertheless, they have contributed substantially to our understanding of many of its perplexing aspects. Perhaps, now that the sound of conceptual gunfire has died away, we might all get back to the far more important task of understanding the real complexity of the Thatcherism phenomenon, the better to defeat and destroy it.

[*As published in spring 1985*]

6

Thatcherism and the Politics of Hegemony: A Reply to Stuart Hall

We are glad that Stuart Hall regards our article (reproduced here as chapter 4) as a significant contribution to contemporary debates on Thatcherism. In that article we examined his work on authoritarian populism (hereafter AP), sketched an alternative approach to Thatcherism in terms of its two nations effects, and outlined some guidelines for future research. Here we consider Hall's response,[1] and try to clarify our disagreements with his approach. We feel sure that he understands the respect for his work which prompted our detailed and lengthy critique, and which now prompts us to elaborate it in these pages. Indeed, we have the highest regard for his prescient and timely analyses of current conjunctures and tendencies, as well as for his more general contributions to a critical social science. We are all the more sorry, therefore, that our motives should be portrayed as academic point-scoring and polemical contestation, for we had actually hoped to intervene in the debate over socialist strategy in the face of Thatcherism. It is a measure of our respect for Hall's work that we discussed its implications in our article and dismissed at the outset various fundamentalist, catastrophist and economistic analyses. We agree with Hall that the left must take the forms of hegemonic politics more seriously. But we also believe that, if hegemony is understood too narrowly or is isolated from other dimensions of economic, political and ideological relations, then the left could adopt mistaken strategies.

Political Theory and Socialist Strategy

It must be said that Hall's conjunctural analyses are neither theoretically nor strategically innocent. They have attracted considerable interest inside and outside the left largely because they have deliberately emphasized the hegemonic project of Thatcherism and the hegemonic dimension of left strategy at a time when both have been neglected by the mainstream of the labour movement. However, whatever his own stated intentions in underlining the wider implications of *hegemonic politics*, others have certainly read his conjunctural analyses and strategic conclusions as more narrowly *ideological* in focus. We argue that Hall's continual emphasis on the successes of Thatcherism has encouraged such readings. He has frequently ascribed two interrelated forms of success to Thatcherism – the articulation of a new common sense, and the shifting of the balance of forces decisively to the right. Yet he never really establishes whether the first of these successes is limited to the articulation of many different elements into a novel populist *discourse*, or whether it extends to deployment of this discourse in mobilizing effective popular support within and beyond the electoral field. Moreover, since he does not really explore other factors which might have contributed to this change in the balance of forces, Hall implies that it has occurred because the new common sense is ascendant. Even if he has never claimed that Thatcherism is actually hegemonic, such achievements play a crucial role in the struggle for hegemony as Hall defines it.[2]

In stressing the discursive successes of Thatcherism and its capacity to shift the balance of forces on many different fronts, Hall provides the basis for an ideologistic reading of his work. In particular, it could be invoked to justify a strategy largely restricted to a long, slow campaign to reconstruct popular common sense at the expense of other strategic initiatives. It is quite legitimate to counsel against such simplistic responses and to identify the *risks* entailed in Hall's approach. We still maintain that, whatever his own intentions, Hall's analyses are inherently liable to such misuse, and his reply has done little to allay our doubts.

Stuart Hall confirms our general account of how the AP approach developed and adds some fresh elements. What emerges most clearly is his concern with the politics of hegemony and with the way in which AP has reshaped the balance of forces in Britain. Many approaches can be taken towards hegemony, however, with very different political and strategic implications.[3] Accordingly we should consider what is involved in Hall's general concern with the forms of hegemonic politics and in his specific claim that Thatcherism is dominant but not yet hegemonic. We begin with his self-confessed intellectual debt to Nicos Poulantzas, and his attempt to differentiate his own views on how the modern state restructures hegemony. Our motive here is not to swap interpretations of Poulantzas's work but to establish how various approaches to hegemony can generate different strategic conclusions.

Hall and Poulantzas on the Modern State

Hall records how he was struck by the similarities between his own arguments in *Policing the Crisis*,[4] and Poulantzas's accounts of authoritarian statism (hereafter AS). But while he criticized the latter for paying insufficient attention to the *ideological* aspects of the modern state, Poulantzas considered that the authors of *Policing the Crisis* 'did not seriously discuss the new *form of the state*'.[5] Both charges were justified when first made. But whereas Hall has not significantly remedied this gap in his work, Poulantzas did subsequently analyse the ideological reorganization of the state and relate it to the generic crisis of hegemony in modern capitalism. Poulantzas argued that this hegemonic crisis stimulates the role of the mass media in political legitimation and mobilization. For the rise of authoritarian statism involves a significant restructuring of the dominant ideology as well as new forms of open and/or symbolic violence. Poulantzas noted how the right actually disguises the growth of repression by adopting certain liberal and libertarian themes dating from the sixties. In addition, the instrumental rationality and technocratic logic of experts displace notions such as the general will and legality; neo-liberal, anti-statist themes are deployed against the *social* functions of the Keynesian welfare state; there is an emphasis on authoritarian themes such as 'law-and-order'; and racism is inspired by the pseudo-scientific theses of 'biological inequality'. Poulantzas also argued that the channels which elaborate and diffuse the dominant ideology have been restructured. The mass media have taken over from the school, university and publishing house; and, within the state system itself, the administration has assumed the legitimation functions traditionally performed by political parties. Furthermore, the mass media typically draw both their agenda and their symbolism from the administration, falling under its growing and multiform control. Finally, Poulantzas noted that new plebiscitary and populist forms of consent have developed alongside the new technocratic and/or neo-liberal forms of legitimation.[6]

Thus Poulantzas was well aware of the ideological components of authoritarian statism and discussed both its anti-statist and its populist aspects. Indeed, he noted a range of ideological and political shifts among which AP could at best be seen as one (albeit important) element. Yet he also insisted that, whatever such anti-statist and neo-liberal trends might suggest, it is far from easy for the modern state to withdraw economically or politically, for all its activities are being reorganized and subordinated to its economic functions, and the state can no longer avoid the resulting contradictions simply through disengaging in the name of anti-statism or the social market economy. Thus, if the state decreases its interventions in one area, it must increase them in other areas. In fact, the AS state is constantly oscillating between the two terms of the alternative: withdraw or get further involved.[7] This suggests that one cannot simply choose, *pace* Hall, to emphasize either statism or populism as the most important feature of the modern state. For both stem from a central contradiction which can only be understood in the light of complex interrelations among various economic, political and ideological functions of the modern state.[8] A proper account of the contemporary nature and limits of hegemony must consider questions of political leadership in their interconnection with such structural problems.

Poulantzas was also clear on two further issues about which Hall is unsure. Firstly he distinguished among levels of analysis. Poulantzas treated authoritarian statism as a new form which characterized metropolitan and dependent capitalist states alike, and which could be associated with different forms of regime, for example, more neo-liberal in France, more authoritarian in Germany.[9] In contrast, Hall sometimes appears to treat AS and AP as equivalent terms (especially when he describes AP as a new form of state or as the ideological complement to a more directly disciplinary form of state); and at other times suggests, more accurately, that AP is a concept developed to analyse specific conjunctures of class struggle in a given country, and not to characterize an epoch.[10] Hall must decide whether AP provides an analysis of a new form of (exceptional or democratic?) state, or just a descriptive, partial and incomplete account of the current conjuncture. Very different strategic conclusions are surely implied in these apparently contradictory interpretations.

Secondly, although they share a concern for the dynamics of hegemony in the modern state, Poulantzas and Hall certainly do not derive identical strategic conclusions from their analyses. Both would seem to advocate a supra-class popular front embracing new social movements as well as two or more political parties. But there are clear differences within this overall perspective. Poulantzas himself advocated a threefold strategy: rank-and-file movements would be linked together at the base in united and popular fronts, intensifying the internal contradictions of the state, and transforming the state so that it could intervene to support popular movements. He was particularly concerned with how the struggles of state employees related to struggles beyond the state, and with the specific institutional changes needed to democratize the modern state. For his part, Hall recognizes that Thatcherism has successfully exploited contradictions and struggles within the Keynesian welfare state system; but he does not analyse comparable difficulties within Thatcherism and articulate them to an alternative left strategy. Nor does he really consider how the state might be democratized. Thus, although Poulantzas shared Hall's commitment to popular-democratic struggles and ideological contestation, his strategic recommendation went well beyond a long-term ideological campaign for hegemony.[11]

The Politics of Hegemony

In his reply to our critique, Hall argues that we 'have profoundly mis-read the entire Gramscian terrain in which, from beginning to end, the whole AP discussion has been rooted'. He claims to have developed the concept of AP in an 'attempt to characterize certain strategic shifts in the political–ideological conjuncture. Essentially it refers to changes in the "balance of forces". It refers directly to the modalities of political and ideological relationships between the ruling bloc, the state and the dominated classes. It attempts to expand on and to begin to periodize the internal composition of hegemonic strategies in the politics of class democracies.' In so doing, it deliberately foregrounds the political-ideological dimension of Thatcherism. Hall then suggests that we have mistaken this tactical emphasis for a general explanation and therefore fundamentally misdirected our critique.

We certainly share Hall's interest in Gramsci as well as his broader aim of analysing the forms of hegemonic politics. Thus we welcome Hall's clarifications regarding the unrealized hegemonic *intent* of Thatcherism and his new account of AP's appropriate field of application. It is now clear that we paid insufficient attention to Hall's *obiter dicta* on the limitations and contradictions within Thatcherism and also defined too broadly the domain to which he intended AP to refer. In our view, however, there is a systematic gap beween Hall's aims (as defined in his reply and summarized above) and his published work. Hall has consistently emphasized the importance of ideological contestation in political strategy, and the left is deeply in his debt for this. But this must not be allowed to pre-empt rational debate over the adequacy of Hall's own formulations. We too take seriously the political–ideological field and hegemonic politics, but this does not mean that we have to share Hall's approach to them. If our method of analysis is somewhat different, it is not an adequate response to dismiss us as fundamentalists, whatever that might mean in this context.

More generally, one should note that the Gramscian heritage is problematic for all those inspired by him. Gramsci focused mainly on the politics and ideology of class leadership and neglected the structural determinations of hegemony. Hall shares this neglect. This emerges clearly in his argument that he is concerned with hegemony and not with 'changes in the more structural aspects of capitalist formations'.

Yet the long-term stability of hegemony is rooted in specific forms of state, with their own structural or strategic selectivity, as well as in specific forms of organizing the system of production and the mental–manual division of labour. If there is a connection between hegemony and the decisive nucleus of economic activity, as Hall himself has stressed so often, it is surely necessary to explore it. And, in doing so, one must surely consider not only those ideological struggles which alter the balance of economic forces but also those structural changes which help to recompose class relations within and among the working class, petty bourgeoisie and fractions of capital. Gramsci's own understanding of the historic bloc certainly involves much more than political and ideological leadership. It also refers to the non-necessary, socially constructed *correspondence* between base and superstructure. Thus it would be quite wrong to restrict an analysis of the forms of hegemonic politics to questions of political and ideological leadership – let alone to the manner in which the ruling bloc exercises its ideological leadership over the people.

Hegemony versus Dominance

Even more important is Hall's new claim that Thatcherism has managed to become dominant but has not won hegemony. If this is the case (and we believe it is), one must ask what in general is involved in winning dominance and how Thatcherism in particular has secured it. Hall does not help his case here when he appears to confuse hegemony and dominance. Thus, in his debate last year with Tony Benn, he argued that political leadership is not really a question of commanding universal assent on the political scene or of resolving the basic problems of the society and economy.[12] For Hall the crucial questions are: Can it lead the key sectors? Can it win the strategic engagements? Can it stay in front when challenged? He then argues that Thatcherism's ability to do these things has involved a profound reversal for the left in Britain.[13] We are not convinced that Thatcherism has won the strategic engagements and stayed in front when challenged simply because it can exercise political leadership over the key sectors; nor that it has done so by virtue of 'its capacity to develop, between 1975 and 1984, a form of hegemonic politics, that is to say, a form of politics which, while not universally popular, was able to fight and establish its position on one front after another'.[14] In addition to its hegemonic project (which, Hall assures us, has failed) there must be other elements at work in this series of Thatcherite successes. Hall implies that these can be understood in terms of the *domination* which Thatcherism enjoys.

Gramsci also distinguished between hegemony and domination, but it is not fully clear what he meant by this distinction. Sometimes he contrasted *hegemony* as active consent by the dominated classes to the rule of the dominant classes with *domination* as the coercive imposition of that rule. Sometimes he operated with a more complex set of concepts ranging from coercion through 'force, fraud and corruption' to 'passive revolution' and thence to 'expansive hegemony'. In both cases he focused on political and ideological *practices* and neglected the *structural underpinnings* of class domination in the dull compulsion of economic relations, the structural selectivity of different state forms, or the nature of the mental–manual division of labour. Although Hall seeks to characterize the limited success of Thatcherism in terms of its domination, it is difficult to see what this means. We cannot tell whether such domination stems from coercion, 'force, fraud and corruption', a passive revolution, or from structural changes in economic, political and ideological life.

Thus, if we turn from Thatcherism's unrealized hegemonic project to the conditions which favour its dominance, Hall's approach becomes seriously misleading. A rightward shift in the balance of forces need not be due to the success of the AP project in organizing positive support for Thatcherism among the people or within the power bloc. It could also be due to the disorganization of the resistance to Thatcherism (which is not necessarily just an effect of the new common sense); to basic institutional obstacles to such resistance (which need not all be located in the political–ideological realm); or to strategic errors on the part of the left in an otherwise favourable conjuncture. In particular, we believe that the dual crisis of the state mentioned in our article (chapter 4) has played a key role here, as have the forms of the current economic crisis. But other *structural* factors and more *conjunctural* elements would also be relevant.

Hall and Leys on Hegemony

Hall claims to have 'repeated *ad nauseam* Gramsci's argument about hegemony being impossible to conceptualize or achieve without "the decisive nucleus of economic activity"'. Such repetitions are not enough to avoid the risks of ideologism. The crucial question is how far Hall actually considers the decisive nucleus of economic activity as a determining element in hegemonic politics. In this respect there is an interesting contrast between Hall's approach and that adopted in Colin Leys's account of hegemony in the ruling bloc.

Leys considers how the values and demands of British manufacturing industrialists are related to current economic strategies. He discusses why British manufacturers, faced with the absolute decline of industrial output, have been so muted in their response to Thatcherism. He correctly insists that manufacturing interests are constructed within specific historical conditions and expressed through particular institutional channels. He therefore explores how capital gets represented, paying special attention to the structure and power of the Confederation of British Industry. He notes the existence of divisions within manufacturing along the lines of scale and import/export orientation; degree of monopoly; and national versus multinational status. He also discusses the impact of the 1974–6 political crisis on business attitudes. More generally, he emphasizes the historic absence of a hegemonic ideology favourable to manufacturing capital.[15]

The value of this approach is twofold. Firstly, it considers the calculations made by the leading sections within manufacturing industry and explains the circumstances which led them to make such calculations. Secondly, it explains why those sections are dominant within manufacturing industry. It thereby affirms Gramsci's arguments that forces must struggle for hegemony and that, although hegemony is rooted in the economic–corporate, it goes beyond it. In particular, Leys relates hegemony to forms of representation and political organization in the British state, as well as to the changing structure of the British economy. His analysis demonstrates that the concept of hegemony can be used differently – and in our view more effectively – than it is in the work of Hall.

This highlights the gap between Hall's intent and his practice. He claims that hegemony concerns the modalities of political and ideological relationships between the ruling bloc, the state and the dominated classes. Yet instead of actually exploring these issues, he has described the production of a new common sense which appeals to the dominated classes and has neglected the relations within the ruling bloc and between that bloc (if there is one) and the state. Moreover, whereas Leys considers institutional and material factors in accounting for the failure of manufacturing capital to establish its hegemony, Hall explains ideological tendencies and strategies largely in terms of factors located on the ideological level itself.

Such criticisms are related to the foregrounding of political–ideological analysis in Hall's work. In itself, this is a perfectly legitimate choice. But there is an important distinction between a theoretical project which conceives ideology as one region to be analysed alongside others and one which seeks to grasp it from the outset in its complex relationships with other aspects of society. Let us consider this point more closely.

Foregrounding the Ideological

Hall suggests that analysts can properly foreground different issues or moments and that their analyses can then be combined to produce a rounded account. Whilst himself focusing on the ideological, he recognizes that until 'other dimensions are in place *alongside* the concept of AP, the analysis remains partial and incomplete' (Hall's emphasis). But it is not at all clear that one can disaggregate a phenomeron such as Thatcherism into a series of discrete dimensions or aspects (such as the ideological region or the role of AP), which can be studied in isolation and then juxtaposed to other dimensions or aspects (also studied in isolation) to produce a full and complete account. This does not do justice to the complex interrelations and compenetration which character-ize the different moments of a societal system. Hall himself does not actually advocate such a one-sided approach, but this sort of argument does illustrate the *risks* of ideologism involved in foregrounding the ideological in this way. Indeed, Hall does not even pay equal attention to the various aspects of the political–ideological level. He largely ignores political and ideological *structures* and also focuses on ideological rather than political *struggles*. Hall may be right to insist that 'I have long ago definitely dissociated myself from the discourse-theoretical approach to the analysis of whole social formations'. Yet there can be no doubt that his analyses of hegemony – which certainly concern whole social formations – emphasize the discursive strategies and types of subjectivity involved in articulating the new common sense. At the same time, they ignore the material conditions of transmission and reception of ideologies.

Hall further charges that we missed his tactical purpose in bending the twig away from the economic dimension and thereby robbed ourselves of insights from which our analysis might have benefited. We are happy to admit the latter error and to round out the interconnections among economic, political and ideological relations in Thatcher's Britain. Indeed, if our arguments about the dual crisis and about the corresponding resort to populism and *raison d'état* are correct, then the role of the mass media and ideological appeals sketched by Hall makes much sense. In fact, our analysis would help to establish the mediations between the trends towards authoritarian populism discussed by Hall and those towards authoritarism statism identified by Poulantzas. The twin failure of parliamentarism and corporatism to secure the institutional and social bases for a legitimate representative state helps us to understand why Thatcherism should seek to address and mobilize the people through the mass media and ideological discourse rather than through party-political organization and corporatist channels. Thus, the dual crisis and the populist political response which it has engendered correspond to (and help to explain the material basis for) the increased importance of the mass media and the populist ventriloquism to which it has given rise. Such an analysis would provide some support for the arguments put forward on a more abstract level by Poulantzas and reviewed above. It would also suggest that Hall's emphasis on the mass media, moral panics etc. is more justified that we initially recognized.

But the converse is also true. Rather than dismiss our account of the dual crisis as merely a throwback to the sixties concern with corporatism, Hall might have learnt something about the roots of populism and the impact of the mass media. His failure to do so reinforces our suspicion that he is still locked within a regionalist approach to the political–ideological sphere in which ideological phenomena are explained in terms of other ideological phenomena. This is one area where the proper distinction between the organic and conjunctural and the complex relations among different spheres of struggle could be explored in a most fruitful way.

The Strategic Implications of AP

Hall states that his analyses deliberately bend the stick towards the political and ideological, are intentionally concrete and conjunctural, and have a strategic purpose. In chapter 4 we discussed the *potential* for ideologism in Hall's work and its attendant risks. Here we have considered some problems involved in a conjunctural focus at the expense of organic or structural features of particular periods and crises. This is especially important in considering the *structural determination* of hegemony and its relation to hegemonic *class leadership*, as also in examining the relative weight of domination and hegemony in Thatcherism. We now turn to the different strategic implications of the AP and 'two nations' approaches.

Hall has consistently emphasized the failure of left strategy to recognize the fundamental rightward shift in the balance of forces during the last decade. He has also devoted a great deal of attention to the role of Thatcherism's hegemonic project in articulating a new common sense and fighting ideological struggles on a wide range of fronts. In turn this leads him to stress how important it is for the left to take seriously the struggle for hegemony. We basically agree with these arguments but differ from Hall in four crucial respects.

Firstly, whereas Hall seems to ascribe the rightward shift primarily to the effects of Thatcherism's allegedly successful articulation of a new common sense and its commitment to hegemonic politics, we would want to consider the broader structural context in which this ideological intervention has occurred. We would also question how far Thatcherism has not only articulated a new common sense but also mobilized popular support behind it.[16] If this mobilization is only temporary and conjunctural, then we must explain why.

Secondly, whereas Hall bends the stick in the political and ideological direction, we have pointed out that juridico-political dimensions are important in accounting for the dominance of Thatcherism and for its continued economic and political weakness. Hall correctly notes that Thatcherism has not actually solved the crises affecting British society or the British economy. These failures cannot be attributed to the fact that Thatcherism is not yet hegemonic (as if all would be put right if key sectors of the power bloc and/or the people subscribed to AP or the doctrines of the social market economy). Indeed, these failures derive in part from the decisional autonomy enjoyed by the Thatcher 'party' in pursuing its less-than-hegemonic project to restructure Britain and adapt it to the post-Fordist stage of global capitalism. The left should exploit the resulting contradictions and try to intensify the difficulties of the Thatcherite state.

Thirdly, Hall's justified concern with the politics of hegemony has led him to exaggerate the ideological successes of AP in particular and Thatcherism more generally. In this sense he is not merely bending the theoretical stick but giving a distinctive bend to discussions of strategy. Intentionally or not, he is prioritizing a long-term ideological struggle to articulate a new common sense.

Fourthly, although Thatcherism has not won the battle for hegemony, it is certainly dominant politically and ideologically. This suggests that long-term political and ideological strategies need to be articulated with shorter-term strategies in the economic and political as well as ideological fields. In particular, we believe that the increasing contradictions of Thatcherism (in reorganizing the state and economic policies, and, above all, in making a final assault on the welfare state) constitute key areas of resistance and struggle. We touched on these issues in chapter 4 and return to them here.

Authoritarian Populism and Two Nations

Hall claims that it is too obvious to argue that AP cannot bear the full weight of explaining Thatcherism. Maybe so. But he does then say that AP 'refers directly to the modalities of political and ideological relationships between the ruling bloc, the state and the dominated classes'. Even this domain is extensive and AP would be stretched to cover it. This is why we introduced further concepts for analysing the ruling bloc and its relation to the state. Such an analysis will reveal other strategic issues and options which may not hinge directly on the level of support from the dominated classes. We also discussed the economic and political implications of the policies pursued by the Thatcher government – with particular reference to their two nations effects.

Our 'two nations' analysis was intended neither to capture Thatcher's discourse nor to provide a general and definitive account of Thatcherism as a global phenomenon. We merely tried to offer an account to *complement* and *integrate* the economic and political-ideological dimensions discussed in other studies. We hoped to establish some, but not all, relevant links among economic, political and ideological relations rather than to focus on just one 'region'. Thus we analysed the political and institutional context of Thatcherism (especially the dual crisis); assessed how this affected the series of economic and political projects pursued by Thatcherism; and weighed the two nations effects produced in and through such projects. These inter-related projects can be characterized as follows.

Firstly, Thatcherism does have an explicit economic strategy. This goes well beyond control of the money supply and aims to restructure the British economy as part of a reinvigorated, post-Fordist international capitalism. In particular, Thatcherism has adopted a neo-liberal accumulation strategy premissed on the deregulation of private capital, the privatization of significant parts of the public sector and the introduction of commercial criteria into the residual activities of the state sector. This strategy also implies commitment to an open economy. Indeed, the government has encouraged outward investment and an export drive. Recent calculations indicate that 48 per cent of the sales of the top fifty British multinationals are attributable to overseas production and that 39 per cent of their employees are located overseas.[17] More generally, the oil and invisibles surplus has allowed a huge build-up of assets overseas: from £75.1bn in 1979 to £172.5bn in 1983. Overseas assets net of external liabilities have also risen from £13bn to £56bn.[18]

At the same time the government has encouraged multinationals to invest in Britain. Typically these will draw upon and reproduce the low-wage economy of postwar Britain and exploit its accessibility to the rest of the European Community. Thus industrial capital in the UK is 'regrouping around a new set of key industries (oil, chemicals and high-technology advanced engineering) and services (consumer goods and services)' and 'the key areas of industrial growth . . . are among the areas in which foreign capital is most powerfully represented in the UK.'[19] Moreover, the rise of Eurodollar banking in the 1970s and the internationalization of banking and commercial capital have ensured that 'leadership by the City of London is not the same as leadership by *British* financial operators.'[20]

The government clearly hopes that rentier incomes will sustain a low-wage service sector when the oil runs out. But this entails a major dilemma involving likely trade-offs between wages, productivity and the balance of payments. If the trade-off between the average wage and unemployment levels retains its present balance, the prospects for a significant fall in unemployment in the medium term are grim. Conversely, current 'supply-side' measures seem quite unable to rectify the low productivity of the UK economy. Behind this lies a fundamental contradiction in the neo-liberal strategy. These supply-side policies are meant to promote neo-classical *allocative* efficiency. But long-term growth of manufacturing productivity and international competitiveness depend mainly on *dynamic* efficiency. Allocative efficiency requires flex-price markets (especially for labour) as well as labour mobility. But dynamic efficiency depends upon cooperation in the use of labour within the firm. With depressed demand and without planned policies for industrial restructuring, the logics of allocative and dynamic efficiency are in direct conflict.[21] Whereas there are certainly short-term gains in productivity from such policies, they also reduce long-term efficiency and competitiveness. This is already evident in the severe loss of manufacturing capacity, the erosion of infrastructure, and the re-emergence of balance-of-payments constraints on full-employment levels of demand.

Secondly, Thatcherism has a complex political strategy. It is attempting to restructure the state system and its relations with civil society and the economy in the sphere of the politics of state power. It is also seeking to consolidate an electoral coalition through redistributive policies and to create new bases of political support whilst resorting to coercion and/or denying basic rights to those outside this electoral bloc.

In restructuring the state Thatcherism may be more vulnerable than we originally suggested. We argued that the Cabinet's increased decisional autonomy was associated with a decline in the economic and political efficacy of state intervention. But we also confused the growing *centralization* of state power, at the expense of parliamentary, functional and local representation, with its effective *concentration*, which would follow from increased control over different parts of the central state and their associated policy networks. Recent events illustrate the problematic unity and efficacy of the Thatcherite state and the continued resistance at both central and local levels to various Cabinet initiatives. These problems can be seen in recurrent dissent in the House of Lords, Tory backbench revolts, judicial reversals in domestic and European courts, opposition from spending ministries to further cuts, continuing difficulties in controlling local government, a series of unfavourable reports from officials such as Audit Commissioners and education inspectors, and the increased resort by state employees to 'leaks' and passive resistance. A proper discussion of these issues depends on a careful delimitation of the postwar power bloc and state system – which we have *not* yet attempted. Nonetheless, the growing evidence of institutional inertia and resistance in the face of attempts to recast the state also suggests real constraints on the government's ability to restructure the economy and civil society.[22]

Nor is it obvious that the second part of the political project has succeeded. The Falklands war was most beneficial in restoring the fading electoral popularity of the Thatcher government as well as its political unity. The miners' strike has not delivered the same medium-term benefits, despite concerted authoritarian-populist manipulation of public opinion and the problems originating in the NUM's conduct of the strike and in the more general leftwing response. Even so, the government might succeed in its political aim of consolidating an electoral coalition around the new growth industries, the tradable service sector, and the consumer industries dependent thereon. Our analysis (and much other complementary work) indicates a real danger that 'two nations' effects will penetrate deep into the organized labour movement. If the trade union movement were also to recompose itself around the 'privileged nation', then the prospects for the left would be dire.[23] To win the next election with the present electoral system and the continued divisions within and among the opposition parties, Thatcherism only needs to consolidate support among some 40 per cent of those who vote. A successful campaign for a left common sense might not be enough to prevent this. Something more is clearly required.

Alternative Strategic Recommendations

Democratic socialists must struggle on the terrain of the contradictions generated by Thatcher's policies towards the state, economy and civil society, and must do so within an overarching left project to bridge the two nations gaps in both electoral and policy terms. There is clearly a great need for serious thinking about the democratization of the state. The abolition of the Greater London Council and metropolitan authorities, and the left's failure to prevent this, have heightened the importance of rethinking strategy towards the local state. Many local initiatives (for example, the GLC and Sheffield) involve important and creative forms of socialist practice. They provide real opportunities for cooperation with Liberals and, more importantly, with CND, and the feminist, black and ecological movements. But such initiatives cannot be sustained and realize their full potential without a left government with a clear alternative programme. In turn this depends on transforming the central state system so that such a government could mobilize popular-democratic support. Serious theoretical and political work in this area is crucial.

Secondly, whilst having no sympathy for Thatcherite economic policies, we do urge the left to develop a coherent 'supply-side' programme. Only in this way can mass unemployment be seriously reduced and resources generated for a new socialist commonwealth. This requires a new productivist orientation to left economic policies – not in the Bolshevik sense of 'production for the sake of production', but in the common-sensical sense (currently misappropriated by Thatcherism) that 'wealth must first be produced before it can be distributed'. This does not mean indifference to the relations within which wealth must be produced. Sustained debate over an alternative economic strategy (AES) must be resurrected. It must also be linked not only to current local AES initiatives (whose active supply-side approach is undermined by their lack of central government support) but also to those new social movements whose concerns are compatible with democratic socialism.

In this context corporatism should not be unequivocally rejected by the left. A supply-oriented corporatism in which there is a genuine political exchange (not merely a policy of wage restraint in return for nothing) would provide an important basis for extending economic democracy and deepening political representation. Such corporatist relations should *prefigure* socialist forms of economic and political organization rather than reproduce the bureaucratic corporatism and elitist tripartism of earlier experiments. The development of democratic corporatism (or concertation) would help to refute Thatcherism's equation between workers' control, state ownership and centralized planning. The false choice of liberalism or statism must be rejected, and the ideas of syndicalism and democratic corporatism must be introduced as major elements into economic management.

These suggestions may well appear banal but they are worth repeating. Three further points should also be made. In developing an AES the Labour Party still seems preoccupied with the external orientation of the City and neglects the problem of transforming the capital–labour relation at home to encourage innovation and productivity growth. Nor has it grasped the nettle of a socialist incomes policy. This will probably involve short-term sacrifice for more privileged workers, so that those who have lost out in the two nations system can be recompensed and a socialist welfare state be established. In addition, any serious discussion of an AES must be articulated with an alternative state strategy. The experience of Benn's Industry Act, the failure of 'Planning Agreements' and the fate of Bullock's proposals for industrial democracy do not augur well for a future socialist programme that ignores the problem of political reform.

Thirdly, the debate on an alternative social policy must also be extended. The survival of the welfare state remains a major obstacle to a full-blown neo-liberal strategy and constitutes a continuing source of resistance. This is evident from the mixed reception given to the recent reviews of social security. Moves to selectivity and targeting must be opposed in order to undercut the government's strategy of 'maintaining the support of a docile majority through their fear of the immiseration to be imposed on a dependent minority'.[24] But this does not mean that one should simply defend the welfare state in its current or pre-Thatcher forms. These transmute welfare recipients into isolated individual or family units and reinforce self-centred attitudes towards, and experience of, welfare. This is inimical to public participation in welfare provision and also undermines the collective defence of welfare. Likewise, the most bureaucratic sections of welfare, such as social security, are not only the least popular with welfare recipients but are also very expensive to administer. Welfare has also become residualized through the piecemeal transformation of a one nation into a two nations system. This has helped to consolidate the 'productive/parasitic' cleavage in society.

As well as reassessing priorities the left must consider who are the immediate political allies in the struggle against Thatcherism. Should these be understood purely in party-political terms (Liberals, SDP, Greens, Nationalists etc.), or should we extend the notion of alliances to encompass old and new social movements? Should they be restricted to electoral or parliamentary pacts or be built from the base? What economic, political and cultural fronts can be established without falling back into opportunism and undermining the prospects for long-term advance? Given the hostility of the professions to aspects of Thatcherism, should the left accept their priorities in attacking Thatcherite proposals on medicine, law, journalism and so on? Or should the left attempt to mobilize those who have been more quiescent on these issues? What problems are posed by the growing division of Labour's residual support between inner-city minorities and the skilled, unionized blue-collar workforce in hardcore industrial regions? Can one seriously argue that combining minorities and/or mobilizing around particular discontents will add up to a majority? There is a real danger of committing a mechanistic fallacy here and neglecting to prioritize issues around a unifying theme which identifies the movement as *socialist*. Without such a theme any majority could be highly unstable. The left needs to develop a new socialist *general will* within which conflicting economic–corporate interests can be negotiated and mutual sacrifices agreed.

[*As published in autumn 1985*]

PART III

The Highest Stage of Thatcherism?

7

Introduction to Part III

Both chapter 8 and chapter 9 in this concluding Part III of the book address the question of whether Thatcherism has consolidated a rational strategy for the reconstruction of the British economy as well as a durable social and political settlement to back it. Chapter 8 was an immediate response to the 1987 Conservative election victory, with its pre-election commitments to eliminate socialism from the British political scene. In this provisional assessment of 'Popular Capitalism, Flexible Accumulation and Left Strategy' we urged the left not only to study the narrow electoral reasons for its defeat but also to consider how its analysis and project might move beyond the defence of social democracy towards a realistic strategy for the 1990s and beyond. Here we suggested that the political and economic project of Thatcherism might be consolidated through a radically new accumulation strategy combining flexible accumulation with an hegemonic project of two nations, popular capitalism.

   Given the wide variety of meanings attached to the related terms 'post-Fordism', 'flexible specialization' and 'flexible automation', however, we must be careful how we apply them in our theoretical and political analyses. Recent anglophone discussions about post-Fordism have focused on two key issues: the Fordist pattern of postwar growth and the related claim that we are now witnessing a transition to post-Fordism. Some analysts justify these claims by focusing on changes in the labour process and the leading growth sectors in the economy. But others operate with a broader conception of the typical Fordist or post-Fordist society which comprises a more or less coherent set of economic, political, welfare and ideological institutions. In both cases the Fordist core is found in the conjunction of mass production and mass consumption, the post-Fordist future in more flexible forms of production and more differentiated forms of consumption.

In the first, narrow sense 'Fordism' refers to the combination of semi-skilled, machine-paced labour processes with scientific management (assembly-line production) to produce standardized commodities for the mass consumer market. In the Fordist sectors, the spectacular advances in mechanization after the Second World War formed the material base for a virtuous circle of growth wherein rising productivity, growing living standards and consequently buoyant demand and profits were the order of the day. This is then contrasted with an emerging regime of post- (or neo-) Fordism which is defined by the production of specialized commodities for luxury and/or niche markets. The latter's material base is to be found in the application of micro-electronics and information technology to the operations of the firm. The result – sometimes termed 'flexible specialization' – is an integration of small-scale production with design, stock control, marketing and retailing.

Many questions can be asked of these accounts. At best the characterization of postwar growth as Fordist can only be applied to certain leading sectors. And even if such a description is accepted, there was still considerable national variation in the forms of labour process organization and the broader institutional structures of accumulation. In addition, the Fordist literature pays remarkably little attention to one of the key developments of postwar growth in the metropolitan economies: the massive expansion of multinational corporations in the manufacturing sector. Finally, the close focus on the manufacturing sector tends to direct attention away from equally significant realignments in the organization of commercial and financial capital and the service sectors (both public and private).

Equally, with regard to the post-Fordist future, several important questions remain unanswered. Are the core markets for consumer goods saturated? What is the empirical evidence for such a claim? Are the apparent moves to segmented consumer markets a secular trend or merely the result of economic crisis and the specific distribution of social demand? Is there any reason to suppose that what are currently identified as niche and/or luxury markets will remain so? If market saturation is not the sole or even the primary cause of the crisis of Fordism, why precisely has productivity growth slowed down? In the absence of a clear answer to the question of the origins of the slow-down in productivity growth, what is the reason for a belief that the age of Fordism is over and that flexible specialization offers a way forward?

'Flexible automation', on the other hand, carries no heavy theoretical baggage and merely purports to describe the general impact on manufacturing of micro-electronics and information technology. In this more limited, descriptive sense there are clearly many examples of such developments in manufacturing. Whether this, in itself, can provide the base for a new period of sustained accumulation is far more doubtful.

In sum, we can conclude at this stage that flexible specialization, and more clearly flexible automation, exist, but their weight in specific national economies and/or the international economy remains unclear. And in particular, the thesis that flexible specialization offers an historic alternative to the crisis-ridden mass production of the Fordist era is theoretically weak, empirically dubious and strategically misleading.

As noted above, there is a second, broader usage of the 'Fordist/ post-Fordist' couplet. In this context the focus is placed on the pattern of institutional regulation of economic growth and social conflict. Fordist patterns of regulation involved such institutional forms as: regularized collective bargaining; the importance of expanding norms of collective consumption; the central role of credit (private and public) in anticipating productive increases; the practice of monopolistic pricing by leading corporations; and the increased salience of state intervention in securing both full employment and social welfare for all. By contrast, post-Fordism might come to involve: a decline in the scope and effectivity of collective bargaining; a shift to private and individualized forms of welfare consumption; a decreased role for the state in securing traditional social democratic, or inclusive national, objectives; a growing polarization of the population along occupational, regional, ethnic and gender lines; and the consolidation of exclusionary, or two nations, forms of mass integration. Once again, however, this model must be heavily qualified by the many national variations within the advanced capitalist societies. Nevertheless, at a broad descriptive level we find it accurate enough as a heuristic device to uncover some powerful trends now operating in many (but not all) advanced capitalist societies.

From this point the argument concerning Thatcherism and post-Fordism might be taken forward in one of two ways. On the one hand, it might be suggested that the emerging state strategy of Thatcherism is adequate for the promotion of post-Fordist growth in manufacturing industry operating in the UK economy. In turn, the rest of the government agenda would be interpreted as the social and political shell for such an economically rational strategy. On the other, it could be argued that Thatcherism is post-Fordist in the sense that it plays up increasing social and geographical polarizations in order to construct a politically exclusionary (two nations) strategy. This latter approach is the one we argue for in chapter 8. Thus we write:

> The primacy of the political class struggle in Thatcherite policy is often astonishing. Whereas the last Labour government tended to subordinate political strategy to economic crisis-management, the Thatcher governments have often treated economic policy as a sub-field for the politics of hegemony ... The general rationale seems to be that if the government

can modify the balance of forces in the short term, it will gain sufficient time to restructure society and to allow a market-generated recovery.

We find the first approach unconvincing for substantive and theoretical reasons. Theoretically, we would argue that economic developments and/or crises do not act as automatic steering mechanisms for state action, and it is therefore illusory to suggest a more or less direct link between the requirements of a post-Fordist economy and state policy. Rather, economic forces – in whatever form: direct influences, structural constraints, agenda setting etc. – are always *politically* mediated. Substantively, two points are of considerable importance. The core–periphery divide, which does so much work in theories of post-Fordism and/or flexible specialization, is neither new nor primarily a phenomenon of the manufacturing/industrial sector. As all the detailed empirical surveys show, the core–periphery divide is an economy-wide development of long-standing importance; and it is located primarily in the *service* sector, and increasingly in the *state* services. What is new about Thatcherism is not so much the actual existence of these divisions, but the fact that the Conservative Party has sought to construct a 'post-recession settlement' through politically institutionalizing them. As Leadbeater has noted: 'What is important is that these divisions have created new and conflicting interests, and as a consequence set up a new distributional dynamic for politics. Thatcherism has set about managing and moulding these divisions and conflicting interests to form the stable base for a coherent political order.'[1] Moreover, he also points out that the Labour Party has implicitly accepted this through its belief that its employment goals should be constrained by what the *market* can deliver, and through its electoral inability to challenge seriously the tax and earnings privileges of the 'insiders'.[2]

Finally, there is a second, and perhaps more profound, set of issues that confounds the attempt to see Thatcherism as a rational promotion of post-Fordism in the economic sphere. This partly relates to the neo-liberal, financially driven nature of the Thatcherite agenda treated elsewhere. (Here we merely note that the UK manufacturing trade deficit continues to deteriorate and successful post-Fordist industries have not yet emerged in the British economy on a significant scale.) But perhaps of even greater importance are the continuing international uncertainties. Many authors have argued that a new world economic order is emerging on the back of the shift from Fordism to post-Fordism in the capitalist metropolises. Through the multinational corporations and (increasingly) the transnational banks, there is emerging a new international division of labour (NIDL) which is based on the increasing globalization of production (GOP). (Technically the theories of the NIDL and the GOP are separable: the former stresses a North–South divide; and the latter focuses on the increased importance of decentralized production sites (in both North and South) and their increased coordination through new technology – above all information technology.)

A useful summary of this general perspective has been provided by Gordon.[3] In the first instance it is argued that productive capital is being re-located on an increasingly global scale, thus increasing geographical specialization and interdependence. Secondly, it is suggested that the multinational corporations (MNCs) have developed new structures of control based on recent developments in communications, transport and managerial strategies. And thirdly, the internationalization of the financial and money markets in combination with the increasing fusion of MNCs and banks have resulted in the global enforcement of the law of value and increased competition.

However, it is arguable that this whole approach is fundamentally misconceived, for a basic assumption of such perspectives is that these trends (which undoubtedly exist) presage the emergence of a new stage or phase of capital accumulation on a global scale. But another way of looking at the very same developments is to see them as a defensive response to the crisis of the seventies: not a 're-ordering of world capitalism'[4] but rather 'global decay, not transformation' (Gordon's view). Thus in a powerful and carefully documented critique of theories of the NIDL/ GOP, Gordon has argued that recent developments are still part of the crisis, not a solution to it. The fall in corporate profitability in the sixties in most of the advanced capitalist economies led to a phase of 'paper investment' and the accumulation of financial assets. This trend was then exacerbated by the move to floating exchange rates, and the consequent increase in volatility of exchange and interest rates, which augmented the preoccupation with financial assets and the rapidly growing short-term financial flows across borders. From this perspective, the apparent dominance of circulation over production is but a symptom of the continuing crisis – not a resolution of it. In particular, Gordon's review of much of the relevant empirical evidence suggests that: 'we have *not* witnessed movement toward an increasingly "open" international economy, with productive capital buzzing around the globe, but ... we have moved rapidly toward an increasingly "closed" economy for productive investment, with production decisions increasingly dependent upon a range of institutional policies and activities and a pattern of differentiation and specialization among the less developed countries'.[5] If this is so, then to attribute an emerging post-Fordist economic logic to Thatcherism is, to say the least, somewhat premature.

Thus there are many ways in which to interpret the role of the Fordist labour process and the likely pattern of flexibilization; and it is far from clear that a distinctive Fordist or post-Fordist pattern of society exists. Indeed, once we move away from broad heuristic frameworks and engage in more nuanced analyses, the notions of Fordism and post-Fordism could become misleading if not carefully specified.

In the article which forms chapter 8 we paid insufficient attention to these protocols. Here we were misled for two main reasons. Firstly, we mistook the Thatcherite (and much business) rhetoric of 'flexibility' for the diverse and often unrelated social and economic changes that are really occurring. We now see that this rhetoric is better interpreted as an attempt to make sense of and impose some coherence on a highly complex reality, as part of an active and creative hegemonic project and accumulation strategy, rather than as the real, underlying changes themselves. And, secondly, given that some forms of flexibilization are undoubtedly occurring, these must be understood in terms of (a) nationally specific modes of growth, rather than identified with abstract regimes of accumulation, and (b) their specific insertion into a changing international economic order. Here, too, we would reinterpret rather than reject our arguments. Thatcherism is clearly seeking a new role for Britain in the global economy, which is distinct from that played during the postwar boom, and is more attuned to those areas of services and financial intermediation where the UK economy has a certain comparative advantage.

These qualifications are consistent with the more general approach we have tried to adopt throughout. We distinguish different strategies through which Thatcherism has sought to master and direct broader patterns of political and economic change. What we see in the current conjuncture (for all that it could be broadly characterized as post-Fordist) is a distinctive neo-liberal accumulation strategy, a specific pattern of state action premised on the political conjuncture, and a novel two nations hegemonic project. None of these is inconsistent with a transition to post-Fordism; but, equally, these phenomena can neither be reduced to a general logic of post-Fordism nor subsumed under a simple claim that Thatcherism is the British road to post-Fordism.

Chapter 9, the concluding essay, aims to serve several purposes. In the first instance, we briefly present the theoretical approach and concepts which we have found useful in the analysis of Thatcherism. Here we explore the notions of the social basis of the political order, the accumulation strategies of capital and the state, the state strategies pursued by political forces, and the hegemonic projects and power blocs that long-range political programmes seek to construct. In this section we are particularly concerned to move beyond the increasingly sterile divisions often encountered between sociology, politics and economics. In part this is the result of our different interests, but more fundamentally it is a reflection of our belief that theoretical progress in the social sciences requires this kind of research programme. In passing we note some of the points of convergence between our own work and that of other theorists who are often from very different theoretical traditions.

Our second principal aim is to demonstrate the power of these concepts through a provisional assessment of the degree to which Thatcherism has consolidated a new social, political and economic settlement. Here we suggest that the broad outlines of a new settlement are reasonably clear. But as with the postwar settlement, this new order is neither free of contradictions nor unchallengeable by alternative strategies and projects. Specifically, we draw attention to the failure of the Thatcherite accumulation and state strategies to reverse the UK's relative economic decline. This weakness has combined with a continued inability to resolve a long-standing ambivalence in British foreign policy between European integration and Atlanticism to create the space for a competing project from the centre. In outline at least this can be seen in the alternative recommendations urged by Michael Heseltine.

Unlike our earlier pieces in the *New Left Review* we do not offer here any strategic recommendations for the left. On this occasion our intent is strictly explanatory rather than strategic. We continue to believe, of course, that an adequate assessment of the Thatcherite strategy and project is a necessary precondition for combating its divisive and authoritarian drift. To this end, finally, we offer some suggestions for further research into the strengths and contradictions of, and alternatives to, Thatcherism.

8

Popular Capitalism, Flexible Accumulation and Left Strategy

Three years ago we presented an anatomy of Thatcherism, but today we are witnessing Margaret Thatcher's vivisection of the Left.[1] Her third successive general election victory has intensified the crisis in the labour movement and is likely to precipitate both a merger and a split in the Alliance. It has also given her the time and room for manoeuvre to prepare fresh onslaughts on already demoralized and disorganized leftwing forces, whose various strategies are often at odds with one another and incapable of overcoming a sense of disorientation. But has the Thatcher government consolidated its own position within the country as a whole? Talk of 'two nations', the 'North–South' divide and the Prime Minister's own election-night commitment to bring Thatcherism to the inner cities and the North suggest that much is still to be done. Now seems a good time to take stock of Thatcherism and consider its future. In our previous article we started with a critique of Stuart Hall's well-known account of Thatcherism as a form of 'authoritarian populism', and then moved on to develop our own analysis of it as a political movement, accumulation strategy, hegemonic project and attempt to recompose the state. In particular, we focused on four areas: the political and institutional preconditions for the rise and consolidation of Thatcherism in the 'dual crisis of the British state' and the crisis of the postwar social democratic settlement; the 'two nations' character of its political strategy and its effects on the redistribution of resources and the recomposition of electoral forces; the neo-liberal post-Fordist accumulation strategy which began to emerge after Thatcherism had consolidated its hold over government in 1982;[2] and the continuing reorganization of the British state and its relations to civil society and the political economy. Four key points are worth noting.

Our work has argued that Thatcherism had created neither a new national-popular consensus nor a new organic power bloc. For us its novelty lay in two areas. Firstly, Thatcherism had closed the gap between the electoral ideologies of grassroots Tories and the political perspectives of the leadership – dislodging the old 'one nation' and 'right progressive' Tories from control and reconstituting the Conservatives' electoral base after the failures of the Heath administration. Secondly, in linking 'authoritarian populism' and 'neo-liberalism' to a new *productivist* ideology, Thatcherism was developing an implicit two nations strategy. This would benefit those who belonged to the productive core of the market economy through state benefits and the rewards of the market. In contrast, those who were marginal to (or lived outside) the market economy would experience deteriorating economic conditions and reduced social welfare. This two nations strategy would have a complex and uneven impact on such societal cleavages as productive/parasitic, rich/poor, North/South or employed/unemployed; and would lead to an opposition between the favoured nation and contained, subordinate forces (including much of the non-skilled working class as well as ethnic minorities, single parents, poor pensioners etc.) outside the South-East and in the inner cities everywhere. This emergent strategy could powerfully consolidate Thatcherism and leave the Labour Party to defend the weak and marginal sections of society. The fundamental political choice would then become one between a new, two nation Toryism and the one nation, rightwing social democracy of the Alliance. This forecast has only partly been realized. The danger for the Labour Party still exists but, at the time of writing, the Alliance's future role is uncertain.

In addition we noted that Thatcherism had an explicit strategy to restructure the British economy as part of a reinvigorated, post-Fordist international capitalism. It adopted a neo-liberal accumulation strategy which involved the deregulation of private capital, the privatization of significant parts of the public sector, the introduction of commercial criteria into residual state sector activities, and the promotion of an open economy. Its post-Fordist components included the furthering of flexible accumulation based on new technologies, products and services; and a dual labour market in which a high-waged, skill-flexible core was opposed to a low-waged, time-flexible periphery.

Finally we suggested that, through their impact on the working class, petty bourgeoisie and fractions of capital, these structural changes in 'the decisive nucleus of economic activity' would be crucial in the struggle for hegemony. But we also pointed out that the reliance on market forces to secure sustained recovery eschewed substantial state direction and coordination, and thus ignored the fact that the long-term growth of manufacturing productivity and international competitiveness depend mainly on *dynamic* efficiency, active cooperation from labour within internal labour markets, and the facilitative and supporting role of the state. Nonetheless, the Conservatives' warrant of autonomy persisted with general support from the City, mixed blessings from industry, and only muted opposition from organized labour in the private sector and divided opposition in the public sector.

In this context we argued that the Conservatives might succeed in consolidating an electoral coalition around the new growth industries, the tradable service sector, and the consumer industries dependent thereon. If the trade union movement were also to recompose itself exclusively around the 'privileged nation', then the prospects for the left would be dire. To win the next election with the present electoral system and the continued division within and among the opposition parties, Thatcherism would only need support from some 40 per cent of those who voted. In the event it secured 43 per cent and further strengthened its position among the crucial skilled working class in the private sector.

The Electoral Record

Labour had probably lost the election before the first shots of the campaign were fired, as it is now clear that some 60 per cent of voters had already made up their minds. Even so, with around 40 per cent of electors still to decide, the Labour Party could have mobilized a majority for a short-term electoral coalition. After capturing 3–4 per cent of voters from the Alliance in the first week of the campaign, however, Labour was unable to make further gains. Apart from the Tory gutter press (which is always with us), there are no obvious scapegoats for this failure. Indeed, in contrast to 1983, the campaign itself was one of the most professional and disciplined since the war; the leader was credible, and the activists were united, at least for the duration.

The campaign material comprised a monthly *Briefing* during the pre-election period plus a *Local Election Special*, weekly background briefings for target seats, various editions of *Key Statistics*, information packs on the Tories' broken promises, on defence and on local elections, an election briefing book, a brochure from Trade Unions for a Labour Victory (TULV), and draft press releases for candidates. There was also an *Election Briefing* almost daily during the campaign. These materials, generally of a very high quality, were backed by a computer link-up to many constituencies so that responses to any campaign developments could be immediate and coordinated. Labour Central Office also produced twenty-one leaflets on all major policy issues, together with eight posters/car stickers, nine different clipsheets, seven direct mail drafts, and seven booklets; TULV issued a further six leaflets. Clear propaganda roles were given to *Labour Weekly*, *Labour Party News* and *New Socialist*; and there was a national press advertising campaign. Five television party political broadcasts were also prepared, the first of which (repeated on 5 June) was widely regarded as being state-of-the art. Party headquarters succeeded almost beyond hope in managing the agenda so that, as far as possible, pre-selected issues were discussed. To this end individuals such as Scargill and Benn were carefully hidden, and national figures were sent to specific places to support the day's theme. It is hard to imagine how Labour could have conducted a more professional campaign. This strongly suggests that the problem had more to do with the message than the medium and that any future advance of Labour will depend on developing a new programme together with the organizational, institutional and strategic changes needed to support it. This impression is reinforced by looking behind the campaign to the sociology and political economy of electoral support.

The 1979 election, which first brought the Thatcherite Tories to power, was a 'normal' election held in 'exceptional' circumstances. Many cast their vote against the Labour Party, the 'Winter of Discontent', and the unions rather than for the Thatcherite programme: inflation, taxation and crime were also key issues. Nor did a realigning election really occur in 1983. The 'Falklands factor' appears to have had only limited impact.[3] The majority of voters were motivated more by dislike of other parties than by support for their chosen party.[4] This was linked to the sense of economic optimism and individual prosperity among Conservative voters – especially among skilled blue-collar workers – and the fear that Labour might ruin it. Uneven development of the British economy under Thatcherism had aggravated the North–South divide and promoted regional polarization rather than the traditional uniform swing. There were clearer divisions between the South, suburban, and rural constituencies and those in the North and inner-city areas; and New Towns and 'affluent worker' constituencies had higher pro-Tory swings than university towns or areas of Asian and Afro-Caribbean settlement.[5]

This pattern was reinforced this year (1987). Real gains in individual or family prosperity for the majority, and an increasingly widespread belief that the economy was looking up, dovetailed with the Tory campaign to persuade people that Labour could not manage the economy. Moreover, neither Labour nor the Alliance parties attacked the Conservatives' economic record as such – only its social repercussions. The outcome of the June election has strengthened the impression that two political nations now exist in Britain, well beyond merely regional differences in party support. Although this has often been expressed in terms of the so-called North–South divide, such a catchphrase can be misleading.

Finally, we do not believe that authoritarian populism played a major role in the Conservatives' electoral success. Since 1979 there has been a 'gradual moving left' among the electorate. This has not yet reversed the 'great moving right show' of the seventies, but it does show steady support for the welfare state system.[6] Indeed, the 1987 election highlighted the paradox that, although the three most salient issues for voters (jobs, health and education) all revealed a Labour lead, a campaign built around them had little impact without narrow appeals to self-interest and/or a record of apparent success in managing the economy in the past.[7] It is material concessions which have been crucial in consolidating pragmatic Conservative support in the working class, albeit strongly reinforced by the mass media and the 'moving right' ideological organizations.

The Changing Party System

Psephologists have encountered major problems in interpreting the shifts in voting behaviour in Britain.[8] For they ignore the fact that structural crises undermine familiar parameters and that societal restructuring usually extends to a reorganization of party systems. Thus the emergence of an allegedly impossible 'stagflation' in a Keynesian welfare state system in crisis was matched by both class and partisan de-alignment in the two-party political system which lasted from 1945 until 1970. In the present transition to a post-Fordist economy, we are now witnessing a parallel reorganization of the party system which, by no means automatic, involves contrasting political responses on the part of the two main components. So far Labour has failed to adapt organizationally and strategically to the current changes. Since 1983, however, the Conservatives have identified, interpreted, and given some political and ideological coherence to the complex and disparate socio-economic changes involved in this period of transition.

As familiar class boundaries began to dissolve in the sixties, political parties lost both their electoral bearings and their programmatic clarity. In particular, the manual/non-manual distinction was overlaid by three further cleavages. The postwar boom generated affluence for the Fordist 'mass' or semi-skilled worker (reflected in the ill-founded *embourgeoisement* thesis) as well as more instrumental unionism and electoral behaviour and a new division between the private and public sectors and among non-manual workers.[9] Class de-alignment was particularly marked in the working class because the Labour Party failed to represent the interests (as defined within the Keynesian welfare state system) of its traditional supporters or to resolve the emerging crisis in its flawed Fordist economic base.[10] The Conservative Party also lost ground as a result of its Keynesian commitment (including its solicitous concern for full employment and the social wage). But its traditional petty bourgeois support responded not so much with new electoral allegiances (apart from Liberal protest votes) as with a sense of petty bourgeois *ressentiment* which flowed as a subterranean current to re-emerge in the river of Thatcherism.

The crisis of Fordism and the Keynesian welfare state system laid the basis for a new politics both in the inner cities (reflected at local government level) and in social movements (often strongest in the inner cities). This new politics, opposed as much to Butskellite consensus as to the emergent neo-liberal crisis-management of Labour and Tories alike, served to fragment the Labour Party especially between inner-city Constituency Labour Parties (with their concern for non-affluent workers, the public sector, and various rainbow minorities and social movements) and the national organization (which was more oriented to the skilled male union member and the maintenance of the postwar settlement). In turn this was associated with a process of partisan de-alignment tending to narrow Labour's working-class base to 'traditional' sectors in Scotland, the North, the public sector, and the council estates.[11] The emergence of the SDP was initially inspired by an urge to resurrect and preserve Keynesian social democracy against a Bennite Labour Party and corporatism. Under Dr Owen it then evolved in the direction of a 'progressive', neo-liberal party oriented to 'Thatcherism with a human face'. However, this shift has helped to undermine the Alliance – which was, in any case, becoming more and more a movement based upon professional and managerial workers. Only the Conservative Party has a true cross-class base, having consolidated its support among the skilled working class. The latter is the biggest single group in the electorate and, in material terms, has done well under Thatcherism.

The post-Fordist division of the workforce between a skill-flexible core and a time-flexible periphery, which is now replacing the old manual/non-manual distinction, underlies a shift from the postwar vision of a one nation mass consumption system to a two nations model based on the affluent flexible worker plus a social security state. Whereas the Labour Party, *qua* social democratic, could gain from the Fordist system with its Keynesian welfare state politics, it is the Conservative Party which is pioneering the transition to post-Fordism and identifying itself with the class interests of workers at its core.

The Labour Party is only now beginning to debate whether to adapt to the post-Fordist realities at the expense of traditional one nation commitments – a debate all the more necessary because of changes in the class structure. Not only has the manual working class shrunk from around half of the electorate in 1964 to around a third in 1983; but even this class is being more heavily polarized into core and periphery. Clearly this transition and recomposition are proceeding unevenly across Britain. This explains the paradox that, 'while class forces have waned among individual voters, they appear to flourish in the regions – and even within constituencies'.[12] Thus a strong manufacturing presence correlates with Labour voting in the North and Tory voting in the South. Moreover, since this divide continues a trend pre-dating 1979, it cannot just be explained away as an effect of Thatcherism. In a sense North and South have become metaphors for Fordism and post-Fordism, and Labour's hold on the 'North' could prove uncertain, especially if the Tories succeed in pushing Thatcherism and post-Fordism beyond their current strongpoints. Unless the Labour Party adapts to the fundamental social and economic changes, future elections will merely determine whether we have a majority Conservative government or a hung Parliament.[13] Even the alternative bases of Labour's support in the seventies and eighties (in the inner cities, rainbow coalitions and social movements) could turn out to be unstable. Not only is it difficult to reconcile the interests of such minorities with a broader electoral base, but their political commitments are also liable to change. This is not to suggest that Labour has only to identify itself with the 'white heat' of the post-Fordist revolution to make a decisive breakthrough at the polls. But it does pose a series of strategic dilemmas which need serious debate on the left.

The Thatcherite Strategy

These dilemmas must be considered from at least two viewpoints: firstly, the likely changes in British political economy and social structure during the Conservatives' third term; and secondly, the current strategy, function and organization of the Labour Party. As we have seen, Labour's campaign in 1987 did not properly address the issues of flexible accumulation and popular capitalism around which the Conservatives are organizing their accumulation strategy and hegemonic project for the 1990s. There is a real danger that the Labour Party (with or without the Alliance) will concentrate its efforts on forming an anti-Thatcherite bloc for the next election when it is far from clear either that Thatcher will remain as leader, or that the Tories are incapable of presentational adjustments. The real tasks for the next election are to develop a socialist version of flexible accumulation and a socialist alternative to popular capitalism.[14]

The principal lines of conflict within the Conservative Cabinet have changed at least twice since 1979. The tussle between 'wets' and 'dries' is now past history and that between 'consolidators' and 'radicals' – which precipitated the 'mid-life crisis of Thatcherism' – has now been resolved in favour of the latter.[15] The inertia and drift which characterized much of the second term is to be banished from the third. This time round the main point of contention concerns the degree and forms of state intervention necessary to advance the transition to a post-Fordist economy. On this issue Thatcher seems to be in a minority in her Cabinet, and much will depend on whether the neo-statists have more success than did the wets or the consolidators. Certainly the growing centralization of state control in existing areas – as well as the new forms of intervention through the Manpower Services Commission, the

Urban Development Corporations, new technology programmes, or state support for the allegedly self-starting, self-financing small business sector – belie the government's claim to be rolling back the frontiers of the state. In fact, of course, Thatcherism is merely rolling back the frontiers of the social democratic state; disengagement here is accompanied by deeper involvement in other areas of post-Fordist promotion.[16]

The agenda outlined in the Queen's Speech and the Conservative Manifesto gives indications about the future course of government policy. Four main themes have been announced for the beginning of the third term: changes in the management of the inner cities; a radical restructuring of the state education system; changes to the ownership structure of public rented accommodation (and the decontrol of private rents); and the abolition of the domestic property tax (rates) in favour of a regressive poll tax. The most significant omission from public statements thus far is, of course, government plans for the NHS. The proposals have a threefold objective: to extend the neo-liberal strategy to the depressed, low- or no-growth urban areas and parts of the welfare state; to undermine Labour's electoral base in the second nation; and to alter significantly the modes of representation, internal organization and intervention in the state system.

Spearheading the attack on the inner cities will be the Young–Clarke team at the Department of Trade and Industry (DTI) and Ridley at the Department of the Environment (DoE). The latter has been Whitehall's main arm reaching directly into the urban arena, and its favoured (if hitherto largely experimental) mode of operation under Thatcherism has been the Urban Development Corporations (UDCs).[17] These are dominated by business and finance and have only two local authority representatives; they have abrogated local authority planning powers and enjoy total control over designated areas of urban deprivation. Their responsibilities include: buying land, preparing industrial infrastructure, developing land for private industry, attracting private investment and selling land to business. The most celebrated example is the London Docklands Development Corporation, which has built a transit system, a city airport, housing and industry. For a government supposedly committed to rolling back the frontiers of the state and opposed to quangos these powers are breathtaking.

The DTI seems most unsuitable as a ministry for urban intervention and devotes the bulk of its (drastically reduced) spending to general, regional and specific industrial support. This may explain why struggles continue among the departments of employment, trade, health and social security, and the environment over who is to play the chief coordinating role in the new urban initiative. At the same time, however, ministers are generally agreed that no increases in total public spending are required – although political pressure and existing demand-led programmes clearly limit the scope for reductions. This suggests that it is change in the institutions allocating funds (and the political forces able to influence them) which is thought to be decisive for the inner city programme. This point is crucial for understanding the Thatcherite strategy. For, during the long postwar boom, Britain along with many other capitalist democracies saw a rising share for local government in a rising total public expenditure. This occurred because of the growing weight of socialized consumption patterns under Fordism and the role of local and/or regional agencies in welfare delivery. These agencies were not always democratically accountable to local electorates and were prey to influence from the professions, business interests, the unions and the local authorities' own peak organizations. Quasi-government agencies also proliferated, removed from local control. In this sense, the removal of local government powers significantly pre-dates the Thatcher era.[18] But this long-term trend is now reinforced by two phenomena more directly related to Thatcherism: its neo-liberal strategy and its attempt to restrain, cut and redirect public expenditure.

The post-Fordist mode of accumulation places a lower value on mass individual and collective consumption and creates pressures for a more differentiated production and distribution of health, education, transport and housing. In earlier capitalist regimes the majority of the population were 'have-nots' and a minority could be described as 'have-lots'.[19] The one nation Keynesian welfare state was intended to grant this majority access to mass consumption through transfer payments and/or collective provision. Ostensibly this occurred at the expense of the 'have-lots', but in reality it mainly depended upon inter-generational redistribution within the same class. The transition to post-Fordism is associated with an emergent division between, on the one hand, subordinate groups who have come to depend on the public provision of these goods and services, and, on the other, privileged sectors who can take advantage of new forms of private provision, often encouraged by fiscal subsidies. A majority now belong to these privileged sectors in terms of transport and housing and to the subordinate groups in terms of health and educational provision. This has already produced an electoral alliance of the privileged majority against the 'have-nots', and the Conservatives want to encourage this through their policies for 'popular capitalism'.

Centralization and Devolution

In the third term this will involve further attempts to undermine the Labour Party's base in public housing and to consolidate the Conservatives' own base through differential access to education and health. At first this need not involve a major transfer of activities to the market sector proper, but could proceed through a two-pronged strategy of centralization from above and devolution to consumers below. This would erode the power of local authorities and public-sector producer groups and the overall legitimacy of public provision. According to the balance of forces and the precise institutional arrangements, it might then be possible to contemplate a further stage in which the central state would be able to carry through actual privatization. The anti-bureaucratic, anti-egalitarian thrust of the first stage, with its intra-class redistributional implications, might have considerable electoral appeal to groups of privileged wage-earners – especially if Labour merely confines itself to defence of the status quo.

Tax cuts are intended to assist the shift from public to private provision and to sustain the general ideology of public expenditure control – a traditional obsession of the Treasury – that legitimates attacks on local authorities. But the growth of privatization, contracting-out and deregulation of local services will also strengthen capital vis-à-vis organized labour and the state. More generally, the shift from locally accountable to centralized and/or consumer-driven services alters the institutional allocation of social spending in favour of productive investment and at the expense of unproductive consumption. Insofar as it weakens the legitimatory and mass-integrative functions of the welfare state, it could also lead to greater emphasis on policing the crisis through a range of repressive measures.[20]

These issues can be illustrated by a brief look at secondary education and housing. The political space for Thatcherite policies in education was opened by Labour's failure to offer a principled defence of collectivism or to propose convincing reforms to secure its democratic provision. The (not so) Great Debate on teaching standards and the curriculum initiated by Callaghan in 1978 paved the way for identifying young people as a political and employment problem and the teaching profession as responsible for the crisis of the education system. Education cuts were also begun under the last Labour government in response to IMF pressures and forecasts about falling enrolments. These developments enabled the Conservatives to present their policies as responding to a *nationally agreed* set of problems rather than a business-inspired agenda. The softening-up moves of the first two administrations included: removal of the compulsion on local authorities to reorganize along comprehensive lines; the establishment of parental rights to express a preference for a school; the appointment of parents and teachers on governing bodies; and the assisted places scheme. However, it was clear that no further progress could be made until the teachers' unions were beaten decisively. Therefore a second round was scheduled to effect the unilateral introduction of greater DES control over teacher training, the publication of HM Inspectors' reports, changes in teachers' working conditions, and the by-passing of local authorities and unions in matters of pay. Soon a single education bill will break local authority monopoly over public education provision, devolve power from administrators to heads and prescribe a nationwide core curriculum. Local authorities will thus be squeezed between heightened central control and devolution to independently governed schools (or business-funded city technical colleges) able to compete for per-pupil grants. Even if spending on education were significantly increased (above the 5.3 per cent of GDP in 1978–9 and 4.7 per cent in 1985–6), these changes could not fail to yield a markedly more inegalitarian, two nation state system. If in time the balance of forces proves favourable, a final step might be to privatize the state's role through overt selection and additional fee-paying on top of a minimalist voucher system.

Housing is simpler still. Following the electorally advantageous round of council-house sales, it is now intended that the public rented sector should be privatized (or at least removed from local authority control through state sponsorship of housing associations). This has been pioneered by Tory councils such as Wandsworth, and Conservative Central Office is reported to have been paying close attention. After all, 'if they can win a seat like Battersea they can win many others like it. And if they can break down Labour's power base on the council estates, they equally can break Labour's power base in the inner cities.'[21] Any residue of local spending powers will be further curtailed by the regressive poll tax, under which 18 million ratepayers (6 million of whom do not pay the full amount) will be boosted to 35 million poll-tax payers. The losers will be drawn mainly from the second nation.

In the short to medium term, such strategies for the welfare state and the inner cities are not intended to produce serious changes in the economic prospects of the second nation. The central concern is rather to consolidate political support for the general parameters of the neo-liberal accumulation strategy and the popular-capitalist hegemonic project. Indeed, the primacy of the political class struggle in Thatcherite policy is often astonishing. Whereas the last Labour government tended to subordinate political strategy to economic crisis-management, the Thatcher governments have often treated economic policy as a sub-field for the politics of hegemony. This can be illustrated in four examples: the early restructuring of exchange-rates to win the political battle against inflation, despite the impact on a struggling British industry; the key role of 'popular capitalism' and PSBR considerations, rather than industrial or competition policy, in shaping the privatization drive; the gearing of manpower training to the social and political consequences of youth unemployment as much as to the promotion of neo-liberal flexibility; and the use of public-sector industrial relations to provide macho-management demonstration effects for a far more cautious private sector. The general rationale seems to be that if the government can modify the balance of forces in the short term, it will gain sufficient time to restructure society and to allow a market-generated recovery.

Thus restructuring for capital through Enterprise Zones, Freeports and UDCs is as much concerned with social and political recomposition as it is with job creation. Local Labour authority initiatives have probably created more jobs, at lower costs, than these government schemes. However, as two left critics, Goodwin and Duncan, note: 'Local economic policy is not, directly, about economic change. It is about the *way* in which political demonstration and political mobilization can support economic change, and thus what kind of economic change this will be.'[22] This view is confirmed in a recent comment in *Financial Weekly*, the house journal of the new financial services sector:

> It is not hard to see Government policy as the next and possibly final round in a battle against the Labour local authorities rather than as direct action to relieve the inner cities. Its emphasis on UDCs, central government-appointed bodies that can usurp many of the basic functions of local government, could be taken as corroborating the view that this is a power battle first and a zeal for reform second.[23]

Left Strategy

In our earlier chapters we argued that the British state had been restructured through civil service reorganization and politically motivated promotion to key official posts; through the enhancement of Treasury control over all areas of government; through a much-reinforced policing apparatus, a redefinition of 'subversion' and heightened manipulation of the media; through the radical centralization of government power and the assault on local government; through a programme of denationalization and competition which would be difficult to reverse; through privatization in the welfare state – thereby constructing new interests in private provision both among clients and within the professions and supply industries; and through radical restructuring of education and the expansion of the Manpower Services Commission, etc.

The reorganization of the state under the past two Thatcher governments has been marked by permanent improvization, trial-and-error experimentation, and institutional Darwinism. This has had three major, and somewhat paradoxical, effects. Firstly, it has lessened (or further removed) the functions and political power, not only of Parliament but also of local and regional government, the institutions responsible for the social democratic delivery of welfare goods and services, and organs of functional representation (particularly the unions). Secondly, in some cases these functions and powers have been (re)concentrated below the central level – most notably through the UDCs – so that they have become more flexible and less accountable to local electorates, their own employees, or traditional clients. But central government has typically reserved the right to redistribute resources across and among these bodies without meaningful prior consultation with the interests affected; and it can pick and choose among different, often competing, experimental models to promote those which seem to be advancing its objectives and then modify or close those which are costly and ineffective or which serve as sites of resistance. In this way the central state hopes to penetrate more effectively into local niches and micro-economic interstices, reinforcing capital's ability to exploit even the smallest areas of surplus production and consumption and to further its reorganization by gaining access to the micro-level of civil society.

Thirdly, in other cases this power has been centralized in the executive branch in Whitehall. This does not mean, however, that it has been subject to any effective concentration and coordination through increased control over different parts of the central state and their associated policy networks. Whether this lack of concentration is rational cannot be assessed purely in administrative terms. It has certainly militated against stable, long-term policy making in many institutions (for example, local government, education and training, health, nationalized industries). But it also enables the government continually to reallocate resources through selective adjustment of financial and manpower budgets, to redirect policy by closing, modifying or expanding specific initiatives and programmes, and to encourage competition by making further support contingent on compliance with the government's (often changing) objectives. This is all the more necessary because Thatcherism has encountered many institutional obstacles and much political resistance as it seeks to find a relatively smooth path towards a post Fordist future. Periods of institutional inertia, political immobilism, electoral unpopularity or economic discomfiture have been broken, circumvented, ridden out and overcome through a mixture of lies, good luck and sharp judgement. Nor have the economic and social costs been negligible as first one, and then another, tactic are mobilized behind a flexible accumulation strategy and a two nations hegemonic project.

Through this kaleidoscopic movement within the state system two key elements of continuity stand out: one political, the other administrative. Thatcher clearly personifies the political commitment to the radical, neo-liberal popular-capitalist strategy which has gradually taken shape over two periods in office, while the continued administrative dominance of the Treasury as the guardian of the public purse has served as a key instrument in the financially driven reorganization of the state. Together with the step-by-step recomposition of the top civil service to promote people who are 'one of us' (or sufficiently chameleon to appear so), this has helped to consolidate the political gains of the 'Thatcher revolution'.

All these changes could still prove temporary, of course, if the overall accumulation strategy proves unworkable. We have already offered reasons to question how rational this might be in the long term, especially for domestic capital and its workforce.[24] Nor can there be any guarantee that the hegemonic project of popular capitalism can cement a bloc of electoral support for Thatcherism around the 'haves' in the economic core and the most-favoured-nation owning homes, shares and private pensions. Changes in the state, however dynamic, cannot be the only key to success. Not only hegemony but also the state need a 'decisive economic nucleus'. In turn this suggests that a successful challenge to Thatcherism must organize on all three fronts and offer an alternative institutional design for the state as well as for flexible economic organization and a democratic pluralist civil society.

The *New Statesman* has now joined *The Economist* in arguing for a realignment in party politics that would involve some kind of pact between the Alliance (minus its Owenite Front) and the Labour Party. The logic of this argument, as with its pre-election versions, derives primarily from electoral considerations. Thus the paper's political commentator, Peter Kellner, after surveying the awesome scale of Labour's defeat, has argued that the Labour Party is faced with only two, mutually exclusive options: either come to terms with the Alliance or attempt to marginalize it.[25] The former policy, which is favoured by Kellner, would imply a commitment to PR, policy changes, Party reorganization (suggestions include: one member one vote for candidate selection, a non-policy-making role for Conference, etc.) and an acceptance that Labour will never govern alone again. The latter orientation, which appears to have the support of Kinnock and Hattersley, would involve even more profound changes of policy and structure as the Party would have to shift to the centre ground in the hope of displacing the Alliance. This line of analysis is premissed on the correct observation made by Anthony Arblaster, from a rather different position, that 'the notion of an anti-Thatcher majority has just as much, and as little, substance as its opposite: the existence of an anti-Labour or anti-Socialist majority.'[26] In terms of the *electoral* logic of the *pre*-1987 period there was little to fault this argument: the result in 1987, despite Labour's numerically higher poll, was a more serious defeat than in 1983. Indeed Raymond Williams, again within a dissenting perspective, made a similar point in early 1984 during the 'Hobsbawm debate'.[27] But Williams went on to ask the question that many of the current enthusiasts refuse to face: What kind of party is the Labour Party to be? On what terms would such a pact be possible?

Those on the left who have advanced the pact/PR argument hope for a break with the competitive party duopoly, presaging moves to a more open, decentralized and democratic political system within which a genuine socialist politics could begin to be constructed.[28] Michael Rustin has argued that this would involve not a *general* political pact but a '*specific* pre-election agreement, on a minimal programme of democratization including electoral reform', regional/national devolution, strengthened local government, freedom of information, and so on.[29] It presupposes the defeat of Owen & Co. within the Alliance and would not preclude electoral competition around other issues. This view has much to commend it and the changes and strategy we have described above would have been impossible in a state with constitutional protection for local and/or regional government. Hilary Wainwright has argued for a similar strategy for the Labour left which would focus on the widespread democratization of the institutions of British society.[30] In our view such a strategy is unlikely to succeed on its own, but it would begin to provide an opening to the privileged nation through the Alliance constituency committed to constitutional reform. But is it wholly realistic? The Alliance would use the pact to shift the boundaries of 'moderate' policies to exclude many from the left. Similarly, the Labour Party and its union allies would reinforce the politics of 'balanced ticket' leadership 'wherein a paramount concern for defensive unity is conjoined to the tenacious belief that the key to electoral success lies in marginalizing the left.'[31] The failure of the joint Tribune–Campaign Group slate and the Centre–Right dominance of Kinnock's shadow cabinet are only the most recent demonstrations of this. In other words, besides marginalization of the Owenite Front such a strategy would require a decisive reorientation of the strategy of the *Labour* leadership.

Moreover, since we cannot have PR before the defeat of the Conservatives, the space for a genuine left politics would not arise until 1991 at the earliest, perhaps not till the mid-1990s. In the interim the requirements of the pact would surely stifle independent left initiatives for fear of pushing the Alliance contingent towards a non-Thatcherite Conservative Party, that is, where David Owen has always wanted it. It was this kind of consideration that led Williams, Arblaster and others to conclude that such a pact would be the worst defeat that *socialists* could suffer. Furthermore, Conservative politics will be very different in 1991 from 1987, just as they were different in 1987 from 1983 or 1979. The left all too often fights in terms of the previous election, which results from the organizational inertia of the labour movement and the failure to analyse Thatcherism as a constantly evolving politico-economic project. This has one immediate consequence. If the Conservative Party perceived an 'anti-Thatcher' alliance in the making they would move to outflank it by seeking to detach its SDP contingent. It is therefore doubtful whether the narrow political basis for such a pact exists anyway. A 'progressive Thatcherism' *à la* Heseltine & Co. is uncomfortably close to the right of the Alliance for optimism on this score. Finally, and most importantly, we would argue that such calculations do not address the real basis of Thatcher's success to date.

The New Agenda

The Conservative Party has convinced much of the privileged core that its material interests as both workers and consumers are best secured through policies of popular capitalism: at present this includes ownership of the home, shares and pensions, and it may come to embrace a degree of private entitlement to education and health provision. Privatized incorporation of the worker/consumer, however, can only be sustained if the bases of collectivist politics are simultaneously eroded. This is not just a matter of changing the social profile of the class structure – the pace of change has been dramatically hastened by rapid de-industrialization and government policy – but also requires the erosion of the organizational and relational bases for collectivism and democratic politics. The defeat of oppositional trade unionism, the far-reaching diminution of the powers and autonomy of local government, the recasting of state institutions (abolition and/or restructuring of quangos, changes in personnel and operating criteria, etc.) and the demobilization of new social movements have all sustained a new form of statism. In parallel with the widespread privatization and deregulation, there has been an unprecedented arrogation of central state powers which has openly short-circuited established mechanisms of participation and/or account-ability. In this final elimination of corporatist collaboration, individuals are protected by the strong state as long as they have no wish to participate in, or initiate, policy on their own behalf. The aim is thus to construct a robust yet flexible institutional order which precludes political 'interference' in business activity and forcibly imposes market criteria on wide areas of state provision.

The Conservatives won in 1987 because of their economic record, not in spite of it. It is too easy to blame this on the undoubted difficulty that Labour faced in convincing the electorate that Thatcherism was economically irrational while those in work had seen their real incomes steadily rise. The images of decline and decay in Labour's rhetoric (however accurate for the second nation) failed to reflect the apparently market-led growth of the leading sectors in the neo-liberal project; and the images of controls, constraints and bureaucratic redistribution conveyed negative, backward-looking connotations. Moreover, the long-announced economic crunch has not materialized. The re-emergence of a balance-of-payments constraint on domestic expansion is real enough, but it does not follow that there will be an identifiable moment when the left can seize the initiative from any crisis. Given the demobilization and passivity induced under Thatcherism, combined with the erosion of the left's organizational base, any opening may well prove to be one for the right. But all of this merely reflects the central problem that the left lacks an alternative strategy of reconstruction – one that could unify and defend the second nation while appealing to the industrial core in both its worker and consumer status.

What, then, are the political obstacles to the two nations project? And what kind of politics of power is required if the left is to bridge the divide between the second nation and the privileged core? In the realm of education and health care, over 90 per cent of the population remains entirely dependent on collective provision, but even here the potential for Thatcherite advance should not be underestimated. For while there is widespread popular support for a politics of redistribution, this must both be non-bureaucratic and ensure economic growth for the privileged core. In this sense the key barrier lies less in people's perceptions than in the absence of the organizational structures that might provide an arena for the two nations to find common cause. This situation will be aggravated to the extent that the Conservative attack on Labour's remaining power bases is successful. And such causes, to constitute a politics of the *left*, must involve an extension of democracy at the level of the state and the enterprise. A continuation of Labour's traditional centralism and statism is doomed to failure, while pure market-based solutions merely pave the way for an Owen-style 'progressive' Thatcherism. The weakness of market-based proposals is not simply their economic logic, it is rather that without a significant extension of democracy and popular participation the social base for a redistributive politics cannot be constructed.

Thus if the left is to take advantage of opposition to, and contradictions in, the statism and market polarization induced by Thatcherism, it must recognize that only a democratic collectivism can avoid the demobilization and political passivity that both marketization and bureaucratic–collectivist solutions engender.[32] For the Labour Party there are only two possible partners with whom to build a coalition around such concerns: the Alliance or the trade unions, and neither offers any easy options. We have argued that an anti-Thatcher pact with the Alliance, cast at the level of the politics of support, is deeply problematic. But some form of appeal to the Alliance, in the politics of both support and power, must be made for Labour to reconnect with the privileged core and the public sector professionals and managers. Recent experience is hardly encouraging. Despite real cooperation at the grassroots, the Alliance has been split apart by policy disagreements and strategic differences among the leadership. The open, post-election wrangles have simply made plain the two contesting visions that have always constituted the Alliance: the Jenkins–Steel project to build a non-union party of the centre–left that would accomplish the aborted Gaitskellite design outside the Labour Party; and the Owen Front strategy of a plebiscitarian-leadership party of the centre that could play a power-broking role in a partially de-aligned party system. Aside from this, any workable cooperation between Labour and Liberal (let alone SDP) activists will be very hard to achieve. In the Labour camp the constituency parties have become infamous for their capacity to devote heroic amounts of time and energy to organization and internal matters. Among the Liberals the activist concern with community politics, opposition to union involvement and a basically liberal social philosophy all militate against cooperation with Labour. The position and role of the trade unions are equally uncertain.

Over half of the declining trade union membership did not vote Labour. This poses another acute dilemma: Labour can retain something like its existing relationship to the unions and hope that they win a wider membership; or it can distance itself from the unions and make an alternative appeal to these union (and non-union) voters. It is true that an overwhelming majority of union members support a political role for their union, but this is no longer necessarily a Labour politics. For the fastest-growing sections of the movement have been in those unions which have not affiliated to the Labour Party. Moreover the traditional industrial and general unions have been weakened by the massive job loss in manufacturing, altered management and ownership in the public sector, industrial relations legislation, the freezing out from corporatist bodies and the longer-term restructuring of employment patterns. The last includes the formation of a post-Fordist core of company unionism, internal labour markets, relative job security and rising living standards, and a periphery (both new and old) of high-turnover, part-time/ temporary work with limited employment rights and low pay. Unity among trade unions is obstructed still further by the difficulties of organizing the periphery and overcoming inter-union rivalry in the core. On the one hand, the new 'strike-free' unionism shows no sign of developing a concern with industrial democracy; it is rather the old strategy to secure craft monopoly and increased membership in conditions of restructured labour processes and markets. On the other hand, the membership drive of the TGWU, GMB and others is explicitly premissed on an assessment of the 'new individualism'. Finally, a fourth (but not final) round of legislation will weaken the closed shop, further regulate union finances and balloting, and institute a blacklegs' charter by preventing disciplinary action against those who continue to work after a ballot to strike.

Concluding Remarks

We do not see it as our purpose to provide detailed recommendations for the Labour Party or the left. Rather we are concerned to outline the broad issues that any successful strategy must confront, and which seem to have been passed over in much of the immediate post-election analysis and prescription. If the broad outlines of the above analysis are correct, then we would suggest that Thatcherism is a highly flexible, rapidly changing phenomenon, with a formidable capacity to work with, rather than against, powerful social and economic trends. This has involved giving them a particular shape and allocating benefits and losses in order to reshape constituencies of support. The two nations divide was not simply an intention of Thatcherite politics but a consequence of its neo-liberal strategies. Once emergent, however, its significance was recognized and its consolidation has become more deliberate. The left cannot wait for this dynamism to expire but must elaborate and pursue alternative strategic choices to confront the consequences of neo-liberalism.

Beyond narrow electoral speculations and internal constitutional debates, it is necessary to grasp the nature and likely evolution of Thatcherism, its weaknesses and contradictions. In particular, the structure of the Labour Party needs to be reconsidered in terms of the function it is expected to perform – which, in turn, can only be specified in the light of the strategy adopted by the left. The current subordination of most discussion in the Party to the concerns of immediate electoral politics, and an assessment of the *last* election, can only result in a perpetuation of Labour's inability to challenge Thatcherism on the new political and socio-economic terrain. We have felt obliged to reiterate one of our earlier arguments: that Labour appears always to be committed to fighting the previous election. Yet the evidence is clear that Thatcher's three elections have so far been very different. While it may be true that the institutional structure of the Labour Party inhibits quick-footed responses and that a new campaigning capacity is required, a fetter at least as great is the unwillingness to abandon past touchstones of Labour Party analysis and action. The solution is not simply to hand more decisional autonomy to the Party leadership, nor to develop a more effective campaigning approach with the help of increasingly fetishized opinion polls. Without an alternative projected in a convincing way, the chase after opinion polls may lead Neil Kinnock to Number 10 – only to discover that he is Mrs Thatcher's tenant.

Left strategy must start from a recognition of the irreversible changes wrought by the crisis of a nationally based Fordism, now superseded by an internationalized post-Fordism. First of all, the left must promote an alternative to the neo-liberal path to flexibilization, involving renewed concern with industrial strategy to underpin a domestic employment project. Second, such a strategy will provide for an enhancement of the role of the state and other publicly-owned economic bodies – and there is thus an urgent need to devise new institutional mechanisms that promote democratic, decentralized collective decision making in the economy and the state delivery of services. Here we strongly endorse the arguments of Robin Murray that the case for macro-economic planning and industrial restructuring has lost none of its force, and that the relationships between socially-owned enterprises and the (increasingly international) market must be at the centre of strategic thinking about the public sector.[33] This would dovetail with a commitment to a partnership within Europe to promote an independent third force – as the German SPD, for example, has increasingly advocated – rather than the Conservative vision of a strengthened Euro-Thatcherite pillar for the Atlantic alliance.

Third, the social base for such a politics of power will have to reach into the privileged core of wage-earners while simultaneously unifying the second nation. A rainbow coalition of the unemployed, blacks, women and other marginalized constituencies lacks the organizational and programmatic coherence to serve as the basis of a left politics. This is not to say that social movements are an irrelevance. On the contrary, many of the issues they raise – determined policies against institutionalized racism, the marginalization of women in the labour market, the lack of adequate child-care facilities, measures for disarmament etc. – must be major priorities for any left force. But they cannot substitute for political parties. Fourth, and finally, left strategy must also offer policies which lie outside the boundaries of Thatcherism. To offer a more progressive and humane brand of Thatcherism would not necessarily be electorally advantageous; when offered the choice between *ersatz* and the real thing, it is unlikely that the electorate would choose the former.

[*As published in autumn 1987*]

9

Analysing Thatcherism

Part I critically reviewed a range of competing definitions, periodizations, and interpretations of Thatcherism and suggested that even the best provided only a partial account. In this chapter we try to justify the alternative approach to political analysis that informed our work in Part II. We identified two general problems with much of the literature on Thatcherism. First, a wide range of accounts – both academic and journalistic – merely described the surface events of British political life after 1979 without seeking to explain them. Second, those analyses which have tried to develop a deeper understanding of Thatcherism – through various theoretical models – concentrated one-sidedly on its economic, political or ideological aspects. All would probably agree that a rounded account must be sensitive to each dimension: but the central question is how this can be achieved without simply presenting a more or less random mix of factors. In this chapter we outline some ways in which current approaches to political economy and the anatomy of civil society can be combined to offer analyses whose multiple strands offer both *breadth* and *depth*. By 'breadth' we refer to the diverse range of institutional sites within and through which social struggles are conducted; and by 'depth' we refer to the way in which the manifest (surface) events of political life are related to underlying institutional and organization settings, which in turn are located within broader structural principles of the social system.

This means, above all, that the fetishized disciplinary boundaries between sociology, political science and economics must be transcended. The institutional clusters of civil society, state and economy interpenetrate one another in complex ways. It is therefore artificial and arbitrary to attempt to explain a phenomenon such as Thatcherism from just one standpoint. It is not sufficient, however, simply to mix together elements from each discipline. What is required is a set of concepts whose reference spans the range of these analytically separable dimensions, and for each region has depth. This problem has been recognized by Stuart Hall in defending himself against the charge of one-sided concern with the ideological.[1] He suggested that it would not have been advisable for him to combine a sophisticated ideological analysis with a naive economic one, and that traditional disciplinary boundaries discouraged such an attempt. We agree with his diagnosis but nonetheless believe that this problem can be overcome by combining analyses with a similar degree of depth. The key to our approach lies in an attempt to develop a range of concepts which identify the institutional forms through which civil society, the state and the economy are linked to one another.

Marxist approaches to political science are often (and misleadingly) placed in either an instrumentalist or a structuralist camp (after the Miliband–Poulantzas debate). In these terms the state is either seen as acting at the behest of class interests located, constituted and organized outside of the state system – in the economy and civil society – or else is held to act on behalf of capitalist interests willy-nilly through the constraints imposed on its operation by the wider structures of social and economic power. There is clearly some truth in each of these approaches. As an institutional and organizational ensemble the state *is* a set of instruments, with powers and resources, but these are not equally accessible and available to all forces; nor are these forces fully constituted outside the state but are also formed and organized through state structures and agencies. For example, a range of business interests have successfully lobbied and/or given active support to Thatcherism; equally the constraints imposed by the financial and money markets over government macro-economic policy were considerable during the emergence and subsequent consolidation of Thatcherism. But both of these accounts are vitiated by similar weaknesses. To begin with they each lie at one pole of a false dichotomy. Instrumentalist accounts allocate a primacy to the agency of social forces at the expense of their structural conditions: structuralist accounts assert the priority of social structures over individual or collective agency. Of equal importance is the fact that each approach ultimately reduces political power to economic power: in other words, political phenomena are held to be wholly explicable in terms of the interests they represent or the structures they reproduce. We share the aim of such approaches to link state activities to the economy, but we reject the claim that the political level is somehow derivative from the 'real' (underlying) base.

Our Approach

An alternative approach would focus on both the specific institutional form of the connections between the state, civil society and the economy, and the distinctive organization of the state system itself. This entails the development of concepts to grasp the forms of representation through which economic and social forces relate to the state and the patterns of intervention through which the state seeks to regulate economic and social processes. It also implies the need for a further set of concepts by which to describe the internal ordering of the state system itself. Moreover, since such a theoretical project recognizes that neither the economy nor civil society are self-regulating and self-reproducing domains, it is also necessary to develop concepts which account for their internal differentiation and layering.

Specifically, we suggest that the notions of 'social base', 'accumulation strategy', 'state strategy' and 'hegemonic project' are helpful constructs through which to organize political analysis. Although the meaning of these terms may already have emerged above, we now provide some more precise definitions before employing them to analyse the durability of Thatcherism.

The Social Base of the Political Order

We begin with the social base of the state and political system. This notion refers to a set of social forces which support – within an accepted institutional framework and policy paradigm – the basic structure, mode of operation and objectives of the state system in its role as the official representative of civil society. Support involves not so much normative consensus around a set of beliefs and values (in line with the so-called dominant ideology thesis),[2] but rather institutionalized modes of mass social and political integration and the management of conflicting material demands. Several approaches for analysing different types of social base have been advanced. Thus Przeworski has developed a powerful analysis of the cross-class, material compromise upon which postwar social democracy rested.[3] Another approach, developed with great insight by Burawoy, focuses on the forms of consent generated within specific 'factory regimes'.[4] And, lastly, we would cite the rich and complex analyses of the structuring of popular culture by civil society offered by Gramsci (for example, his analysis of Americanism and Fordism).[5]

This issue is further complicated because the objective social patterns do not have an unmediated impact on the political scene. On the one hand, lived experience must be interpreted and organized through some ideological framework; and political forces in turn seek to rework such popular sentiments into their own distinctive ideologies. And on the other, the expression of material interests in the political sphere is never direct and unmediated. For the formation of interests and the specific programmes adopted by social forces are often shaped in powerful ways by the structure of the political and state system which they seek to operate on and through.

Social structures are therefore major determinants of political outcomes. But this does not occur in a simple manner, nor without the reciprocal reshaping of the social base by the outcomes of the political process. While such propositions may seem self-evident when expressed so baldly, they have major implications for all those approaches which assume a more direct determinism. So-called society-centred approaches – pluralist or Marxist – all presume that the political process involves the crystallization and transmission of socially-determined divisions of interest into specific forms of political processes. In this manner, not only do many orthodox Marxists identify Thatcherite policies with particular objective class interests, but many political scientists also feel confident that changes in the British class structure spell doom for any political movement based on the working class.

Finally, one must not allow a concern with the social base of politics to slide into a general and undifferentiated concern with consent and support, for not all groups in society can mobilize power to the same extent, and therefore the consent and support of some forces counts for more than that of others. The identity of powerful groups clearly changes over time and can be founded on differing structural and organizational capacities. Within the political process itself the most important organizational bases of power are pluralist interest groups, corporatist arrangements and political parties. On such a reading, traceable involvement in the policy process is the main focus of attention and strategies must be understood in terms of their attempted resolution of the balance of political forces as they appear in the political arena.

However, there are also indirect – yet perhaps more powerful – ways in which power can be exercised by interests located in civil society and the economy. Thus a form of structural power is inscribed into institutional structures themselves through their differential impact on access to centres of power and their implications for different strategies. Thus the capacity to withdraw resources and/or consent from the state and the political system is a very powerful mode of sanctioning. Within the economy this capacity is held at various times by industrialists, trade unionists or the financial markets. Here we find the notion of a power bloc (see below) very useful. But let us first explain more fully what we mean by the notion of an accumulation strategy.

Accumulation Strategies

'Accumulation strategy' refers to a specific pattern, or model, of economic growth together with both its associated social framework of institutions (or 'mode of regulation') and the range of government policies conducive to its stable reproduction. Of course, nobody, whether in the CBI, the City, Smith Square or Downing Street sits down to devise a fully coherent strategy that is then unproblematically implemented. Rather we are referring to an emergent pattern that is provisionally mastered by political forces. In order to specify the parameters of an accumulation strategy one would have to answer such questions as: what are the leading sectors of the economy; what is their mode of capital accumulation (competitive, monopoly or state monopoly); how do they relate to the national and international economy (are they primarily exporters, producers for the home market or multinationals); what are the societal preconditions for their continued expansion; and how is their growth facilitated by the actions of the state. Accumulation strategies are always premissed on specific forms of state intervention as well as the balance of forces and the organizational form of the economy. Although it sounds paradoxical a state may have an accumulation strategy by default. For there are circumstances where openness to the increasingly international markets is consciously promoted. But even such an apparently liberal strategy often requires a considerable mobilization of state power and/or an increase in the power of other apparatuses of the state, specifically a strengthening of the institutions of social regulation and control.

Thus, for example, a state may seek to promote – through directly controlled institutions and/or channels of corporatist concertation – the modernization of specific sectors of the economy, the provision of high-quality infrastructure for economic growth in the form of generous funding for scientific and technical education, worker re-skilling and research and development funds etc. In addition it may commission or conduct studies to identify areas of the economy's strengths and weaknesses in home and international markets the better to rationalize in areas of weakness and expand in those of strength. Alternatively, where the mechanisms for such intervention are absent and/or the balance (and organization) of class and other forces is such that social cooperation proves difficult to maintain, the state may seek to facilitate the options chosen by the market combined with specific and general, but uncoordinated, disbursements of aid etc. There are, of course, many other variations that could be envisaged and we include these schematic accounts here only for illustration.

State Strategies

Thus far we have introduced the concepts of social base and accumulation strategy, and in each case we have found it necessary to refer to the specific institutional form of the state system and the strategies pursued through it. By 'state strategy' we refer to a pattern of intervention in the economy which: (a) favours the course of an accumulation strategy and the flow of material benefits to the requisite social base; and (b) constructs forms of representation that systematically favour the access of the key sectors and social groups to sites of political and economic power. In addition, one must ask what are the implications of the institutional form of the state for its strategic selectivity, for the state is not equally accessible to all social forces. The state cannot be controlled, mobilized or resisted to the same extent by all strategies, and it is not resourced and empowered to secure all possible policy goals. Different political regimes inevitably favour the access of some forces, the conduct of some strategies and the pursuit of some objectives other others. One important theoretical divide in the literature which occurs in this context is that between functionalist-Marxist notions of relative autonomy and the very different perspective of those who focus on the institutional specificity and autonomy of the state.

Some Marxist accounts argue that the inherent structural forms of the capitalist state guarantee its functionality for capitalist interests; whereas others – often influenced by the work of Weber, de Tocqueville and Hintze – seek to 'bring the state back in' as a political force in its own right. Let us now consider the former approach.[6] In general this 'state-derivation' perspective locates the capitalist bias of the state in a range of features. Thus:

1   the state is excluded from the productive core of the economy and so depends on privately-generated tax revenues and the purchase of government debt by the private sector;
2   the liberal democratic form of the state and the operation of the rule of law disguise class domination and class membership through the 'isolation effect' – that is, individuals are constituted as free sovereign citizens with equal political weight;
3   the very operation of national politics (parliamentary or corporatist) depends on a minimum degree of class collaboration;
4   the bureaucratic insulation of the state from anything like full democratic accountability facilitates access to the state by powerful groups;
5   the indirectness of legal and monetary forms of intervention necessitates a degree of business compliance for their successful operation; and
6   the insulation of the economic and repressive functions of the state from democratic control enables them better to serve minority capitalist interests.

This approach has considerable merit. In particular it begins to establish the state itself as an object of analysis. However, it does assume that such structural features of the state always favour capitalist interests.

Against this Offe has often argued that the very de-commodified form of much state intervention, under conditions of parliamentary democratic representation and bureaucratic policy making, constantly acts to subvert the logic of the market.[7] This in turn prompts economic tensions (for example, fiscal crises of the state) and political pressures (anti-inflation and tax revolts) to re-commodify parts of the state sector. Moreover, there is no reason to assume that the form of the state necessarily favours capitalist interests; in particular attention must also be placed on the balance of class and popular forces. The effects of a particular institutional arrangement cannot be calculated in isolation from a knowledge of the balance of forces mobilized. Thus, for example, where the peak organizations of capital and labour are unified (Sweden), or where the organizations of labour are excluded (Japan), corporatist institutions can often facilitate the pursuit of nationally-agreed accumulation strategies. (The British experience with corporatist strategies without underlying corporatist structures is by no means typical.)

Nor does our position assume that capital accumulation proceeds in a crisis-free manner. Indeed, we stress the problems deriving not only from the basic contradictions of capitalism but also the conflicts and uncertainties introduced by competing strategies of accumulation, their articulation and temporary stabilization. Thus, whatever the balance of forces between capital and labour in general, the interests of particular capitals may be tendentially unified under some strategies but not under others. Equally, specific state structures may facilitate some strategies and not others. In these and other ways, the recent development of Marxist state theory clearly moves away from any simplistic society-centred determinism – wherein the prime mover is either the class struggle or the structures of capital. But the degree to which these accounts actually take seriously the structures of state institutions themselves and the power that these generate varies considerably. There is much to be learnt in this regard from the recent anti-Marxist effort to 'bring the state back in' and develop a more grounded institutional and historically-informed perspective than that of most of mainstream political science.[8]

The distinctive and innovative changes in perspective envisaged by those engaged in this project cover six major themes:

1   the geo-political position of different modern states within the international system of nation-states and its implications for the situational logic of state action;
2   the dynamic of military organization and warfare in the development and orientation of the modern state;
3   the distinctive powers of the modern state – especially those rooted in its

capacities to produce and enforce collectively binding decisions within a centrally administered, territorially-bounded society – and its consequent strategic reach in relation to all other institutional orders of society (including the economy), organizations (including capitalist enterprises), and social forces (including classes) within its domain;

4   the nature of the state as a distinctive factor in shaping the character of institutions and social forces beyond the state, in the economy and in civil society – the aspect that Skocpol has called its Tocquevillian moment;

5   the specific pathologies of the modern state – above all the danger of authoritarian degeneration ever present as a result of its distinct and increasing powers of surveillance; and

6   the particular interests and capacities of 'state managers' as opposed to other social forces.

Different 'state-centred' theorists have emphasized different factors, but the general conclusion is shared: the state is a force in its own right and does not simply reflect the dynamic of the economy and/or civil society. This leads 'state-centred' theorists to advocate a radically different approach to the question of state autonomy. They have drawn particular attention to two dimensions of autonomy: (a) state autonomy as the ability of state managers to exercise power independently of (and even in the face of opposition from) social forces located in civil society – a power rooted in the state's own specialized capacities and/or in the room for manoeuvre which state managers enjoy vis-à-vis a pluralistic universe of social forces; and (b) state capacities or infrastructural power, that is, the state's ability to penetrate, control, supervise, police and discipline modern societies through its specialized capacities even when these are controlled directly or indirectly by forces beyond the state.[9]

Clearly these themes are diverse and not all of them have so far been taken up in the analysis of Thatcherism; and we would not claim to have offered a full account of it in these terms. In particular, the international dimensions of the British state under Thatcherism need much greater attention. Nor have we paid sufficient attention to the genuine and pressing problems of expanding state surveillance and the rise of authoritarianism in contemporary Britain.

To summarize, in our view there is no intrinsic incompatibility between the approaches we have just outlined so long as the more deterministic formulations of the state-centred approaches are rejected. Equally, it is necessary to reject the residual class reductionism of many Marxist accounts. This commits us neither to the strong state-centric claim that state managers enjoy a significant degree of irreducible autonomy, nor to the reductionist society-centred assertions that political outcomes are predetermined, or guaranteed, by the structure of the economy and civil society. Instead, we must pay attention not only to the social forces acting in and through the state but also to the ways in which the rules and resources of political action are altered by changes in the state system itself. Let us turn, finally, to the notion of a hegemonic project.

Hegemonic Projects

By 'hegemonic project' we mean to refer to a *national-popular* programme of political, intellectual and moral leadership which advances the long-term interests of the leading sectors in the accumulation strategy while granting economic concessions to the masses of the social base. Here we are essentially asking whether political forces are able to unify their social base, accumulation strategy and state strategy into a coherent whole. We would suggest that such a task requires the creation of a 'power bloc' that unifies – around a common political and economic programme – the most powerful social forces in the society, and also the establishment of a broader complementarity between the institutions and forces of civil society and the polity, on the one hand, and those of the economic order, on the other – that is, a 'historic bloc'. It is often overlooked that, in addition to the well-known and widely used concept of hegemony, there are two other concepts in Gramsci's work which are particularly useful in analysing politics in liberal capitalist polities. These are historic bloc and power bloc. Both concepts are located principally at the level of the whole society, although one can also discuss historic blocs and power blocs by analogy at the regional and international levels.

An historic bloc is an historically constituted, socially reproduced structural ensemble characterized by a contingent correspondence between the economic 'base' (with its specific accumulation regime and mode of growth) and the political and ideological institutions (state form, civil society). The consolidation of an historic bloc depends on the mutual, reciprocal conditioning of economy, state and civil society: it is not to be analysed according to the model of pre-given economic base and epiphenomenal superstructure but more in line with the contingent co-evolution and structural coupling of different institutions and practices as reinforced and mediated through specific economic, political and ideological practices.

Similarly a power bloc is also an 'institutional' as well as 'strategic' category.[10] It refers to a stable, structurally determined, and organized bloc of dominant classes (or class fractions) and dominant social and political categories (for example, top bureaucrats, military elites, intellectuals). This bloc is typically organized around a specific accumulation strategy, state strategy and hegemonic project. Its stability derives not only from the organic character of these projects but also from the structural constraints patterned in the society and economy which privilege the pursuit of these interests and their associated objectives over those of groups outside the power bloc. In this sense, a power bloc should not be confused with temporary alliances for specific goals, or purely defensive rassemblements, etc. For the stability over time of a power bloc depends on its relations to a specific state form, the leading sectors of the economy, and a shared ideological outlook. Nor, then, should it be reduced to organization or alliances in the political sphere: party politics, tripartism, and other political groups may often be the mediated reflections of the power bloc (or of its crisis), but the political sphere has its own irreducible properties and dynamics.[11]

For present purposes it is useful to distinguish between a one nation and a two nations type of hegemonic project. The former involves an inclusive and expansive conception of the social and political community wherein all interests in the society are ideally able to share its material and symbolic rewards. The latter refers to an exclusive conception of the society in which only those who are part of the privileged nation can share in its benefits. Of course, in reality the one nation social democracy of many postwar settlements was marred by pronounced degrees of inequality and effective social and political exclusion; and equally, even a divisive, two nations hegemonic project allows some benefits to 'trickle down' to the poor and marginalized sections of society. Nonetheless, we insist that there is a fundamental difference between a political strategy which consciously plays on the divisions in society to mobilize a majority of the satisfied at the expense of the dissatisfied, and a strategy which, at least in intent, seeks to transcend such differences and to share necessary sacrifices and benefits. Finally, we should note that a one nation hegemonic project may become a two nation project if the underlying level of economic growth is insufficient, and, equally, a two nations project, initially adopted in defensive circumstances, may still be pursued in better economic conditions. We now apply this broad conceptual framework to an analysis of the Thatcherite social, political and economic project in order to assess its relative durability.

The Background to Thatcherism

We have argued that the origins of Thatcherism must be understood in terms of the Conservative Party's changing response to the continuing relative decline of the British economy and, more particularly, to its political repercussions.[12] Thus its response was mediated through crises in the Keynesian welfare state regime, its associated party system, and the social bases of support for the social democratic postwar settlement. Underlying this decline and overdetermining the forms of crisis were the mode of growth of the British economy, the capacities of the state system to regulate economic and social relations, and the ideologies of the postwar settlement. Before considering the nature of Thatcherism and its longer-term future we must first review the problems which brought it to power. Only then can we assess whether Thatcherism is a response to the crisis or just one more form in which this crisis is continuing to unfold.

The Postwar Settlements

A combination of structural constraints and political decisions taken in the mid-forties entrenched the British economy into a distinctive mode of growth. Essentially Britain acquired a position within the international division of labour which privileged financial capital and externally-oriented commercial and industrial capital and weakened domestic capital. Even the relatively privileged sectors suffered handicaps, however: the City was largely confined within the overseas sterling area and sterling itself played second fiddle to the dollar. Much of Britain's export trade was with slower-growing areas in less advanced goods or in areas where American competition and/or European and Japanese recovery would soon reduce market share, and slow domestic growth proved increasingly restrictive for the capital base of financial institutions. But this mode of growth was sustained by the nature of the postwar settlements at home and abroad. Indeed, in contrast to many analyses of the postwar settlement, which focus on its domestic aspects, we would suggest that the international postwar settlement and the external aspects of the domestic settlement were the dominant factors influencing the development of the British economic and political scene.

Thus we have already argued that this settlement at home was compromised by the dual external commitments to an open financial and trading policy (which largely if not unambiguously benefited the City and MNCs operating in the UK) and to an Atlanticist military–diplomatic posture which involved a junior partner role in support of the United States as well as an imperial role East and South of Suez. Indeed we would even suggest that the cross-party, state-sponsored commitment to *Churchillism* was perhaps the dominant level of the postwar state strategy, overarching the better-known contradictions within the domestic postwar settlement. This consensus around Keynesianism, international liberalization, and Atlanticism was as significant for what it precluded as for what it included: above all, it ruled out any serious attempt by the state to coordinate a domestically focused strategy of industrial regeneration. This was because, *inter alia*, such a strategy would have involved the subordination of interest rate policy to the requirements of domestic investment rather than the defence of sterling; and the necessary powers and responsibilities of industrial sponsoring departments would have been incompatible with the continued dominance of the Treasury within the state.

Moreover, even had a consensus existed in favour of greater state intervention to promote industrial regeneration, it would have encountered obstacles rooted in the limited capacities of the state. The dominant liberal state tradition was pressured by party competition to intervene on an *ad hoc* basis for various politically motivated reasons even though it lacked effective means to steer the economy. Attempts to introduce corporatist concertation foundered on the lack of corporatist organizations able to sustain a tripartite consensus and to deliver the support of their members. Equally, attempts at state direction from above were undermined by the inability or unwillingness of successive governments to challenge the market-based allocation of credit, the misplaced concern with job protection rather than industrial promotion, and the bias of state-sponsored research and development towards aerospace, military uses (especially electronics) and nuclear power.[13]

Economic Decline and Political Crisis

The growing openness of the UK economy posed constant problems for domestic economic management. In time a vicious cycle of cumulative causation – slow growth of demand, poor productivity improvements, creeping inflation and low levels (and poor quality) of investment – produced recurrent balance of payments and/or sterling crises. Further, the maintenance of a post-imperial world policing role imposed still more costs on the balance of payments and diverted resources from civilian production. Once the UK economic crisis deepened in the late 1960s it was the domestic commitments to full employment, the welfare state, and cooperation with the trade unions which were increasingly called into question rather than the basic external orientation of the UK state and externally oriented capital. Indeed this privileging of continuity in foreign economic, diplomatic, and military policy over the domestic requirements for a growth-oriented social democracy was shared by the largest blocs within both major political parties.

Viewed comparatively, the fundamental causes of Britain's relative economic decline are twofold. First, the enduring City–state–industry institutional nexus precluded the coordinated restructuring of productive capital required for success in international markets.[14] And second, the global pretensions of the British state in its post-imperial phase have imposed a burden on the domestic economy that the latter could not bear and which have still further thwarted intervention aimed at international competitiveness.[15] This interaction has facilitated a distinctive pattern of multinationalization and contraction of the industrial base that eventuated in the disintegration of the UK economy as a nationally integrated economic space.[16] On the other hand commercial and financial capital have strengthened their positions in the economy and hence their ability to exert structural constraints over alternative state policies through their power to determine the terms on which government debt and/or any negative foreign balances are funded. Within the state itself the Bank–Treasury axis has reasserted its position of authority (following its wartime demotion) and this has enhanced the structural selectivity of the state towards liberal strategies oriented towards external balance and openness.

It is above all this overarching external context which, despite the specific circumstances surrounding the rightwing mobilization on the domestic scene, must qualify any judgement that Thatcherism (as Party strategy, hegemonic project or accumulation strategy) represents a complete break with the past. For not only have there been significant continuities between the past and the Thatcher era but also many of the significant ruptures in the postwar political-economy pre-date 1979. Nonetheless, there was a domestic crisis. The synchronization of the UK's relative decline with, first, increased international volatility, and second, the world recession of 1974–5 resulted in a corporate trade union offensive between 1972 and 1975. This produced no reorganization of either capital or the state to the long-term advantage of labour. Rather the Labour government of 1974–9 presided over a phase of relative stabilization while the labour movement adopted an economistic and defensive stance, leading to the Winter of Discontent.

The disintegration of the Labour government coincided with a manifold and manifest crisis on the right. The latter could be seen in the increasingly uncertain loss of electoral support for the Conservative Party, the apparent loss of a governing authority by the Tories in 1974, and the 'political crisis of capital' and the growing concern among sections of the Establishment during the events under the Social Contract, Benn's 'Industry Bill' and the Bullock Report.[17] But the shocks delivered in the 1970s prompted an alignment of rightwing forces around a political project to roll back the economic and social gains of the working class and to impose an austerity programme in which capital and the state could regain the autonomies which they had enjoyed before the postwar settlement drew them into a series of compromises and alliances whose dynamic they could not control. Thatcher was significant here as the rallying force not only for worried sectors of the bourgeoisie and Establishment but also for many discontented and alienated sectors of the petty bourgeoisie and working class. Once the Tories were in office the dual crisis of the state gave Thatcherism a measure of decisional autonomy which allowed it the time to consolidate its position despite initial unpopularity and resistance.[18]

The Project of Thatcherism

In consolidating power the Thatcher government pursued a strategic line oriented as much to the politics of support as to the politics of power. Regarding the first, Thatcherism seeks both an end to the electoral decline of the Conservative Party, through the creation of a new social base around 'popular capitalism' rather than the welfare state, and a reassertion of the Party's governing authority through the creation of a neo-liberal state form. In each case restructuring of the state system plays a crucial role, for the creation of a new social base is in part to be achieved through the private appropriation of public assets and the individualization of collective forms of welfare provision (opting out in pensions, education and health). In addition sites of opposition where social democratic and/or Labour forces are strong are undermined and then removed from the ambit of state intervention (unions and local government). And finally, a significant minority of the population which is unable to participate in popular capitalism is to be contained and, where necessary, repressed with the new powers and instruments at the disposal of the police.

As to the politics of power, the Thatcherite strategy aims to aid the internationalization of the UK economy, which disproportionately benefits the financial and service sectors concentrated in the South-East, and seeks to achieve a significant class-based redistribution of income and wealth towards the privileged nation and to expand this sector of the population – from which a new electoral base for the Party is to emerge. This not only responds to the political crisis of capital of the late seventies, by radically altering the balance of class power within industry as unions are weakened and unemployment raised, but also divests the state of the social democratic responsibilities of maintaining employment and facilitating corporatist concertation.

It is worth noting here that such a project could not have been envisaged in the absence of North Sea oil. The revenues to the state and the contribution to the economy from this source have protected the balance of payments, served as a major site of capital accumulation throughout the recession and permitted the pursuit of a strategy of de-industrialization that would have imposed costs on the privileged nation in its absence. The presence of this temporary 'windfall' has also disguised the true picture of the underlying performance of the rest of the UK economy, on which future national prosperity will increasingly depend.

A New Settlement?

Besides describing its broad strategy we must also ask how far has Thatcherism constructed a new social, economic and political settlement. This is best answered in terms of four sets of issues. First, is there a new *social base* for Thatcherism? Is there a set of social forces which support – within an accepted institutional framework and policy paradigm – the basic structure, mode of operation and objectives of the state system? Here we need to know the answers to such questions as:

(a) has the electoral decline of the Conservative Party been arrested and reversed; (b) have other powerful institutions and/or social forces in civil society been won over to a Thatcherite agenda, not only through support for the Conservative Party but also through institutional ties to the Thatcherite state and its allies in the economy and civil society; (c) how far have the old social bases of social democracy been fatally weakened and/or displaced; and (d) as a consequence of the foregoing, to what extent has the party system been recomposed around a new Thatcherite agenda?

Second, we must see how far Thatcherism has encouraged and benefited from a new model of economic growth. Is there a new *accumulation strategy* which will both advance the long-term interests of British capitalism (or, more accurately, capital operating in Britain) and provide material rewards to any emergent social base. Here we must ask such questions as: (a) what is the overall pattern of growth in the economy and can it be sustained; (b) which sectors of the economy are likely to prosper; (c) where are these leading sectors located geographically; and (d) what kinds of work do these sectors provide?

Third, has the Conservative Party so restructured the state system as to have solved and/or by-passed the dual crisis of the state? Is there an emergent *state strategy* which will both intervene in the economy so as to favour the continuation of any putative accumulation strategy and the flow of material benefits to the emerging social base, and construct forms of representation that systematically favour the access of the leading sectors/regions to places of political and economic power? Here we need to know: (a) what are the dominant forms of state intervention at a European, central, regional and local level; (b) how have the channels of representation been restructured; (c) in what ways has the internal organization of the state system been altered; and (d) what are the overall implications of any changes for the strategic selectivity of the state system?

Fourth, has a new power bloc and/or historic bloc emerged and unified around the Thatcherite project to secure its *hegemonic project*? To answer this would involve replies to the following: (a) do the leading sectors in the economy identify with and support the Thatcherite accumulation strategy; (b) has Thatcherism won over the state and intellectual elite to the current state strategy; and (c) has it succeeded in restructuring the institutions of civil society (schools, churches etc.) such that they articulate its agenda? In addition, we must see if Thatcherism has been able to impose an overall national-popular unity on any new social base, accumulation strategy, state system, power bloc and historic bloc. Has Thatcherism a new *national-popular* programme of political, intellectual and moral leadership which advances the long-term interests of the leading sectors in the accumulation strategy while granting economic concessions to the masses of the social base? Here we are essentially asking whether the answers to all the above questions in sum form a coherent political and economic project that can be more or less stably reproduced over an extended period of time, even after Margaret Thatcher is replaced as Conservative leader, and even when the Conservative Party is no longer in office.

The Thatcherite Agenda

This is a long list of questions and we cannot hope to provide a full range of answers here. Instead, we shall attempt to outline the broad parameters of what appears to be a reasonably coherent, if fragile, arrangement of institutions and forces which might support a new political settlement. Another complicating factor which we must take into account is that much of what has thus far passed for Thatcherism has in fact involved the dismantling, displacement and restructuring of social democratic institutions and forces. This has been a necessary clearing operation for the success of the more ambitious Thatcherite project sketched above. But whatever the degree of its success, it is not – by itself – equivalent to the creation of a new settlement. Thatcherism has proved to be extremely effective at the pursuit of crisis management and the roll-back of social democracy; but whether a viable alternative has been constructed is another issue and is altogether less certain.

The Social Base of Neo-Liberalism

Schematically, we might say that Thatcherism first arrested (but has not yet reversed) the long-term decline of Conservative electoral support through profiting from the uneven impact of the recession and the subsequent growth of the 'South'; the tendency of non-Tory voters to support the Alliance parties in this area of prosperity; and the increased restriction of Labour's electoral base to the 'North' of the old working class and those dependent on public employment and/or provision. More recently, an attempt to discover a *new* social base, as opposed to shoring up a traditional one and disorganizing the opposition, is evidenced in the project of 'popular capitalism'. The latter involves a range of policies such as the private appropriation of public assets through the privatization programme and/or the sale of council-owned housing, and the individualization of collective forms of provision through the abolition of SERPS, the creation of private pension plans, the opting out of affluent parents from the local authority-controlled education system, the increasing support for private health care and so forth.

The uneven economic development of recent years (see below), which both preceded and was promoted by Thatcherism, has had profound electoral consequences. Thus Johnston et al. show that 'on a broad scale, elections in the south have become a Conservative : Alliance affair in many seats, with Labour a poor third, whereas in the north they are more likely to be dominated by the Labour and Conservative contestants, with Alliance candidates occupying respectable third places.'[19] This state of affairs is especially serious for the Labour Party. The Party will gain few electoral benefits from further advance in the North, and in the South Labour has never been strong – 1945 was the exception here and this gain was never consolidated through either strong party organization or favourable social milieux – and now this region is in general highly prosperous, with many people having good reason to feel optimistic about the future. Moreover, the Tories are not standing still.

A range of policies from trade union reform, local government and housing through to education and health changes are in part designed to erode Labour support. As Johnston et al. put it: 'The Tories are not letting Labour keep hold of its heartland, therefore: they are invading it, in a variety of ways.'[20] This policy of eroding Labour's social base has often been pioneered by Conservative local authorities such as Wandsworth and Rochford. And even a half-way, moderately successful restart for the Social and Liberal Democratic Party in the South would seal off the already limited chances that Labour might have of winning power alone.

The representational bias inherent in the British electoral system combined with the increasing regionalization of UK electoral behaviour has resulted in large parliamentary majorities for the Conservative Party. This apparently unchallengeable dominance has had a more general impact on the party system: for politicians in the Alliance parties and many in the Labour Party have argued that this Conservative dominance can be challenged only if they shift their policies towards those adopted by the Tories. In other words, the dominance of the Conservative Party within the electoral system has exerted pressure on the other parties, through the logic of electoral competition, to move on to the Thatcherite terrain. To some extent, then, Thatcherism has recomposed the party system. It has also been the case that other forces and institutions have been under pressure to adapt in a similar manner: examples stretch from the BBC to the TUC. Of particular importance here for the Labour Party has been the emerging new realism in those unions most heavily represented in the expanding sectors of the economy, the weakness of trade unionism in general in the service sectors, and the splits in the TUC over the suspension (and later expulsion) of the EETPU.

Equally, if not more, successful has been the Conservative Party's strategy for displacing, restructuring and/or undermining those social institutions and forces which had provided the social base for social democracy. Of central importance have been the policies adopted towards the trade unions: the legislative environment has changed enormously since 1979, to say nothing of the impact of high unemployment. Much the same is true of local government, where the role of professionals and unions in the determination of service provision has been increasingly replaced – if the services have not been turned over to the market or centralized to Whitehall – by that of managers brought in from the private sector. (Since the role of the state here is crucial, we consider this aspect in more detail below.)

A Neo-Liberal Accumulation Strategy

The strategic line of the Thatcher administrations has been determined by the position of the British economy within the international division of labour as well as by the constraints imposed by past failures to establish an effective corporatist representational regime, or more directive forms of state intervention, which might have sustained neo-corporatist or neo-statist strategies. Specifically, the economic strategy has four components. First, there is a commitment to privatization, deregulation and the introduction of commercial criteria into any residual state activities. Second, the City was deregulated in an attempt to establish London as the centre for international financial capital and to secure an export role for Britain through its specialization in financial services. Third, the government has weakly sponsored a market-generated industrial recovery which has focused on the encouragement of inward investment, the promotion of a small business sector, the expansion of new technology and the transformation of the MSC into an agency concerned with enhancing labour flexibility. Fourth, in the longer term, the Thatcherite strategy is hoping that the synergic effects of a tricontinental multinational presence will transform the UK economy into a dynamic multinational space.

Without in any way minimizing the serious nature of de-industrialization in the UK, we think it is important to recognize the international nature of the present restructuring.[21] Between 1962 and 1983 inward investment to the UK tripled in real terms. By the early eighties 60 per cent of inward investment was located in the 100 largest foreign-owned firms, and of the largest 1,000 firms 402 were foreign-owned (some four times the proportion of the late sixties). Moreover, the rise of Eurodollar banking in the seventies and the internationalization of banking and commercial capital have ensured that the continued dominance of the City as an international financial centre is no longer equivalent to the pre-eminence of *British* financial capital.

The complement to this is the high degree of international spread by British companies. But although this is still large by comparative standards, four key points should be borne in mind. First, in the industrial sector some 40 per cent of overseas production by UK MNCs is located in the United States. This has advantages in so far as the

US market is still the largest, but it limits the UK's ability to participate in any potential European integration. Second, in technology-driven industries the UK market is too small to sustain the necessary research and development and productive infrastructure expenditure to remain competitive, and European firms are both divided among themselves and are collaborating (1992 notwithstanding) with Japanese and US capital. (In this context the UK appears to have pipped Germany as the site for the growing Japanese multinational presence to enter the EC.) Third, the consumer-oriented firms have done well, with an overseas production some twenty times their UK exports, and many have gained a stronghold in the US market. But, once again, they have been less successful in Europe. Fourth, although the City's large banks and insurance companies are well placed internationally and the recent rounds of deregulation have reinforced London's role as the prime centre in the European time zone, the smaller firms (merchant banks, brokers, jobbers etc.) are ever less able to compete on an independent basis with the American giants. This process is reinforced by the current phase of internationalization in the securities industry.

No other major capitalist economy exhibits such a high degree of internationalization in its leading sectors. Indeed, the UK now has very few significant sectors of manufacturing capital with a secure home market, high levels of investment and research and development and a successful export performance in international competition.[22] (Chemicals and aerospace are something of an exception, but the future even of the latter is precarious.) In short, there is as yet no sign of any industrial renaissance that will be needed both to replace the chronic trade deficit in electronics, cars and other manufactures, and to replace the foreign exchange that will be lost as North Sea oil output declines. This is, as Jessop has pointed out, in direct contrast to the three leading capitalist economies (and, one might add, several of the NICs):

> The three leading capitalist economies have carefully fostered industrial cores through state action. Japan leads in robotics, electronics and high-tech consumer goods; West Germany in chemicals and high-tech capital goods; the US in military hardware, aerospace and information technology. Britain's role in these areas is increasingly that of a branch-plant assembler of their goods. Thatcherism might well be promoting a worldwide post-Fordist age by creating a rentier British economy, with a secondary industrial role in the world economy and a low wage, low-tech service sector at home. This may consolidate the dominance of City *financial* interests but also poses strategic dilemmas. Should Britain become a fifty-first American state? Or the Trojan horse of Japan in Europe? Or a more integral element of the EEC under West German hegemony?[23]

The Conservative Party is now faced with an intriguing dilemma in any attempt to balance the interests of its national political base with the international orientation of the key growth sectors of the economy.

For one of the most dramatic components of Thatcherism's economic agenda is its open recognition, indeed celebration, that the interests of the British state (and therefore the Conservative Party's statecraft) are no longer synonymous with the interests of British capital. Rather, they are synonymous with capital operating in Britain and the operations of British capital overseas. (And it is far from clear that these two are in any sense coincident.) Thus among the major capitalist economies, what distinguishes the recent UK experience is the complete absence of a *national* strategy for capital restructuring, whether under the auspices of the banks, the state or the 'social partners'. This is not to say that there is no state intervention; on the contrary, there is considerable intervention. But this does not take the form of an attempt to manage the *British* economy.

This is no mere ideological quirk; rather, it reflects the fact that because of the degree of internationalization and multinationalization of the UK economy there is simply no significant bloc of domestic UK capital that might provide the base for such a strategy. And despite significant restructuring of government aid (especially the abolition of regional aid and cuts to the budget of the DTI), the type of intervention remains 'a variant of the classic liberal "tax-subsidy" form'.[24] What is ruled out is either any sustained attempt to coordinate the restructuring of individual firms in a given sector or the identification of weaknesses in the economy and the promotion of adequate remedial activity. There has been, however, a series of detailed studies by the NEDC, the CBI and others which have pointed to areas of concern in the UK economy; but at a central level no coordinated response has been forthcoming. In some contrast, at the local level there has been a range of initiatives pioneered by local authority planning units, the Scottish and Welsh development agencies etc. Finally, there are many forces in the business community, the state system and the Conservative Party (for example, Heseltine) which would support a more robust approach to the promotion of international competitiveness (see below).

But without the adequate infrastructural support of the state for re-skilling and skill flexibilization together with market specialization in new technologies, processes and products, the market-led recovery will fail to reverse British de-industrialization and lead to the short-run balkanization of Britain's industrial core among sectors integrated into the circuits of American, Japanese, German and UK multinational capital. The fact that this pattern of activity does not amount to a coherent *national* accumulation strategy for the UK does not mean that there will be no growth. On the contrary, there has been some growth after the depth of the recession of the early 1980s was turned, but this has been highly specific to particular sectors and has been extremely regionalized in its distribution.

Thus by geographic reason there has been a clear North–South divide in the levels of unemployment. (Only Inner London and to some extent Devon and Cornwall in the South and rural areas in the North failed to conform to this pattern.) In addition, by functional region there were even larger variations of unemployment: from half the average in the most prosperous regions to double it in the poorest immigrant areas. Over the longer period of 1965–85 'six of the ten standard regions in Great Britain ... experienced declines in their percentage of the country's manufacturing jobs, whereas the other four – the Southwest, the Southeast, East Midlands and East Anglia – experienced increases, clearly indicating a north to south shift in the relative prosperity of the manufacturing sector.'[25] (It should be remembered that these shifts took place within a context of overall absolute decline in manufacturing job totals after 1966.) A similar geographical disparity can be seen in the movement of house prices: at its most extreme, prices rose nearly four times as fast in London as in the North between 1983 and 1987.

Typically, the growing regions contain within them the M4 corridor, projects linked to the Cambridge science park, most of the defence contractors (with good links to London/Heathrow), a large proportion of government, private sector and university/polytechnic research establishments, etc. These same privileged regions have witnessed the fastest growth in service employment, particularly in producer services. This alone also demonstrates the crucial importance of state infrastructural provision for successful economic growth. Not the 'free-market' but a fortuitous concatenation of geographical proximity to continental Europe, state support, high-quality infrastructural provision, skilled and educated workforces, and local initiative have been the driving forces behind the South's success.

A Liberal and Authoritarian State

Traditional Conservative statecraft had to resolve the central dilemma of Conservative politics in the age of mass democracy: how to secure the stable management of the interests of British capitalism and the British state in the presence of a well organized working class. Essentially the strategy adopted was threefold in character: try to win office alone; adopt a broad, national, cross-class appeal around the symbols of authority in order to do this; and once in office seek to insulate government from outside pressures as far as practicable.[26] The tactics appropriate to such a strategy involved the use of Parliament as a powerless but ideologically central intermediary for outside interests, the removal of potential conflict-ridden issues from the political agenda, and the devolution of many of the less important political questions to sub-central government agencies. But these tactics required a careful management of the balance of class and popular forces for success. In particular, for these tactics to be efficacious in terms of the strategy, external pressures had to be limited, the subjects had to be docile and the opposition (primarily the Labour Party) had to play by the rules of the established constitutional order. By the seventies this strategy had broken down. The question for Thatcherism here, then, is has it reconstituted an appropriate state system to order its accumulation strategy and secure its social base?

We have argued above that the dual crisis of the state gave the Thatcherite clique a high level of decisional autonomy, but we also argued that the long-term stability of this form of rule was far from clear. Decisional autonomy allows considerable room for manoeuvre but does not in itself give direction to – or a capacity for – the state to consolidate a new project. Thatcherism has proved exceptionally adroit in circumventing, riding out and abolishing the social democratic apparatuses of intervention and representation. The Thatcher governments have clearly taken great care to reconstruct central state authority in several fields.[27] The pattern of interest representation has been altered through the abolition of previous corporatist channels and the emasculation of local government, and there has been a regular resort to *raison d'état* and populism. Macro-economic policy has been transformed through a shift to a focus on monetary policy to control inflation, rather than a fiscal policy for full employment, and an increasing concern with the supply-side of the labour market through the MSC, moves to regional pay differentials etc. The management of the public finances has also been significantly changed through attempts to cut and restructure the state budget away from traditional social democratic welfare and employment concerns. Finally, in the sphere of social order, we have witnessed an enhanced policing and surveillance of the population, intimidation of opposition and dissent, and the manipulation of authoritarian sentiments. To date this has certainly been a successful strategy with which to confront and dismantle the social democratic aspects of the state form – notably in its set-piece confrontations: Miners, Teachers, Local Authorities (Liverpool) etc.

In this manner the loss of governing authority has been repaired through the construction of an increasingly authoritarian-liberal state. This entity is only a contradiction if one takes an overly rationalist view of the role of ideology. As Gamble has so forcefully argued, a liberal state in its economic mode all too often requires an authoritarian shell in order to deny political representation to oppositional forces and to police dissent. And the Conservatives have also overcome the *political* crisis of capital through a substantial weakening of the power of the trade unions, the privatization of large parts of the public sector, and the creation of a more general political climate in which a corporatist, interventionist Labour Party (1970s-style) is unelectable.

It is important to emphasize that many of the key institutional changes to the state system engineered under Thatcherism have never had majority popular support – abolition and emasculation of local authorities, opting out in welfare, wholesale redistribution of income towards the rich, benefit cuts for the poor etc. (Of course, once done such policies attract powerful minority interests for their continuation and expansion.) Rather the mechanics of the first-past-the-post electoral system, the elective dictatorship of prime ministerial power under the British constitution, and the divided opposition have together provided the crucial political preconditions for Thatcherism. But this is not all. For the Thatcher governments have been particularly astute in designing new forms of representation and intervention which underpin the interests of the political coalition that they are seeking to mobilize through popular capitalism for a neo-liberal accumulation strategy.

Of particular importance in this context are the new forms of articulation of business groups and privileged consumers to the state system. Here recent reforms in education provide a striking example. In secondary education popular accountability is now to operate through the direct mediation of governing bodies, rather than through the elected representatives of local councils. But the statutory composition of governing bodies not only enforces minority representation for educational professionals, it also stipulates that governors co-opted from business and the community must outnumber parents and teachers combined. Meanwhile, central control over the form and content of educational provision will be strengthened through the national curriculum and compulsory testing procedures. Finally, the opting-out provisions are likely to function as a powerful means of subordinating local education authorities to middle-class pressure, even where the school remains within the authority's jurisdiction. Those schools that do leave the LEA, however, will come under the central authority of the Department of Education and Science.

More generally, we have identified three major trends in the overall pattern of state system restructuring under Thatcherism. First, there has been a widespread weakening and/or removal of functions and powers from those parts of the state system concerned with the delivery of welfare and collective services – the drastic reduction of local government powers and funding; the erosion of a range of corporatist bodies, from the NEDC to local wages councils; the privatization programme which has administratively re-commodified large areas of the state sector; the creeping privatization of such institutions as the universities as budgets are restrained and the private sector steps in; and the gradual but steady introduction of commercial criteria into the remaining welfare sectors. Second, many of these powers have been reconcentrated below the central level in unelected (usually ministerially-appointed) and unaccountable – except to the minister and local business interests – bodies, for example, the UDCs. Other functions and services have been devolved to the market. Third, there has been a centralization of functions and powers in Whitehall, often beyond effective parliamentary scrutiny, and not necessarily rationally coordinated in any simple administrative sense.

This framework has conferred considerable flexibility on the government and sustained its decisional autonomy, while simultaneously eroding the institutional forms that generated the dual crisis of the state. But its overarching unity is somewhat precarious and we consider below whether a new power bloc is now emerging. The dual crisis was initially ridden through a resort to *raison d'état* and populism and this is still a common mode of operation for the Thatcherite state. The social democratic institutions have been weakened and their linkages to the state have been eroded. At the same time new types of functionally-based policy networks and communities have been established (typically excluding organized labour but embracing both private and public bodies) to play analogous roles in many areas. And the crisis of the party system is being resolved as the Thatcherite agenda increasingly takes the form of a new common sense. Thus the 'dual crisis of the state' is now perhaps over.

To begin with, however, such unity as there was in this state strategy derived from the political determination of the Thatcher clique in the Cabinet to impose a neo-liberal, popular capitalist strategy on social, political and economic change, and from the enhanced administrative dominance of the Treasury over all branches of the state. This unity was secured through a series of other more or less irreversible developments: politically motivated appointments in the civil service and the quasi-state organizations; the restructuring and reduction of the state's tax base; and the increased openness of the UK financial and money markets, which enmeshes the state deeper into the structural constraints of footloose international capital.

A Two Nations Hegemonic Project

For a while the emergence of a new power bloc was precluded by Thatcher's distaste for concessions, divisions among those forces which supported and/or were prepared to grant a warrant of autonomy to the government, and the very complex of neo-liberalism and authoritarianism the Conservative Party is seeking to promote. This is so because the very notion of a popular capitalism implies that individuals (or, at most, families) participate in the new order through their atomized consumption of benefits and values. This is why the Conservative Party can claim to speak for the whole people while simultaneously eroding those remaining representative structures with any real power. In the broad range of institutions of civil society (churches, schools, media etc.) Thatcherism has attempted to restructure them around its preferred agenda of the pursuit of possessive individualism and the attachment to an increasingly authoritarian definition of the national interest in moral and political affairs.

Regarding the power bloc itself, the rise of Thatcherism corresponded to a crisis in the social democratic power bloc determined both in and through structural crises and through the economic and political disorientation of its constituent elements. But Thatcherism in its first stage did not constitute a new bloc: at most it represented, in the face of an acute crisis, a defensive alliance of forces in the pursuit of rolling back the gains of the postwar settlement. During the second stage of Thatcherism there was an intermittent (but cumulative) destruction of the structural underpinnings of the former power bloc and its continued disorientation, but little progress was made in creating or consolidating a new power bloc. Indeed, once the immediate crisis was resolved through the election of a Conservative government, disputes grew within the Establishment about the appropriate direction of economic, political, and social strategy. Only in the period of consolidated Thatcherism have we seen signs of a new power bloc emerging on the basis of a new accumulation strategy, involving a new niche for MNCs, international finance and traded services in the international economy, a new liberal and authoritarian state form appropriate to this strategy, and a hegemonic project which both defines the common interests of a reconstituted capitalist class and offers a chance of winning some measure of hegemony over society as a whole. This leads us, finally, to a consideration of the prospects for the overall hegemonic project of Thatcherism.

The evidence of the growing social and economic polarizations in British society since 1979 is extensive and will not be repeated here (we have noted its geographical specificity above). Rather, we want to draw attention to the fact that these developments are not the inevitable consequence of painful economic and social changes. They are, in fact, the product of a two nations hegemonic project.

The essential character of social democracy, with its commitment to Keynesian techniques of employment maintenance and a welfare state for all, was a one nation, expansive form of hegemony. In the British case the weak domestic base and the external constraints always meant that such commitments were more often honoured in the breach; but such a hegemonic project – even though it was never fully institutionalized – nonetheless set the political agenda and provided the broad framework of party competition. The collectivism of such arrangements was ostensibly underpinned by cross-class transfers through a progressive tax system and equal entitlements to universal welfare provision; in reality, the transfers were predominantly of an inter-generational, but intra-class, kind. Once again, however, the very rhetorics of equality – let alone the genuine elements of progressivity in the system – were real in their effects in so far as they set some of the terms of public debate on the national terrain. For, whenever research or political protest revealed failures in this area, attempts were made to incorporate the marginalized through some form of collectivism (for example, the community development programmes or the educational priority areas). In Thatcher's new model social security state, similar discoveries are more likely to provoke an attitude of indifference or a lecture on the culture of dependency.

Thatcherism rejects this social democratic, one nation logic in its entirety: the economic and state strategies pursued since 1979 have accentuated a latent two nations polarization of British society. To begin with, such polarizations might have been interpreted as the unavoidable (and even regrettable) consequences of the inability to maintain an expansive one nation hegemony in conditions of economic crisis. But it has become increasingly clear that many Thatcherite policies have consciously played on and reinforced such divisions. (The high risks associated with such a strategy were the main cause for concern among the so-called Conservative 'wets' and 'consolidators'; the consequences explain much about the worries expressed by large sections of the churches.) In other words, the balance of forces has enabled the Thatcherites to continue to pursue a clear – and increasingly transparent – two nations strategy even as a degree of economic growth has returned.

The electoral victories of 1983 and 1987 were both premissed on an alliance of the privileged nation, which reaped the benefits of the rising real wages of those in employment and the private provision (often tax-subsidized) of goods and services, against the subordinate nation, which comprised the long-term unemployed, those employed in the secondary labour market, and those largely dependent on (diminishing) public provision of goods and services. A two nations hegemonic project aims, first, to *expand* the numbers of those in the privileged nation in areas where its privileges are well entrenched – namely, transport and housing – and, second, to *widen* the scope of their privileges – to pensions, education and health care. This project is underwritten, above all, by the uneven impact of economic decline and growth (itself mediated by government policies), and by a major redistribution of *income* from poor to rich. This entails the widening of differentials within the wage-earning classes in line with market forces and arbitrary differentials; a shift of public *wealth* to individual rich consumers via privatization; and the political creation of differential access to collectively provided welfare.

It is, of course, debatable as to what extent this project can be described as a *national–popular* strategy of political, intellectual and moral leadership: the rhetoric of nationalism fits ill with the international orientation of the accumulation strategy and the power bloc, while the populism of the hegemonic project builds on divisions among the people rather than reducing them. In addition, as we have stressed above, the privileged nation is not very thick on the ground in the North, the Celtic fringes or the deprived urban locales. Indeed, it is to this 'gap' that much of the third term's legislative programme is directed. Ultimately, the success or failure of such a hegemonic project is dependent on the capacity of the accumulation strategy to continue to provide economic growth. We remain deeply sceptical of the ability of the Thatcherite state strategy to facilitate sufficient growth over the long term to secure such a project in a crisis-free mode. This does not mean that it will fail in the sense of not persisting for a considerable period of time – beyond 2000? A comparison with postwar social democracy might serve to illustrate this.

Already by the late 1950s various analysts had foreseen that actually existing social democracy in Britain was composed of fatally flawed material: but the domestic dominance of social democracy lasted until 1976. Thus Shonfield argued that the external economic strategy that was being pursued was incompatible with the requirements for domestic growth and economic stability;[28] and Worsthorne spoke of the stalemate state, wherein an unstable equilibrium existed between a labour movement with considerable social and economic power and a conservative Establishment that continued to monopolize effective political power.[29] Moreover, in the early-to-mid-1960s there was an attempt to modernize British social democracy, improve Britain's economic performance, and alter its foreign-policy alignments. This posed a limited but real alternative to the dominant pattern of politics as pursued during the 1950s. The final judgement on this *competing* set of strategies must be that they failed, but this was not a completely foregone conclusion.

An Alternative Agenda

In a similar way, the Thatcherite agenda sketched above may be deeply flawed: it is certainly opposed by several competing strategies, and it may yet be partially overturned – or instead it may defeat its challengers and last (albeit with modifications) for some considerable time. We would argue that even within the Conservative Party there is a clear alternative to the Thatcherite line that could still come to occupy a position of dominance. This position is certainly not a reversal of Thatcherism; indeed it accepts many of the latter's tenets, but neither is it simply its continuation under another name. We are thinking of the general position outlined by Michael Heseltine.

Heseltine has come to articulate a set of alternative economic and international projects to those of the Thatcherites. Thus although any alternative hegemonic project from this camp would almost certainly be of an ameliorated two nations kind, his accumulation and state strategies would differ in significant respects from those of the Thatcherites. Moreover, such a position could no doubt command widespread assent not only across the party system – embracing much of the Conservative

Party, the Alliance and significant sections of the Labour right – but also from within the state system and powerful sections of capital operating in the UK. Perhaps the key distinguishing feature of this competing line is its self-conscious Europeanism.

In part Thatcherism's neo-liberalism proceeds from a recognition that the UK economy is too weak as a nationally-integrated space to attempt to 'go it alone'. However, starting from the same perception, an alternative strategy might focus more single-mindedly on the European option. An increasing number of politicians in Europe (across the left–right spectrum) are currently arguing that as American relative power declines Europe will have to take responsibility for more of its own defence, and that in turn this will necessitate an increased level of European integration. Additionally, the moves towards an internal free market in Europe, the growing concern about protectionism, and the continuing competitive challenge to European capital from the US and Japan are also prompting a range of concrete proposals for European cooperation and integration in the economic field. To date, three main strategies have been canvassed. First, there is the position of 'Atlantic Reformism', which argues for a strengthened and more coordinated European pillar for the NATO alliance (established through the West European Union) which could treat with America more equally. Second, there are the 'European Reformers' who focus on a strengthening of the institutions of, and the development of common policies within, the European Community. These two positions are by no means contradictory given a 'separation of powers', with the WEU concentrating on defence and foreign policy, and the EC confining itself to economic and social issues. Third, and possibly emerging as a rightwing backlash to the failure of either of these two strategies, there is the position of 'Euro-Gaullism' which advocates more state intervention, a European nationalism, and an assertive and hawkish foreign and defence policy for an independent Western Europe.[30]

Thatcherism is too attached to the traditional Atlanticism of British foreign policy, with its preference for a special relationship with the US, and too distant from the EC, either as an economic or a political ideal, seriously to countenance either Atlantic or European Reformism. It is here, above all, that Owen and Heseltine present a clear alternative to Thatcherism. This difference in external orientation also has important domestic implications. Thus Heseltine, for one, has consistently argued since his Westland resignation that for Britain to play a constructive role in Europe it must also fashion a coherent industrial policy to regenerate its industrial base. This might comprise an active policy for the promotion of high-tech sectors, a micro-corporatist approach to labour relations where the new realism is encouraged at company level but a national deal with the TUC is ruled out, and a genuine shift towards European defence procurement and planning so that Europe would become more of an equal with the US.[31]

More specifically, Heseltine's arguments may be summarized as follows. Only in combination can the European governments enter a partnership with industry to face the competitive challenge from the US and Japan; there is a need to strengthen the powers of the Department of Trade and Industry to counter the finance-oriented Treasury; the government has a major, and industry a marginal, role to play in the regeneration of the inner cities; and there is a need for a shift of power to restructured local authorities, with real powers of economic planning, to overcome the monopolistic political society centred on London.[32] In the interview with *Marxism Today* where Heseltine expressed these ideas, he was also careful to specify his areas of agreement with the Thatcherite agenda. Thus this competing accumulation strategy, state strategy and ameliorated two nations hegemonic project outlined by Heseltine would operate largely on the terrain set by Thatcherism; but in its Europeanism, its coordinated approach to industrial promotion, and its concern to mitigate the costs of social and economic restructuring for the poor and marginalized it would constitute a genuine alternative to the Thatcherite agenda outlined above.

Finally, the terms of opposition for the left would be significantly altered if Heseltinism were the dominant strategy as opposed to Thatcherism. First, if it were accepted that the mitigation of two nations divisions is the proper concern of government, then it would become easier to argue for the redistribution of the benefits of economic growth to promote a one nation social and political community. Second, once a degree of coordinated restructuring had been placed on the agenda – at both a European and a local level – then the left would be able to argue about its form and scope from a minimum of common ground, rather than being in the position of offering a complete alternative to the dominant agenda. And third, dominant state and accumulation strategies which were oriented towards Europe might reinforce the marginalization of the anti-EC wing of the Labour Party and strengthen the hand of those pressing social issues and economic planning on the EC agenda.

Agenda for Future Research

No doubt future analysts of Thatcherism will, with the benefit of hindsight, wonder at the presumption involved in our attempt to provide a theoretically informed account of the phenomenon even as it unfolds. We are aware of the pitfalls that await such contemporary analysis but we remain convinced of its importance. For if one cannot understand the opposition then attempts to construct a political alternative will remain critically debilitated. The longer Thatcherism persists, the more research must concern itself with the emergent restructuring of the economy, civil society and the state. Some of the relevant questions here have been asked (but by no means fully answered) above. Without a clearer sense of the strengths of the Thatcherite project, its contradictions and its areas of weaknesses, the left is likely to oscillate between a fatal pessimism and a chiliastic faith in a future surge of popular radicalism.

A first priority is to understand better the current (and likely future) pattern of economic development in the UK. This is important not only for an assessment of the fortunes of the Thatcherite accumulation strategy but also because changing patterns of economic growth have manifest political implications. For example, if future employment creation is to be mainly in a thinly unionized service sector, what might this imply for trade union–Labour Party links? Of similar importance are questions concerning the form of relationships between new growth sectors and the state. What forms of intervention and facilitation would be open to a future government which was keen to promote industrial regeneration?

For civil society, the Thatcherite goal of achieving irreversible change in social institutions and their associated forms of consciousness is clear enough. What requires further investigation is the extent to which the lived experiences and power relations (for example, in the workplace and the home) could provide a basis for a culture of opposition. Thatcherism's ideology of possessive individualism and consumerism is well enough documented. Sociological work on changes in class consciousness has already begun, but much more is needed in this area. Equally important, however, are detailed studies of the changing structures and practices of the institutions of civil society, for example in the educational system. We should be on our guard against easy assumptions that institutional change in itself decisively weakens potential sites of resistance.

In the last analysis the potential for alternative political programmes is powerfully mediated by the institutional structure of the state and its various instruments for intervention and representation. Do changes under Thatcherism make it easier or more difficult to implement an alternative set of strategies? What kinds of obstacles to economic intervention have been created by privatization, the restructuring of the tax base, and the increased power and autonomy of the financial and monetary markets? All these questions require further investigation and the answers to them will ultimately be a better guide for left strategy than short-term calculations of electoral mood and party image.

Notes

Notes to chapter 1

1 Two useful examples of this approach are: P. Jackson (ed.), *Implementing Government Policy Initiatives* (1985): and D.S. Bell (ed.), *The Conservative Government 1979–1984* (1985).

2 Andrew Gamble provides a brief example of this approach in his article 'The rise of the resolute right', *New Socialist*, Jan./Feb. 1985. So, too, does M. Biddiss in 'Thatcherism: Concepts and Interpretations', in Minogue and Biddiss (eds), *Thatcherism: Personality and Politics* (1987), pp. 1–21. And Tessa ten Tusscher has reviewed feminist analyses in her essay 'Patriarchy, capitalism and the New Right', in Evans et al., *Feminism and Political Theory* (1986), pp. 66–84.

3 See D. Kavanagh, *Thatcherism and British Politics: The End of Consensus?* (1987), p. 11.

4 Examples of this approach include: A. Aughey, 'Mrs Thatcher's Philosophy', conference paper, April 1983; T. Blackwell and J. Seabrook, 'Mrs Thatcher's religious pilgrimage', *Granta*, 6 (1983); and P. Riddell, *The Thatcher Government* (1983), pp. 6–7 and *passim*.

5 Examples include: P. Hennessey, *Cabinet* (1986), pp. 94–122; A. King. 'Margaret Thatcher: the style of a prime minister', in idem (ed.), *The British Prime Minister* (1985); G. W. Jones, 'Cabinet government and Mrs Thatcher', *Contemporary Record*, 1: 3 (1987); and, for a discussion of Thatcher's Nietzschean style and commitment to politics as dramaturgy, see B. O'Leary, 'Why was the GLC abolished?', *International Journal of Urban and Regional Research*, 11 (1987), pp. 193–217.

6 See Kavanagh, *Thatcherism*, pp. 12–13. Although we criticize its lack of theoretical depth in chapter 2, this ranks among the best books analysing Thatcherism in terms of this fifth approach.

7 For a spirited critique of the authoritarian populist and/or statist theses for idealizing the postwar settlement and exaggerating the novel horrors of Thatcherism in the field of law, order and surveillance, see: P. Gilroy and J. Sim, 'Law, order and the state of the left', in P. Scraton (ed.), *Law, Order and the Authoritarian State* (1987), pp. 71–106.

8 Stuart Hall's work is synthesized in *The Road to Renewal: Thatcherism and the Crisis of the Left* (1988); Andrew Gamble's in *The Free Economy and the Strong State* (1988); our own work is summarized here. See also Bob Jessop, *The Political Economy of Postwar Britain* (forthcoming, 1989).

9 Cf. A. King, 'Margaret Thatcher'.

10 Cf. B. Schwarz, 'The Thatcher years', in R. Miliband et al. (eds), *Socialist Register 1987* (1987).

11 Cf. P. Green, 'British capitalism and the Thatcher years', *International Socialism*, second series, 35 (1987), pp. 3–70.

12 M. Thatcher, *The Sunday Times*, cited in M. Holmes, *The First Thatcher Government* (1985), p. 209.

13 There is nothing inevitable or magical about the number three when defining stages and sub-stages: it just so happens that, for our purposes and based on our reading of the development of Thatcherism, three periods have so far occurred and each can be sub-divided into three sub-stages.

Notes to chapter 2

1 Cf. K. Minogue, 'Introduction: the context of Thatcherism', in Minogue and Biddiss (eds), *Thatcherism: Personality and Politics* (1987), pp. x–xvii (p. x).

2 B. Walden, *Sunday Times*, 17 Apr. 1988.

3 For an accessible account of the methodology of scientific realism, see A. Sayer, *Method in Social Science: A Realist Approach*, London: Hutchinson, 1985.

4 Alternative strategies abound but translating them from intellectually defensible to politically feasible plans has so far proved impossible. For two examples, neither of which is openly critical of Thatcherism, see: I. Gilmour, *Inflation Can Be Cured*, Oxford: Blackwell, 1983; and M. Heseltine, *Where There is a Will* (1986).

5 A recent and highly readable analysis along these lines is Peter Jenkins's book *Mrs Thatcher's Revolution* (1987).

6 The meaning of these terms actually varies from case to case and in using them we are not trying to suggest that they are mutually exclusive and/or exhaustive.

7 The classic in this genre is William Keegan's *Mrs Thatcher's Economic Experiment* (1984); see also D. Smith, *The Rise and Fall of Monetarism* (1987); S Pollard, *The Wasting of the British Economy*, London: Croom Helm (1982); and Lord Kaldor, *The Scourge of Monetarism* (1982).

8 J. Ross, *Thatcher and Friends* (1983), p. 3.

9 Ibid., pp. 40–1.

10 Ibid., p. 43.

11 Since this criticism might seem to beg the question of economism vs. political or ideological explanations, we deal with the issue of relative autonomy below.

12 H. Overbeek, 'Global Capitalism and Britain's Decline', unpublished thesis, University of Amsterdam (1988), p. 254. A revised version of this thesis will be published by Hutchinson in 1989.
13 A. Bhaduri and J. Steindl, 'The Rise of Monetarism as a Social Doctrine', Thames Working Papers in Political Economy. London, 1983, p. 14.
14 Ibid.
15 T. Nairn, 'The crisis of the British state', New Left Review, 130 Nov./Dec. 1981, p. 39.
16 T. Nairn, The Break-Up of Britain (1981), p. 391.
17 Ibid., p. 388.
18 Nairn, Break-Up, pp. 382, 392, 396.
19 J. Foster, 'The Political Economy of Mrs Thatcher's Monetarism', Quarterly Economic Commentary, Oct. 1981.
20 F. Atkins, 'Thatcherism, populist authoritarianism, and the problem of left strategy', Capital and Class, 28 (Spring 1986), pp. 33–5.
21 See, especially, Nairn, 'Crisis', Break-Up.
22 Overbeek, 'Global Capitalism', 1988. On the Amsterdam school, see B. Jessop, 'Regulation Theories in Retrospect and Prospect', International Conference on Regulation, Barcelona, 16 June 1988.
23 See K. van der Pijl, The Making of the Atlantic Ruling Class, London: Verso, 1984.
24 Overbeek, 'Global Capitalism', pp. 233–9.
25 Ibid., pp. 248–55.
26 Ibid., pp. 248–9.
27 Simon Clarke notes that even the economic theories of monetarism are generalizations from the book-keeping principles of the petty capitalist enterprise or the petty bourgeois household. See S. Clarke, 'Capitalist Crisis and the Rise of Monetarism', Socialist Register 1987, pp. 393–427.
28 C. Leys, Politics in Britain (1983), pp. 94–5, our emphasis.
29 Clarke, 'Capitalist Crisis'.
30 Ibid.
31 Ibid., passim.
32 B. Jessop, 'The transformation of the state in postwar Britain', in Scase (ed.), The State in Western Europe (1980); and the articles from New Left Review reprinted in chs 4, 6 and 8 of this book.
33 The following account is drawn from two articles: J. Bulpitt, 'The discipline of the new democracy: Mrs Thatcher's domestic statecraft', Political Studies, 34 (1986), pp. 19–39; and idem, 'Conservatism, unionism and the problem of territorial management', in P. Madgwick and R. Rose (eds), The Territorial Dimension in British Politics, London: 1982.
34 See, especially, Bulpitt, 'Discipline'.
35 K. Minogue, 'The Thatcherising of Neil Kinnock', The Weekend Australian, 8–9 Aug. 1987.
36 J. Krieger, Reagan, Thatcher and the Politics of Decline (1986), p. 199.
37 Ibid., pp. 86–8.
38 This view is more fully developed in A. Gamble, The Free Economy and the Strong State (1988).
39 A. O'Shea, 'Trusting the people: how does Thatcherism work?', in Formations

of Nation and People, London: Routledge & Kegan Paul (198-), pp. 19–41.

40 S. Hall, et al., *Policing the Crisis: Mugging, the State and Law and Order*, London: Macmillan (1978).

41 S. Hall, 'The toad in the garden: Thatcherism among the theorists', in C. Nelson and L. Grossberg eds, *Marxism and the Interpretation of Culture*, London: Macmillan (1988).

42 For three useful overviews of the theoretical background to Hall's work see: S. Hall, 'Cultural studies and the Centre: some problematics and problems' in Hall et al., *Culture, Media, Language*, London: Hutchinson (1981), pp. 15–48; Hall, 'Gramsci and us' in *Marxism Today*, May 1987; and Hall, 'The toad in the garden' in C. Nelson and L. Grossberg eds, *Marxism and the Interpretation of Culture*, London: Macmillan (1988).

43 S. Hall, 'Authoritarian Populism, a reply', *New Left Review* 151, 1985; reproduced here as chapter 5.

44 O'Shea, 'Trusting the people', p. 35.

45 Ibid., pp. 22–3.

46 Ibid., pp. 30–1.

47 Ibid., p. 21.

48 Ibid., pp. 19, 21–3, 32–3.

49 Ibid., pp. 23, 30, 19.

50 Ibid., pp. 35–6.

51 R. Williams, 'Problems of the coming period', *New Left Review*, 140 (July/Aug. 1983) pp. 7–18.

52 R. Williams, *Television: Technology and Cultural Form* (1974).

53 Williams, 'Problems'.

54 G. Therborn, 'The prospects of Labour', *New Left Review*, 145 (May/June 1984), pp. 32–3.

55 For an empirical account of mobile privatization and its possible links to Thatcherism, see R. Pahl and C. D. Wallace, 'Neither angels in marble nor rebels in red: privatization and working-class consciousness', in Rose (ed.), *Social Stratification and Economic Change* (1988), pp. 127–151.

56 B. Campbell, *The Iron Ladies: Why Do Women Vote Tory?* (1987), p. 233.

57 See, for example, J. Gardiner, 'Women, Recession, and the Tories', and L. Segal, 'The heat in the kitchen', both in Hall and Jacques (eds), *Politics of Thatcherism* (1983); E. Wilson, 'Women and Thatcherism' in Miliband et al. (eds), *Socialist Register 1987* (1987).

58 E. Wilson, 'Women and Thatcherism', pp. 206–15, 229–30.

59 *Ruth 1983: 350*, cited by T. ten Tusscher, 'Patriarchy, capitalism and the New Right', in J. Evans et al. (eds), *Feminism and Political Theory* (1986).

60 T. ten Tusscher, 'Patriarchy', p. 67.

61 Ibid., pp. 75–6.

62 Ibid., pp. 78–81.

63 Campbell, *Iron Ladies*, p. 234.

64 This does not mean that Bea Campbell sets out to criticize Hall's method: instead she uses it and shows the limits of the AP discursive strategy in this area. See particularly *Iron Ladies*, pp. 197–8.

65 Ibid., p. 246.

66 Ibid., pp. 276, 294.

67 Cf. ibid., pp. 150–98.

68 Wilson, in 'Women and Thatcherism', *Socialist Register 1987*, pp. 200–1; and Gardiner, 'Women, Recession'.

Notes to chapter 3

1 Later still came the Forum for Business.
2 B. Elliot and R. McCrone, 'The petty bourgeoisie and conservatism in Britain', *Sociological Review*, 1987, p. 486.
3 Ibid., pp. 486–7.
4 Hugh Stephenson gives a useful survey in *Mrs Thatcher's First Year*, London: Norman, 1980.
5 For a useful survey, see P. Jones, 'The Thatcher experiment: tensions and contradictions in the first year', *Politics and Power 2*, London: RKP, 1980, pp. 137–68.

Notes to chapter 4

1 Stuart Hall et al., *Policing the Crisis* (1978).
2 Stuart Hall and Martin Jacques (eds), *The Politics of Thatcherism* (1983).
3 For a review of the Birmingham Centre's work, see Stuart Hall et al., *Culture, Media, and Language* (1981).
4 Hall et al., *Policing the Crisis*.
5 See Stuart Hall, 'The great moving right show', in *Politics of Thatcherism*, pp. 19–39 (originally *Marxism Today*, Jan. 1979).
6 See Hall et al., *Policing the Crisis*, pp. 218–323; cf. Martin Jacques, 'Thatcherism: breaking out of the impasse', in Hall and Jacques, *Politics of Thatcherism*, pp. 40–62.
7 Hall et al., *Politics of Thatcherism*, p. 9.
8 See Hall, 'Moving right show', pp. 22–3; *Policing the Crisis*, pp. 278, 304, 320; and 'Popular-democratic versus authoritarian populism', in Hunt (ed.), *Marxism and Democracy* (1980).
9 Contrast Hall, 'Popular-democratic', pp. 161, 182, with 'The empire strikes back', *New Socialist*, July–Aug. 1982.
10 See Hall, 'Popular-democratic', p. 161 and *Politics of Thatcherism*, pp. 29, 30–1, 34, 35, 37; 'The Battle for Socialist Ideas in the 1980s', *Socialist Register 1982* (1982), p. 15.
11 See Stuart Hall, 'Moving right show'; Introduction to *Politics of Thatcherism*, p. 11; and 'The little Caesars of social democracy', ibid., pp. 302–21.
12 S. Hall, 'Battle for socialist ideas', p. 13; cf. Hall, 'The culture gap', *Marxism Today*, Jan. 1984, p. 22.
13 See Hall et al., *Policing the Crisis*, pp. 218–19, 227–38, 261, 264–72, 309–17; 'Moving right show', pp. 24–7, 33-4.
14 This is recognized in Jacques, 'Thatcherism', in Hall and Jacques, *Politics of Thatcherism*, p. 41.
15 Anthony Barnett, *Iron Britannia* (1982): originally *New Left Review*, 134 (July–Aug. 1982), p. 46.
16 Francis G. Castles, *The Social Democratic Image of Society* (1978).

17 Ian Gilmour, *Inside Right*, 2nd edn, London 1978, p. 20.
18 Hall also notes this in 'Moving right show', p. 20.
19 Ibid., pp. 29, 37.
20 Hall and Jacques, Introduction to *Politics of Thatcherism*, p. 15.
21 Cf. Andrew Gamble, 'Thatcherism and Conservative politics', in Hall and Jacques (eds), *Politics of Thatcherism*, p. 121.
22 Karl Marx and Friedrich Engels, *On Britain* (2nd edn. 1962), p. 345.
23 Eg., Robert McKenzie and Alan Silver, *Angels in Marble* (1968).
24 See Bo Sarlvik and Ivor Crewe, *Decade of Dealignment* (1983), pp. 324–38; Ivor Crewe, 'How Labour was trounced all round', *Guardian*, 14 June 1983.
25 Hall also rejects the image of fascism, 'Moving right show', p. 22.
26 This is also reminiscent of Conservative luck at the turn of the century in having a divided opposition – Gladstone's Liberals splitting over Home Rule for Ireland and then being confronted with the emergence of the Labour Party – to be split in turn by the events of 1931.
27 Cf. William Keegan, *Mrs Thatcher's Economic Experiment* (1984).
28 Cf. Gerhard Lehmbruch, 'Liberal Corporatism and Party Government', in Schmitter and Lehmbruch (eds), *Trends Toward Corporatist Intermediation* (1979).
29 An institutional crisis occurs when the principles of representation are incongruent with the nature and scope of state intervention; a representational crisis occurs when there is a divorce between representatives and represented, such that the activities of representatives no longer reflect the interests and demands of those they represent and the latter's support is lost or becomes volatile; and a crisis of 'rationality' occurs when forms of intervention become less effective (or ineffective) because the structural problems demanding regulation have changed and/or new forms of resistance have emerged.
30 Cf. Bob Jessop, 'The transformation of the state in postwar Britain', in Scase (ed.), *The State in Western Europe* (1980), *passim*.
31 David Edgar has chronicled the rise of the popular New Right in *New Socialist*, Sept–Oct. 1983.
32 On 'populist ventriloquism', see Hall, in Hall and Jacques (eds), *Politics of Thatcherism*, pp. 29, 35, 37.
33 Keith Middlemas, 'The supremacy of party', *New Statesman*, 10 June 1983.
34 For a useful summary of trends, see John Ross, *Thatcher and Friends* (1983).
35 Ibid., p. 80.
36 Hall and Jacques (eds), *Politics of Thatcherism*, p. 15.
37 Cf. Andrew Gamble, 'This lady's not for turning: Thatcherism mark III', *Marxism Today* (June 1984).
38 Ross, *Thatcher and Friends*, p. 39.
39 Andrew Gamble, *The Conservative Nation* (1974), pp. 8–9.
40 Ross, *Thatcher and Friends*, p. 43.
41 Williams, 'Problems of the coming period', *New Left Review* 140 (July–Aug. 1983).
42 Eric Hobsbawm, 'Labour's lost millions', *Marxism Today* (Dec. 1983).

Notes to chapter 5

1 Stuart Hall et al., *Policing the Crisis* (1978).
2 On the conceptual distinction between 'popular' and 'populist' mobilization, which Jessop et al. seem to ignore, see S. Hall, 'Popular-democratic versus authoritarian populism', in Hunt (ed.), *Marxism and Democracy* (1980).
3 Nicos Poulantzas, *State, Power, Socialism* (1978), p. 203.
4 *Marxism Today* (Feb. 1980).
5 See, *inter alia*, 'Recent developments in language and ideology', in Hall et al., *Culture, Media, Language* (1980).
6 E. Laclau, *Politics and Ideology in Marxist Theory* (1977); E. Laclau and C. Mouffe, *Hegemony and Socialist Strategy* (1985).
7 In Hall and Jacques (eds), *Politics of Thatcherism* (1983).

Notes to chapter 6

1 Stuart Hall, 'Authoritarian populism: a reply', *New Left Review*, 151 (May/June 1985); ch. 5 of this book.
2 Stuart Hall, 'Popular-democratic versus authoritarian populism', in Hunt (ed.), *Marxism and Democracy* (1980); 'The great moving right show', in Hall and Jacques (eds), *Politics of Thatcherism* (1983); and 'Faith, hope and clarity', *Marxism Today* (Jan. 1985), pp. 17 and 19.
3 Contrast three very different but equally interesting and provocative analyses: Perry Anderson, 'The Antinomies of Gramsci', *New Left Review* 100 (1977); Peter Gibbon, 'Gramsci, Eurocommunism and the State', *Economy and Society*, 1984; and Hall, in Hunt (ed.), *Marxism and Democracy*.
4 Stuart Hall et al., *Policing the Crisis* (1978).
5 Unpublished reading notes supplied to Bob Jessop by Christine Buci-Glucksmann. Emphases added.
6 On these issues, see: Nicos Poulantzas, 'L'état, les mouvements sociaux, le parti', *Dialectiques* 28 (1979); 'La crise des partis', *Le Monde Diplomatique*, 26 Sept. 1979; and 'Le déplacement des procédures de légitimation', in Vincennes University, *L'Université de Vincennes: ou le désir d'apprendre* (1980), pp. 138–43.
7 See N. Poulantzas, *State, Power, Socialism* (1978), pp. 168–70, 191.
8 For an excellent discussion of the contradictions involved in the Thatcherite attempts at disengagement, see Andrew Gamble, 'Smashing the state: Thatcher's radical crusade', *Marxism Today* (June 1985).
9 See Poulantzas's interview with Stuart Hall and Alan Hunt in *Marxism Today* (May 1979).
10 See, e.g., S. Hall, 'The Legacy of Poulantzas', *New Left Review*, 119 (Jan./Feb. 1980), p. 68; 'Authoritarian populism: a reply', *New Left Review*, 151 (May/June 1985), p. 119: ch. 5 of this book.
11 For a more detailed discussion of these issues, see Bob Jessop, *Nicos Poulantzas: Marxist Theory and Political Strategy* (1985).
12 The latter argument is not one to which Gramsci would have subscribed: he would have dismissed as 'arbitrary, rationalistic, and willed' any hegemonic

project which could not have cemented a new historic bloc.

13 S. Hall, 'Faith, hope and clarity', *Marxism Today* (1985), p. 17.

14 Ibid., p. 18.

15 See Colin Leys, 'Thatcherism and British manufacturing', *New Left Review* 151 (May/June 1985), pp. 5–25.

16 Thus P. Dunleavy and C. T. Husbands's evidence does not support the view that AP issues had a significant impact on Conservative success in 1983: *British Democracy at the Crossroads* (1985).

17 *Labour Research* (July 1984).

18 *OECD Economic Survey: United Kingdom*, Paris 1985, p. 43.

19 M. Spence, 'Imperialism and decline', *Capital and Class* 25 (Spring 1985), pp. 126–7.

20 J. Coakley and L. Harris, *The City of Capital* (1983), p. 59.

21 J. Cornwall, *The Conditions for Economic Recovery* (1983).

22 We are grateful to Rod Rhodes for his comments on this paragraph. See also Gamble, 'Smashing the state'.

23 Cf. Spence, 'Imperialism', pp. 132–4.

24 P. Alcock, 'Welfare state – safety net or poverty trap?', *Marxism Today* (July 1985), p. 14.

Notes to chapter 7

1 Charlie Leadbeater, 'In the land of the dispossessed', *Marxism Today* (Apr. 1987), p. 20.

2 Ibid., p. 23.

3 David M. Gordon, 'The global economy: new edifice or crumbling foundations?', *New Left Review*, 168 (Mar./Apr. 1988), pp. 24–64.

4 Wladimir Andreff, 'The international centralization of capital and the reordering of world capitalism', *Capital and Class*, 22 (Spring 1984), pp. 58–80.

5 Gordon, 'Global Economy', p. 63.

Notes to chapter 8

1 See B. Jessop et al., 'Authoritarian populism, two nations, and Thatcherism', *New Left Review*, 147 (Sept./Oct. 1984), pp. 32–60; idem, 'Thatcherism and the politics of hegemony: a reply to Stuart Hall', *New Left Review*, 153 (Sept./Oct. 1985), pp. 87–101; B. Jessop, 'The mid-life crisis of Thatcherism', *New Socialist* (Mar. 1986).

2 On Fordism, its crisis and the transition to post-Fordism see, *inter alia*, Alain Lipietz, *Mirages and Miracles* (1987).

3 It was certainly significant in consolidating Thatcher's hold over the Cabinet and in the Conservative Party. It also provided a short-term boost to the Conservatives' popularity (some 3 percentage points for three months); but by August economic issues were once again crucial. See D. Sanders et al., 'Government popularity and the Falklands war: a reassessment', *British Journal of Political Science*, 17 (1987), pp. 281–313.

4 I. Crewe, 'The electorate: partisan dealignment ten years on', *West European*

Politics (1984), p. 192.

5 See J. Curtice and M. Steed, Appendix 2: 'An analysis of the Voting', in Butler and Kavanagh, *The British General Election of 1983* (1984).

6 Indices of Thatcherism and 'authoritarian populism' were lower in the 1987 election than in 1983 and lower still than in 1979. I. Crewe's personal communication to Bob Jessop.

7 I. Crewe, *Guardian*, 15 and 16 June 1987. Cf. Sanders et al., 'Government Popularity'.

8 For a review see E. Scarbrough, 'The British electorate twenty years on: electoral change and election surveys', *British Journal of Political Science*, 17 (1987), pp. 219–46.

9 P. Dunleavy and C.T. Husbands, *British Democracy at the Crossroads* (1985).

10 Cf. B. Jessop, 'The transformation of the state in postwar Britain', in Scase (ed)., *The State in Western Europe* (1980); P. Whiteley, *The Labour Party in Crisis*, London 1983. On ideological de-alignment between the Labour Party and its voters and on the collectivist trinity of nationalization, unions and social welfare, see Crewe, 'The electorate', pp. 200–2.

11 Crewe, 'The electorate', pp. 195–6.

12 Cf. Scarbrough, 'The British electorate', p. 237.

13 This is particularly true as the geographical concentration of votes means that the number of marginal seats has declined. Cf. J. Curtice, 'Must Labour lose?', *New Society* (18 June 1987).

14 Cf. R. Murray, 'Benneton Britain', *Marxism Today* (Nov. 1985).

15 The wet/dry conflict involved disputes between one nation Tories committed to restoring the postwar settlement and its pattern of corporatist bias and the hard-liners who trusted in monetarism, austerity, deflation and confrontation as means of economic and political crisis-management; the consolidator/radical divide concerned the debate over consolidating existing achievements or pressing on with the Thatcher revolution. On the latter see A. Gamble, 'Smashing the state: Thatcher's radical crusade', *Marxism Today* (June 1985); Jessop, 'Mid-life crisis'.

16 Following Poulantzas, we stressed this oscillation between disengagement and intervention, statism and populism, in our reply to Stuart Hall. The dynamic of Thatcherism lends further support to Poulantzas's argument here.

17 There are still only six UDCs: London Docklands and Liverpool (1981), Manchester Trafford Park (Feb. 1987), Teesside, Tyne and Wear, Black Country (May 1987). At least five more are to be established.

18 P. Dunleavy, 'The Limits to Local Government', in Boddy and Fudge (eds.), *Local Socialism?* (1984), pp. 49–81.

19 Rentoul argues that British society is now characterized by three groups: the 'haves', 'have-nots' and 'have-lots'. This might suggest that the Thatcherite 'two nations' strategy is better understood as a 'three nations' strategy; but it can also be read as implying that Thatcherism is seeking to create 'two nations' by encouraging the rise of a new class of 'haves' out of erstwhile 'have-nots'. See J. Rentoul, *The Rich Get Richer* (1987).

20 Cf. J. O'Connor, *The Fiscal Crisis of the State* (1973).

21 M. Linton, 'How the Tories rule the roost', *Guardian*, 19 June 1987.

22 M. Goodwin and S. Duncan, 'The local state and local economic policy:

political mobilization or economic regeneration?', *Capital and Class*, 27 (Winter 1986), p. 33.

23 *Financial Weekly*, 2 July 1987.
24 B. Jessop et al., 'Thatcherism and the politics of hegemory'. See also C. Leys, 'Thatcherism and British manufacturing: a question of hegemony', *New Left Review* 151 (May/June 1985).
25 P. Kellner, 'Labour's future: decline or democratic revolution', *New Statesman*, 19 June 1987.
26 A. Arblaster, 'Labour's future and the coalition debate', *New Left Review* 157 (May/June 1986), p. 52.
27 R. Williams, 'Splits, pacts and coalitions', *New Socialist* (Mar./Apr. 1984).
28 See, for example, M. Rustin, *For a pluralist socialism* (1985), pp. 131–46.
29 M. Rustin, 'Can Labour stop Thatcher?', *Chartist* (July-Aug. 1987), p. 26.
30 H. Wainwright, 'The limits of labourism: 1987 and beyond', *New Left Review*, 164 (July/Aug. 1987).
31 L. Panitch, 'The impasse of social democratic politics', in idem, *Working Class Politics in Crisis* (1985), p. 26.
32 Cf. Wainwright, 'The limits of labourism'.
33 R. Murray, 'Ownership, Control and the Market', *New Left Review*, 164 (July/Aug. 1987).

Notes to chapter 9

1 See Stuart Hall, 'The toad in the garden: Thatcherism among the theorists', in Nelson and Grossberg (eds), *Marxism and the Interpretation of Culture* (1988), pp. 35–73.
2 For a valuable discussion of the 'dominant ideology thesis', see N. Abercrombie, S. Hill and B. S. Turner, *The Dominant Ideology Thesis* (1980).
3 Adam Przeworski, *Capitalism and Social Democracy* (1985).
4 Michael Burawoy, *The Politics of Production: Factory Regimes under Capitalism and Socialism* (1985).
5 Antonio Gramsci, *Selections from the Prison Notebooks of Antonio Gramsci* (1971), pp. 279–318.
6 For a collection of contributions to this debate, see John Holloway and Sol Picciotto (eds), *State and Capital: A Marxist Debate* (1978).
7 See, for example, Claus Offe, *Contradictions of the Welfare State*, ed. J. Keane (1984).
8 See the various essays collected in P. Evans, D. Rueschemeyer, and T. Skocpol (eds), *Bringing the State Back In* (1985).
9 See, for example, E. A. Nordlinger, *On the Autonomy of the Democratic State* (1981).
10 For a discussion of the methodological distinction between institutional and strategic analysis, see A. Giddens, *The Constitution of Society* (1984).
11 For a fuller discussion of these issues, see Bob Jessop, *Nicos Poulantzas: Marxist Theory and Political Strategy* (1985).
12 See the article on 'Authoritarian populism, 'two nations', and Thatcherism' reprinted as ch. 4 of this book.
13 See Peter Hall, 'The state and economic decline', in Elbaum and Lazonick

(eds), *The Decline of the British Economy* (1986), pp. 266–302.

14 Of course, the relations involved here have changed over time, but for a general discussion of considerable importance, see Geoffrey Ingham, *Capitalism Divided? The City and Industry in British Social Development* (1984).

15 For an important discussion of these issues, see Malcolm Chalmers, *Paying For Defence: Military Spending and British Decline* (1985).

16 For a highly provocative essay on this subject, see Hugo Radice, 'The national economy: a Keynesian myth?', *Capital and Class*, 22 (Spring 1984), pp. 111–40.

17 For an account of the 'political crisis of capital' during the 1970s, see Colin Leys, 'Thatcherism and British manufacturing', *New Left Review*, 151 (May/June 1985), pp. 5–25.

18 For a more extended treatment of the dual crisis of the British state, see Bob Jessop, 'The dual crisis of the state', in idem, *Essays in the Theory of the State* (forthcoming 1989).

19 R. J. Johnston et al., *A Nation Dividing? The Electoral Map of Great Britain 1979–1987* (1988), p. 282.

20 Ibid., p. 328.

21 The data below are to be found in John M. Stopford and Louis Turner, *Britain and the Multinationals* (1985).

22 See Mark Smith, 'UK manufacturing: output and trade performance', *Midland Bank Economic Bulletin* (Autumn 1986), pp. 8–16; and P. Patel and K. Pavitt, 'The elements of British technological competitiveness', *National Institute Economic Review* (Nov. 1987), pp. 72–83.

23 Bob Jessop, 'The mid-life crisis of Thatcherism', *New Socialist* (Mar. 1986).

24 Grahame Thompson, *The Conservatives' Economic Policy* (1986), p. 184.

25 Johnston et al., *A Nation Dividing?*, p. 77.

26 On this see the important analysis of Jim Bulpitt, 'The discipline of the new democracy: Mrs Thatcher's domestic statecraft', *Political Studies*, 34 (1986) pp. 19–39.

27 A point emphasized in the cogent analysis of Andrew Gamble, 'Smashing the state: Thatcher's radical crusade', *Marxism Today* (June 1985).

28 Andrew Shonfield, *British Economic Policy since the War* (1958).

29 P. Worsthorne, 'Class and class conflict in British foreign policy', *Foreign Affairs*, 37: 3 (Apr. 1959); quoted in Andrew Gamble, *The Conservative Nation* (1974), p. 62.

30 For a discussion of these positions and much else besides, see John Palmer, *Europe Without America? The Crisis in Atlantic Relations* (1987).

31 For a reading of the Westland affair along these lines, see Henk Overbeek, 'The Westland affair: collision over the future of British capitalism', *Capital and Class*, 29 (Summer 1986), pp. 12–26.

32 See the interview with Michael Heseltine in *Marxism Today* (Mar. 1988); 'The Tory opposition'.

Bibliography

This bibliography contains a complete list of those works mentioned in the text or cited in the notes. It is divided into one section on books and another on articles. Where only *one* piece is cited from a book, the full details of the book will appear in that citation. Works containing several pieces will themselves be cited in the book section itself, and only the short title will appear after the relevant articles. Some of the books and articles cited are followed by a few brief comments. We hope that this will help the student reader. The absence of such comments is not an indication of the work's merits. Finally, we have not aimed at a comprehensive coverage but have selected those works that we have found most useful. Our apologies in advance to all those authors whose work we have overlooked.

Books

Aaronovitch, Sam, *The Road from Thatcherism: The Alternative Economic Strategy*, Lawrence & Wishart, London, 1981. An influential statement of the Labour left's alternative to Thatcherism, the so-called 'Alternative Economic Strategy'.

Abercrombie, N., S. Hill and B. S. Turner, *The Dominant Ideology Thesis*, Allen & Unwin, London, 1980.

Armstrong, Philip, Andrew Glyn and John Harrison, *Capitalism Since World War II: The Making and Breakup of the Great Boom*, Fontana, London, 1984. A pioneering study of postwar capitalism which concludes with an account of 'Thatcherism and Reaganomics' in terms of its project to roll back the economic and social gains achieved by the working class during the long boom.

Bacon, Robert and Walter Eltis, *Britain's Economic Problem: Too Few Producers*, Macmillan, London, 1976. Fed into the politics of Thatcherism through its argument that the expansion of the role of the state, and in particular the non-marketed sector, was responsible for Britain's economic problems.

Barnett, Anthony, *Iron Britannia*, originally a special issue of *New Left Review*, 134 (July/Aug. 1982); reprinted in an extended form by Allison & Busby, London, 1982. A spirited polemic against a British political culture that produced a cross-party consensus over the Falkland/Malvinas Islands war. Contains an important analysis of the cross-party consensus around foreign policy which Barnett terms 'Churchillism'.

Behrens, Robert, *The Conservative Party from Heath to Thatcher: Policies and Politics 1974–1979*, Saxon House, Farnborough, 1980. A detailed account of the Conservative Party over this crucial period. One of the few works on the subject.

Bell, D.S. (ed.), *The Conservative Government 1979–1984: An Interim Report*, Croom Helm, London, 1985. A collection of short articles on various government policies.

Beynon, Huw (ed.), *Digging Deeper: Issues in the Miners' Strike*, Verso, London, 1985. Much the best of a spate of books on the major industrial conflict of the second Thatcher administration.

Blake, Robert, *The Conservative Party from Peel to Thatcher*, Fontana, London, 1985. A high Tory peer (ennobled by Thatcher) concludes this standard text with an insubstantial review of the early Thatcher years.

Bleaney, Michael, *The Rise and Fall of Keynesian Economics: An Investigation of its Contribution to Capitalist Development*, Macmillan, London, 1985. A very clear and careful study.

Bosanquet, Nicholas, *After the New Right*, Heinemann, London, 1983. An important and detailed examination of the economic and philosophical thinking of the New Right by a leading welfare economist.

Brittan, Samuel, *The Role and Limits of Government: Essays in Political Economy*, Temple Smith, London, 1983. A highly readable, commendatory series of essays on the political economy of the New Right by the leading economic commentator on *The Financial Times*.

Bromley, Simon, *The Geopolitical Economy of International Oil*, Polity Press, Cambridge, forthcoming 1989. Includes an attempt to situate the political economy of North Sea oil in its international context.

Burawoy, Michael, *The Politics of Production: Factory Regimes under Capitalism and Socialism*, Verso, London, 1985.

Butler, D. and D. Kavanagh, *The British General Election of 1983*, Macmillan, London, 1984. A detailed survey of the election campaign and its outcome.

Butler, D. and D. Kavanagh, *The British General Election of 1987*, Macmillan, London, 1988.

Campbell, Beatrix, *The Iron Ladies: Why Do Women Vote Tory?*, Virago Press, London, 1987. A fascinating and penetrating account of the complex relations of sex and class in Conservative politics.

Castles, Francis G., *The Social Democratic Image of Society*, Routledge & Kegan Paul, London, 1978.

Centre for Contemporary Cultural Studies, *The Empire Strikes Back: Race and Racism in 70s Britain*, Hutchinson, London, 1982. An important collection of studies on the politics of racism in Britain which argues that 'the construction of an authoritarian state in Britain is fundamentally intertwined with the elaboration of popular racism in the 1970s'.

Chalmers, Malcolm, *Paying For Defence: Military Spending and British Decline*, Pluto Press, London, 1985.

Coakley, Jerry and Laurence Harris, *The City of Capital: London's Role as a Financial Centre*, Basil Blackwell, Oxford, 1983. A clear and short account of the important changes in the City of London's financial role over the last twenty years and its relation to the rise of monetarism.

Coates, David, *The Context of British Politics*, Hutchinson, London, 1984. An excellent radical textbook on contemporary British politics.

Coates, David and John Hillard (eds), *The Economic Decline of Modern Britain: The Debate Between Left and Right*, Wheatsheaf, Brighton, 1986. An important and stimulating collection of articles from across the political spectrum.

Coates, David and John Hillard (eds), *The Economic Recovery of Modern Britain*, Edward Elgar, Aldershot, 1987.

Cole, John, *The Thatcher Years: A Decade of Revolution in British Politics*, BBC Books, London, 1987. A witty and detailed account of the daily political routines of the Thatcher years. As to be expected from the BBC stable, the 'balance' swamps the interpretation.

Cormack, Patrick (ed.), *Right Turn*, Leo Cooper, London, 1978. A collection of splenetic rants, which is 'dedicated to Margaret Thatcher', from 'eight men who changed their minds'.

Cornwall, John, *The Conditions for Economic Recovery: A Post-Keynesian Analysis*, Martin Robertson, Oxford, 1983. A powerful critique of, and alternative theorization to, the neo-classical orthodoxy of the 1980s.

Cottrell, Allin, *Social Classes in Marxist Theory*, Routledge & Kegan Paul, London, 1984.

Dearlove, John and Peter Saunders, *Introduction to British Politics: Analysing a Capitalist Democracy*, Polity Press, Cambridge, 1984. A good introductory textbook.

Drucker, H., P. Dunleavy, A. Gamble and G. Peele, *Developments in British Politics 2*, Macmillan, London, 1986. A valuable collection of survey articles on many aspects of British politics, effectively a new textbook.

Dunleavy, Patrick and Christopher T. Husbands, *British Democracy at the Crossroads: Voting and Party Competition in the 1980s*, Allen & Unwin, London, 1985. An important critique of and alternative to traditional models of party competition and studies of voting behaviour.

Evans, P., D. Rueschemeyer, and T. Skocpol, *Bringing the State Back In*, Cambridge University Press, Cambridge, 1985.

Evans, Judith et al. (eds), *Feminism and Political Theory*, Sage, London, 1986.

Finer, S. E., *The Changing British Party System 1945–1979*, American Enterprise Institute, Washington, DC, 1980. A major statement of the adversary politics thesis.

Gamble, Andrew, *The Conservative Nation*, Routledge & Kegan Paul, London, 1974. Still by far the best single history and interpretation of the postwar Conservative Party.

Gamble, Andrew, *Britain in Decline: Economic Policy, Political Strategy and the British State*, Macmillan, London, 1981 (2nd revised edn, 1985). An important and influential account of the long history of UK decline, the alternative political strategies to reverse it and their relation to the state.

Gamble, Andrew, *The Free Economy and the Strong State: The Politics of Thatcherism*, Macmillan, 1988. A major textbook on Thatcherism which reviews debates as to its character on the left and also Conservative accounts. Also presents Gamble's own distinctive interpretation of Thatcherism.

Gamble, Andrew and Stuart Walkland, *The British Party System and Economic Policy 1945–83: Studies in Adversary Politics*, Clarendon Press, Oxford, 1984. A systematic evaluation of the 'adversary politics' thesis. Gamble argues that consensus on external constraints limited macro-economic policy: whereas Walkland argues that industrial policy was undermined by alternating party control over policy making.

Giddens, Anthony, *The Constitution of Society*, Polity Press, Cambridge, 1984.

Gilmour, Ian, *Inside Right: a Study of Conservatism*, Hutchinson, London, 1977. A leading Conservative 'wet' defends the 'one nation' approach.

Gilmour, Ian, *Britain Can Work*, Martin Robertson, Oxford, 1983. An old-style, one nation Tory delivers a powerful indictment of monetarism and proposes an alternative.

Gramsci, Antonio, *Selections from the Prison Notebooks of Antonio Gramsci* (ed. and trans. Quintin Hoare and Geoffrey Nowell Smith), Lawrence & Wishart, London, 1971.

Gurr, Ted Robert and Desmond S. King, *The State and the City*, Macmillan, London, 1987. Stresses the autonomous power of the state to remake the urban environment.

Hall, Stuart et al., *Policing the Crisis: Mugging, the State, and Law and Order*, Macmillan, London, 1978. A seminal account of the drift towards an authoritarian form of state from the late 1960s and through the 1970s. Also to be read as an exemplary demonstration of Hall's approach to political analysis.

Hall, Stuart et al., *Culture, Media, and Language*, Hutchinson, London, 1981. A collection of articles showing the state of development of cultural studies at the Birmingham Centre for Contemporary Studies.

Hall, Stuart and Martin Jacques (eds), *The Politics of Thatcherism*, Lawrence & Wishart, London, 1983. A valuable collection of essays by the left attempting to come to terms with and define Thatcherism. Originally published in the theoretical journal of the Communist Party, *Marxism Today*.

Heath, Anthony et al., *How Britain Votes*, Pergamon Press, Oxford, 1985. An important revision to conventional electoral studies. Adopts a different categorization of social class from the traditionalists and reaches some interesting conclusions on the class basis of contemporary voting.

Hennessy, Peter, *Cabinet*, Basil Blackwell, Oxford, 1986. Some may question the author's belief that the problems of Cabinet government are at the heart of Britain's difficulties but this is simply the best study of the Cabinet we have. Worth ten textbooks on the subject.

Heseltine, Michael, *Where There Is a Will*, Hutchinson, London, 1986.

Hillyard, Paddy and Janie Percy-Smith, *The Coercive State: The Decline of Democracy in Britain*, Fontana, London, 1988. A highly readable account of the myriad ways in which democratic accountability and civil liberties in Britain have been undermined by successive governments.

Hodgson, Geoff, *Labour at the Crossroads: The Political and Economic Challenge to the Labour Party in the 1980s*, Martin Robertson, Oxford, 1981.

Books 199

Holloway, John and Sol Picciotto (eds), *State and Capital: A Marxist Debate*, Edward Arnold, London, 1978.

Holmes, Martin, *The First Thatcher Government 1979–1983: Contemporary Conservatism and Economic Change*, Wheatsheaf, Brighton, 1985. Although based on numerous interviews with key officials and politicians, this superficial and acclamatory book says little that is new. Better to read the government speeches in the original.

Ingham, Geoffrey, *Capitalism Divided? The City and Industry in British Social Development*, Macmillan, London, 1984. A major historical and theoretical reinterpretation of the role of the City in Britain's economic development.

Jackson, Peter (ed.), *Implementing Government Policy Initiatives: The Thatcher Administration 1979–83*, Royal Institute of Public Administration, London, 1985. A collection of detailed studies of policy implementation in the first Thatcher administration. Usefully demystifies notions of a unitary and coherent 'Thatcherism'.

Jenkins, Peter, *Mrs Thatcher's Revolution*, Jonathan Cape, London, 1987.

Jessop, Bob, *Nicos Poulantzas: Marxist Theory and Political Strategy*, Macmillan, London, 1985.

Jessop, Bob, *The Political Economy of Postwar Britain*, Polity Press, Cambridge, forthcoming 1989.

Jessop, Bob, *Essays in the Theory of the State*, Polity Press, Cambridge, forthcoming 1989.

Johnston, R.J. et al., *A Nation Dividing? The Electoral Map of Great Britain 1979–1987*, Longman, London, 1988. A path-breaking study of the increasing regionalization of the electoral map of British politics.

Kaldor, Nicholas, *The Scourge of Monetarism*, Oxford University Press, Oxford, 1982. The definitive Keynesian critique of the technical economic basis of monetary control. Also contains Kaldor's more general reflections on the appropriate role of monetary policy.

Kavanagh, Dennis, *Thatcherism and British Politics: The End of Consensus?* Oxford University Press, Oxford, 1987. An important assessment by a leading political scientist. Thorough and historically grounded but analytically thin and fails to consider the economic project of Thatcherism. The best offering to date from mainstream political science.

Keegan, William, *Mrs Thatcher's Economic Experiment*, Penguin, Harmondsworth, 1984. A leading Keynesian economic commentator (on *The Observer*) interprets Thatcherite macro-economic policy in terms of the capture of the leadership of the Party by ideologues committed to an experiment. As a result conflates Thatcherism with monetarism and its political base with leadership ideology.

King, Desmond S., *The New Right: Politics, Markets and Citizenship*, Macmillan, London, 1987. A valuable study of New Right doctrine and practice.

Krieger, Joel, *Reagan, Thatcher and the Politics of Decline*, Polity Press, Cambridge, 1986.

Laclau, Ernesto, *Politics and Ideology in Marxist Theory*, Verso, London, 1977.

Laclau, Ernesto, and Chantal Mouffe, *Hegemony and Socialist Strategy*, Verso, London, 1985.

Layton-Henry, Zig (ed.), *Conservative Party Politics*, Macmillan, London, 1980. A series of detailed and useful essays on Conservative Party policy making in opposition. It is revealing that this volume did not foresee the depth of antagonism to social democracy that three terms of Thatcherism subsequently made plain.

Levitas, Ruth (ed.), *The Ideology of the New Right*, Polity Press, Cambridge, 1986. An important set of critical essays on New Right thinking in politics, economics and philosophy.

Leys, Colin, *Politics in Britain: An Introduction*, Heinemann, London, 1983. A highly readable and accessible text on the rise and subsequent crisis of social democracy in postwar Britain. Includes a historically grounded treatment, a consideration of the social class base to politics, the structure and policies of the parties, and the character of the state system.

Lipietz, Alain, *Mirages and Miracles: The Crises of Global Fordism*, Verso, London, 1987.

Loney, Martin, *The Politics of Greed: The New Right and the Welfare State*, Pluto Press, London, 1986. A detailed and highly critical account of the social polarizations that have resulted from Conservative welfare policies.

MacInnes, John, *Thatcherism at Work*, Open University Press, Milton Keynes, 1988.

McKenzie, Robert and Alan Silver, *Angels in Marble: Working Class Conservatives in Urban England*, Heinemann, London, 1968.

Marx, Karl and Friedrich Engels, *On Britain* (2nd edn), Progress Publishers, Moscow, 1962.

Miliband, Ralph et al. (eds), *Socialist Register 1987, Conservatism in Britain and America: Rhetoric and Reality*, Merlin Press, London, 1987. A valuable collection of essays comparing the New Right in the UK and the US.

Minogue, Kenneth and Michael Biddiss (eds), *Thatcherism: Personality and Politics*, Macmillan, London, 1987. The Right and Centre of British politics assess 'Thatcherism'.

Mishra, Ramesh, *The Welfare State in Crisis: Social Thought and Social Change*, Wheatsheaf, Brighton, 1984. An excellent comparative study.

Nordlinger, E.A., *On the Autonomy of the Democratic State*, Harvard University Press, Cambridge, Mass., 1981. An influential statement of elite theory as applied to the operations of the modern democratic state.

O'Connor, James, *The Fiscal Crisis of the State*, St Martin's Press, New York, 1973.

Offe, Claus, *The Contradictions of the Welfare State* (ed. John Keane), Hutchinson, London, 1984.

Olsen, Mancur, *The Rise and Decline of Nations: Economic Growth, Stagflation, and Social Rigidities*, Yale University Press, New Haven, 1982. The bible of those who argue that the older capitalist democracies are weighed down by pluralist stagnation.

Overbeek, Henk, *Global Capitalism and Britain's Decline*, Hutchinson, London, forthcoming 1989.

Palmer, John, *Europe Without America? The Crisis in Atlantic Relations*, Oxford University Press, Oxford, 1987.

Pollard, Sidney, *The Wasting of the British Economy: British Economic Policy 1945 to the Present*, Croom Helm, London, 1982. A leading economic historian drops his academic guard to deliver a spirited attack on what he regards as the anti-industrial bias of British economic policy and its fatal apotheosis in monetarism.

Poulantzas, Nicos, *State, Power, Socialism*, Verso, London, 1978.

Przeworski, Adam, *Capitalism and Social Democracy*, Cambridge University Press, Cambridge, 1985.

Rentoul, John, *The Rich Get Richer*, Methuen, London, 1987.

Riddell, Peter, *The Thatcher Government*, Martin Robertson, Oxford, 1983. An early assessment by the leading political commentator on *The Financial Times*. A detailed and balanced account.

Rose, David (ed.), *Social Stratification and Economic Change*, Hutchinson, London, 1988.

Ross, John, *Thatcher and Friends: The Anatomy of the Tory Party*, Pluto Press, London, 1983. An important if flawed account of Thatcherism placed in the context of the long-held but declining Tory dominance of the British political system.

Rustin, Michael, *For a Pluralist Socialism*, Verso, London, 1985.

Sarlvik, Bo and Ivor Crewe, *Decade of Dealignment: The Conservative Victory of 1979 and Electoral Trends in the 1970s*, Cambridge University Press, Cambridge, 1983.

Seldon, Arthur (ed.), *The Emerging Consensus*, Institute for Economic Affairs, London, 1981. A collection of essays from the New Right arguing for a new consensus around the social market economy.

Shonfield, Andrew, *British Economic Policy since the War*, Penguin, Harmondsworth, 1958.

Smith, David, *The Rise and Fall of Monetarism*, Penguin, Harmondsworth, 1987.

Stopford, John M. and Louis Turner, *Britain and the Multinationals*, John Wiley, Chichester, 1985.

Thompson, Grahame, *The Conservatives' Economic Policy*, Croom Helm, London, 1986. A detailed account of the economic thinking, policy making and implementation of the Thatcher governments. Usefully stresses the continuities with past practices, if thereby underestimating the radicalism of the political project being attempted.

Wainwright, Hilary, *Labour: A Tale of Two Parties*, Hogarth Press, London, 1987.

Walker, Alan and Carol Walker (eds), *The Growing Divide: A Social Audit 1979–87*, Child Poverty Action Group, London, 1987. The most detailed documentation to date of the growth of poverty and unemployment, the widening North–South divide, the impoverishment of women and ethnic minorities, and the marginalization of welfare claimants, in short the two nations effects of Thatcherism.

Whitely, Paul, *The Labour Party in Crisis*, Methuen, London, 1983.

Williams, Raymond, *Television: Technology and Cultural Form*, Fontana, Glasgow, 1974.

Williams, Raymond, *Towards 2000*, Hogarth Press, London, 1983.

Young, Hugo and Anne Sloman, *The Thatcher Phenomenon*, BBC Books, London, 1986. Based on a series of Radio 4 programmes involving interviews with and comment from the great and the good in British political life.

Young, Michael and Peter Willmott, *The Symmetrical Family: A Study of Work and Leisure in the London Region*, Penguin, Harmondsworth, 1973.

Pamphlets and Articles

Alcock, P., 'Welfare state – safety net or poverty trap?', *Marxism Today* (July 1985).

Anderson, Perry, 'The antinomies of Antonio Gramsci', *New Left Review*, 100 (1977).

Anderson, Perry, 'The figures of descent', *New Left Review* 161 (Jan./Feb. 1987), pp. 20–77. A major revised restatement of the seminal account of Britain's decline offered by Anderson and Nairn in the 1960s.

Andreff, Wladimir, 'The international centralization of capital and the re-ordering of world capitalism', *Capital and Class*, 22 (Spring 1984), pp. 58–80.

Arblaster, Anthony, 'Labour's future and the coalition debate', *New Left Review*, 157 (May/June 1986), pp. 45–60. One of the clearest contributions to a debate that generated a lot of smoke but little fire.

Atkins, Fiona, 'Thatcherism, populist authoritarianism and the search for a new left political strategy', *Capital and Class*, 28 (Spring 1986), pp. 25–48. An interesting attempt to reorient the left's debate on the character of Thatcherism towards a more international dimension.

Aughey, Arthur, 'Mrs Thatcher's philosophy', paper presented to the Political Studies Association Conference, Newcastle, April 1983.

Barlow, James and Mike Savage, 'The politics of growth: cleavage and conflict in a Tory heartland', *Capital and Class*, 30 (Winter 1986), pp. 156–82. A case study in the contradictions in the Tory social base in Berkshire.

Barratt Brown, Michael, 'Away with all the great arches: Anderson's history of British capitalism', *New Left Review*, 167 (Jan./Feb. 1988), pp. 22–51. A critique of Anderson's account from a more orthodox Marxist perspective on British imperialism.

Bhaduri, Amit and Josef Steindl, 'The rise of monetarism as a social doctrine', Thames Working Papers in Political Economy, Autumn 1983. A 'fractionalist' account of the rise of monetarism in terms of the assertion of rentier interests internationally and domestically.

Biddiss, Michael, 'Thatcherism: concept and interpretations', in Minogue and Biddiss, *Thatcherism*.

Blackwell, Trevor and Jeremy Seabrook, 'Mrs Thatcher's religious pilgrimage', *Granta*, 6 (Cambridge, 1983), pp. 39–52.

Bonnett, Kevin, 'Classes, capital fractions and monetarism', in D. Robbins (ed.), *Rethinking Social Inequality*, Gower, Aldershot, 1982.

Bonnett, Kevin, 'Corporatism and Thatcherism – is there life after death?', in Alan Cawson (ed.), *Mesocorporatism: The State and Sectoral Interests in Policy Formation*, Sage, London, 1985.

Bull, David and Paul Wilding (eds), 'Thatcherism and the Poor', Child Poverty Action Group, London, 1983.

Bulpitt, Jim, 'The discipline of the new democracy: Mrs Thatcher's domestic statecraft', *Political Studies*, 34 (1986), pp. 19–39. An important Tory assessment of Thatcherism. Argues that it should be seen as an attempt to reassert a traditional form of Conservative statecraft albeit in altered circumstances.

Crewe, Ivor, 'How Labour was trounced all round', *Guardian* (14 June 1983).

Crewe, Ivor, 'The electorate: partisan dealignment ten years on', *West European*

Politics (1984). A restatement from one of the originators of the theory of partisan dealignment.

Crewe, Ivor, in the *Guardian* (15 and 16 June 1987).

Curtice, J., 'Must Labour lose?', *New Society* (18 June 1987).

Curtice, J. and M. Steed, Appendix 2: 'An analysis of the voting', in Butler and Kavanagh, *General Election 1983*.

Deakin, Nicholas (ed.), 'The new right: image and reality', Runnymede Trust, London, 1986. A collection of short philosophical critiques of New Right thinking.

Dunleavy, P., 'The limits to local government', in M. Boddy and C. Fudge (eds), *Local Socialism? Labour Councils and New Left Alternatives*, Macmillan, London, 1984, pp. 49–81.

Edgar, David, 'Bitter harvest', *New Socialist* (Sept./Oct. 1983).

Elliott, Brian et al., 'Anxieties and ambitions: the *petit bourgeoisie* and the New Right', in Rose, *Social Stratification*.

Fry, Geoffrey K., 'The Thatcher government, the financial management initiative, and the 'new civil service'', *Public Administration*, 66 (Spring), pp. 1–20.

Gamble, Andrew, 'Thatcherism and Conservative politics', in Hall and Jacques, *Politics of Thatcherism*, pp. 109–131.

Gamble, Andrew, 'This lady's not for turning: Thatcherism mark III', *Marxism Today* (June 1984).

Gamble, Andrew, 'The rise of the resolute right', *New Socialist* (Jan./Feb. 1985).

Gamble, Andrew, 'Smashing the state: Thatcher's radical crusade', *Marxism Today* (June 1985). An excellent discussion of some of the contradictions involved for Thatcherism in attempting to disengage from the economy.

Gardiner, Jean, 'Women, recession and the Tories', in Hall and Jacques, *Politics of Thatcherism*, pp. 188–206.

Gibbon, Peter, 'Gramsci, eurocommunism and the state', *Economy and Society* (1984).

Gilroy, P. and J. Sim, 'Law, order and the state of the left', in P. Scraton (ed.), *Law, Order and the Authoritarian State*, Open University Press, Milton Keynes, 1987, pp. 71–106.

Goodwin, Mark and Simon Duncan, 'The local state and local economic policy: political mobilisation or economic regeneration', *Capital and Class*, 27 (Winter 1985), pp. 14–36. An insightful piece on Conservative strategies in the inner cities.

Gordon, David M., 'The global economy: new edifice or crumbling foundations?', *New Left Review*, 168 (Mar./Apr. 1988), pp. 24–64.

Gordon, Paul and Francesca Klug, 'New right new racism', *Searchlight*, Nottingham, n.d. A detailed chronicle of the anti-anti-racism of the New Right and its connections with more conventional racist notions.

Hall, Peter, 'The state and economic decline', in B. Elbaum and W. Lazonick (eds), *The Decline of the British Economy*, Clarendon Press, Oxford, 1986, pp. 266–302.

Hall, Stuart, 'The great moving right show', *Marxism Today* (Jan. 1979).

Hall, Stuart, 'Popular-democratic versus authoritarian populism', in Alan Hunt (ed.), *Marxism and Democracy*, Lawrence & Wishart, London, 1980.

Hall, Stuart, 'Nicos Poulantzas: state, power, socialism', *New Left Review*, 119 (Jan./Feb. 1980), pp. 60–9.

Hall, Stuart, 'Thatcherism – a new stage?', *Marxism Today* (Feb. 1980).

Hall, Stuart, 'Recent developments in language and ideology', in Hall et al. *Culture Media, and Language*.

Hall, Stuart, 'The empire strikes back', *New Socialist* (July/Aug. 1982).

Hall, Stuart, 'The battle for socialist ideas in the 1980s', *Socialist Register 1981*, Merlin Press, London, 1982.

Hall, Stuart, 'The little Caesars of social democracy', in Hall and Jacques, *Politics of Thatcherism*.

Hall, Stuart, 'The culture gap', *Marxism Today* (Jan.1984).

Hall, Stuart, 'Faith, hope and clarity', *Marxism Today* (Jan. 1985).

Hall, Stuart, 'Authoritarian populism: a reply', *New Left Review*, 151 (May/June 1985), pp. 115–24. Hall's most detailed reply to his 'Gang of Four' critics.

Hall, Stuart, 'The toad in the garden: Thatcherism among the theorists', in Cary Nelson and Lawrence Grossberg (eds), *Marxism and the Interpretation of Culture*, Macmillan, London, 1988, pp. 35–73.

Hall, Stuart and Alan Hunt, 'Interview with Nicos Poulantzas', *Marxism Today* (May 1979).

Hall, Stuart and Martin Jacques, 'Introduction', in idem, *Politics of Thatcherism*, pp. 9–16.

Held, David, 'Power and legitimacy in contemporary Britain', in McLennan et al., *State and Society*, pp. 299–369.

Heseltine, Michael, 'The Tory opposition', an interview with *Marxism Today* (Mar. 1988).

Hobsbawm, Eric, 'Labour's lost millions', *Marxism Today* (Dec. 1983).

Jacques, Martin, 'Thatcherism: breaking out of the impasse', in Hall and Jacques, *Politics of Thatcherism*, pp. 40–62.

Jessop, Bob, 'The transformation of the state in postwar Britain', in Richard Scase (ed.), *The State in Western Europe*, Croom Helm, London, 1980.

Jessop, Bob, 'The mid-life crisis of Thatcherism', *New Socialist* (Mar. 1986). An early attempt to interpret Thatcherism as the midwife at the birth of a post-Fordist future for the British economy.

Jessop, Bob, 'The dual crisis of the state', in idem, *Essays in the Theory of the State*.

Jessop, Bob et al., 'Authoritarian populism, two nations and Thatcherism', *New Left Review*, 147 (Sept./Oct. 1984), pp. 32–60. A detailed critique of and alternative analysis to Stuart Hall's characterization of Thatcherism in terms of its authoritarian populism.

Jessop, Bob et al., 'Thatcherism and the politics of hegemony: a reply to Stuart Hall', *New Left Review*, 153 (Sept./Oct. 1985), pp. 87–101.

Jessop, Bob et al., 'Popular capitalism, flexible accumulation and left strategy', *New Left Review*, 165 (Sept./Oct. 1987). A preliminary attempt to assess the causes and consequences of the third Thatcherite electoral confirmation.

Johnson, R. W., 'Pomp and circumstance', in idem, *The Politics of Recession*, Macmillan, London, 1985, pp. 224–255. A genuinely insightful essay on the roots of Thatcherism in the crisis of the Tory political culture that developed in the mid-1970s.

Jones, G. W., 'Cabinet government and Mrs Thatcher', *Contemporary Record*, 1: 3 (1987).

Kellner, Peter, 'Labour's future: decline or democratic revolution', *New Statesman*

19 June 1987.
King, Anthony, 'Overload: problems of governing in the 1970s', *Political Studies*, 23 (1975), pp. 284–96.
King, Anthony, 'Margaret Thatcher: the style of a prime minister', in idem (ed.), *The British Prime Minister* (2nd edn), Macmillan, London, 1985, pp. 96–140. Through an analysis of Thatcher's premiership offers a contribution to the debate over prime ministerial versus Cabinet government in the British constitution.
King, Roger, 'Petit-bourgeois conservatism', *Parliamentary Affairs*, 34:3 (1981), pp. 308–21.
Leadbeater, Charlie, 'In the land of the dispossessed', *Marxism Today* (Apr. 1987).
Lehmbruch, Gerhard, 'Liberal corporatism and party government'. in Philippe C. Schmitter and G. Lehmbruch (eds), *Trends Toward Corporatist Intermediation*, Sage, Beverly Hills, 1979.
Leys, Colin, 'Thatcherism and British manufacturing: a question of hegemony', in *New Left Review*, 151 (May/June 1985), pp. 5–25. An important argument situating Thatcherite economic policy in the context of the historical political weakness of British capital.
Leys, Colin, 'The formation of British capital', *New Left Review* 160 (Nov./Dec. 1986), pp. 114–20. A short review essay on the relation between industrial capital, the City and the state.
Ling, Tom, 'Comment', *Marxism Today* (July 1985).
Linton, Martin, 'How the Tories rule the roost', *Guardian*, 19 June 1987.
Miliband, Ralph, 'Class war conservatism' in idem, *Class Power and State Power*, Verso, London, 1983, pp. 279–85. A class reductionist account of Thatcherism as an attempt to reverse the gains of Labour through weakering the strength of the organized working class.
Murray, Robin, 'Benneton Britain', *Marxism Today* (Nov. 1985).
Murray, Robin, 'Ownership, control and the market', *New Left Review*, 164 (July/Aug. 1987).
Nairn, Tom, 'Into political emergency: a retrospect from the eighties', Postscript to his *The Break-Up of Britain: Crisis and Neo-Nationalism* (2nd edn), Verso, London, 1981. A brilliant polemic which although flawed by its fractionalist account of Thatcher's economic strategy provides penetrating insights into its relation to the historical trajectory of the British state.
Nairn, Tom, 'The crisis of the British state', *New Left Review* 130 (Nov./Dec. 1981), pp. 37–44.
O'Leary, Brendan, 'Why was the GLC abolished?' *International Journal of Urban and Regional Research*, 11 (1987), pp. 192–217.
O'Shea, Alan, 'Trusting the people: how does Thatcherism work?' in *Formations of Nation and People*, Routledge & Kegan Paul, London, 1984, pp. 19–41.
Overbeek, Henk, 'The Westland affair: Collision over the future of British capitalism', *Capital and Class*, 29 (Summer 1986), pp. 12–26. An attempt to read the significance of the Westland farce in terms of divisions within the British ruling class over a European vs. an American orientation for capital.
Pahl, R. E. and C. D. Wallace, 'Neither angels in marble nor rebels in red: privatization and working class consciousness', in Rose, *Social Stratification*, pp. 127–49.
Panitch, Leo, 'The impasse of social democratic politics', in idem, *Working Class*

206   Bibliography

Politics in Crisis, Verso, London, 1985.

Patel, P. and K. Pavitt, 'The elements of British technological competitiveness', *National Institute Economic Review* (Nov. 1987), pp. 72–83.

Poulantzas, Nicos, 'La crise des partis', *Le Monde Diplomatique*, 26 Sept. 1979.

Poulantzas, Nicos, 'L'état, les mouvements sociaux, le parti', *Dialectiques*, 28 (1979).

Poulantzas, Nicos, 'Le déplacement des procédures de légitimation', in Vincennes University, *L'université de Vincennes: ou le désir d'apprendre*, Paris, 1980.

Radice, Hugo, 'The national economy: a Keynesian myth?', *Capital and Class*, 22 (Spring 1984), pp. 111–40.

Rustin, Mike, 'Can Labour stop Thatcher?', *Chartist* (July/Aug. 1987).

Sanders, David et al., 'Government popularity and the Falklands war: a reassessment', *British Journal of Political Science*, 17 (1987), pp. 281–313. An important corrective to those arguments which suggest that the Falklands 'victory' provided a significant and long-term boost to Conservative popularity.

Scarbrough, Elizabeth, 'The British electorate twenty years on: electoral change and election surveys', *British Journal of Political Science*, 17 (1987).

Schwarz, Bill, 'Conservatives and corporatism', *New Left Review*, 166 (Nov./Dec. 1987), pp. 107–28. A very perceptive discussion of the Conservative historian of corporate bias in the British political system, Keith Middlemas.

Schwarz, Bill, 'The Thatcher years', in Miliband et al., *Socialist Register 1987* (1987), pp. 116–52.

Segal, Lynne, 'The heat in the kitchen', in Hall and Jacques, *Politics of Thatcherism*, pp. 207–15.

Smith, Mark, 'UK manufacturing: output and trade performance', *Midland Bank Economic Bulletin* (Autumn 1986), pp. 8–16.

Spence, Martin, 'Imperialism and decline: Britain in the 1980s', *Capital and Class*, 25 (Spring 1985), pp. 117–39. A clear account of some of the main trends in the development of financial capital in the UK, the internationalization of the UK economy and their relation to divisions among the working class.

Strinati, Dominic, 'State intervention, the economy and the crisis: corporatism, radical conservatism and the state in Britain', in Angus Stewart (ed.), *Contemporary Britain*, Routledge & Kegan Paul, London, 1983. A major attempt to interpret the crisis of the British state and the rise of Thatcherism in terms of the state integration into the economic crisis.

Therborn, Goran, 'The prospects of Labour and the transformation of advanced capitalism', *New Left Review*, 145 (May/June 1984), pp. 5–38.

Tusscher, Tessa ten, 'Patriarchy, capitalism and the New Right', in Evans et al., *Feminism and Political Theory*, pp. 66–84.

Wainwright, Hilary, 'The limits of Labourism: 1987 and beyond', *New Left Review*, 164 (July/Aug. 1987), pp. 34–50.

Waylen, Georgina, 'Women and neo-liberalism', in Evans et al., *Feminism and Political Theory*, pp. 85–102.

Weir, Angela and Elizabeth Wilson, 'The British women's movement', *New Left Review*, 148 (Nov./Dec. 1984), pp. 74–103.

Williams, Raymond, 'Problems of the coming period', *New Left Review*, 140 (July/Aug. 1983), pp. 7–18.

Williams, Raymond, 'Splits, pacts and coalitions', *New Socialist* (Mar./Apr. 1984).

Williamson, Nigel, 'The new right: the men behind Mrs Thatcher', *Spokesman/ Tribune*, Nottingham, n.d. A short account of the various rightwing pressure groups and institutes that form a policy-network for New Right doctrines.

Wilson, Elizabeth, 'Thatcherism and women: after seven years', in Miliband et al. (eds), *Socialist Register 1987* (1987), pp. 199–235.

Worsthorne, P., 'Class and class conflict in British foreign policy', *Foreign Affairs*, 37:3 (Apr. 1959).

Notes on the Authors

Kevin Bonnett is Senior Lecturer in Sociology CCAT, Cambridge. He has published articles on corporatism and monetarism, and co-authored a successful textbook on *Introductory Sociology* (1987). He is active in the Labour Party but still manages to enjoy life.

Simon Bromley lives and writes in Sheffield. He gained his doctorate from Cambridge for a thesis on the international oil industry and is currently working on a book on *The Geopolitical-Economy of International Oil* (forthcoming Polity Press 1989). He is an active member of the Conference of Socialist Economists and in his spare time enjoys walking in the Derbyshire dales.

Bob Jessop is Senior Lecturer in Government at the University of Essex. He has previously published books on *The Capitalist State* (1982) and *Nicos Poulantzas* (1985) as well as many articles and essays on state theory, political economy, and British politics. In his spare time he cycles and collects china cats.

Tom Ling teaches with the Open University, CCAT, and is Director of Studies for Social and Political Sciences at Downing College, Cambridge. He is active in the Labour Party and is currently Deputy Leader of Cambridge City Council. Outside politics he plays Scottish fiddle music and jazz.

Subject Index

accumulation strategy, 55, 120, 135, 158; and AP, 93; a neo-liberal, 171–4; new, 64–5, 168
Adam Smith Institute, 28, 61
aid *see* government
Alliance *see* SDP-Liberal Alliance
alternative agenda, 180–2
alternative economic strategy (AES), 122–3
alternative social policy, 123–4
alternative strategic recommendations, 122–4
alternatives to Thatcherism, 96–8: future research agenda, 182–3
Amsterdam regulation school, 33–4
anti-inflation policy, 84–5
anti-statism, 37–8, 101
arithmetical particularism, 39–40
Association of Independent Businesses, 61
Association of Self-Employed People, 61
'Atlantic Reformism', 181
Atlanticism, 76, 133, 164, 181
authoritarian populism (AP), 12; ambiguities of, 43, 71–2; background to, 70–1; critique and counter-critique, 57–124; debate in context, 65–7; development of the concept, 100–2; genesis of, 41–3;

ideologism of, 72–3; as legitimation technique (Atkins), 33; levels of abstraction and, 102–4; proper scope as an interpretation, 10, 92–5; strategic implications of, 118–19; and two nations, 68–98, 119–22
'authoritarian statism' (AS), 100–1, 111–12
authoritarianism, 161

balance of forces, 3, 43, 100, 110, 113; *see also* class forces
Bank of England, 80
Bank-Treasury axis, 63, 165–6
banking, internationalization of, 120
banks, shift in power from industry to, 31, 33, 91
base/superstructure correspondence, 114
BBC, distrust of, 35
Bennism, 23
Beveridge system of social security, 74
birth control, 13
black movement, 122
black vote, 86
black women, 49
blacks, de-franchising of, 39
bourgeoisie, 166; hegemony, 3; *see also* middle classes

Policing the Crisis (Hall), 41, 43, 69, 70, 100, 107, 111
policy formation centres, 61
political agenda, and AP, 93
political economy, of Thatcherism, 75–83
political order, social base of, 156–7
political power, relations with economic power, 84–7, 130, 142–5, 155
political representation, 81–3, 91
political strategy, 121–2
political theory: and the new right, 28; and socialist strategy, 110–11
politicism, from ideologism to, 95–6
politics, 56; new, 139–40; Thatcher factor in, 26–8; Thatcherism in terms of, 37–41
Politics and Ideology in Marxist Theory (Laclau), 106
Politics of Thatcherism, The (Hall), 69, 70–1
poll tax, regressive, 141, 144
popular capitalism, 65, 134–53, 167, 169
'Popular-Democratic versus Authoritarian Populism' (Hall), 102
populism, 44, 82, 82–3, 101–2; and power bloc, 72
post-Fordism, 55, 119, 127–33, 152; and Thatcherite strategy, 140–2
postwar settlement (PWS), 60, 75–6; petty bourgeois resentment against, 11, 19, 33–5, 82, 96, 138, 166; and Thatcherism, 12, 61–2
postwar settlements, 164–5
Powellism, 60, 61
power bloc, 90–2, 97, 162, 178; decomposition, and AP, 94; recomposition of, 106
power politics, 90–2, 166–7
pragmatism, of Thatcherism, 78–9
presidential system, 83
press: changing role of, and AP, 95; Thatcherite, 63
pressure groups, new, 19

Prison Notebooks (Gramsci), 70, 103
privatization, 91, 142–3, 144, 169, 171, 175; mobile, 46–7; in welfare state, 87
production, politics of 55, 135
productivity, 120–1
professions, hostility to Thatcherism, 124
profits, orientation to, 33–4
protectionism, 181
proto-feminism, 4
psephology, 138
public expenditure, cuts and redirection in, 142
public opinion, 26; *see also* electoral support
public sector, Labour support, 138, 139
Public Sector Borrowing Requirement (PSBR), 36, 144

racism, 4, 111
radicalism, 64, 65
radio, reduction of political independence of, 20
rates, 64, 141
redistribution, politics of, 150
regional government, less power, 145
regions, 74, 174
regulationists, 33–4, 55
relative autonomy, theory of, 73, 83, 159, 161
rentier British economy, 172
repression, 88, 111, 167
research centres, 61
right progressives within Conservative Party *see* 'wets'
rightwing politicians, theories of Thatcherism, 23

Scandinavia, 76
schools, independently-governed, 144
scientific management, 128
Scotland, 139
Scottish Development Agency, 173
SDP-Liberal Alliance, 23, 79, 82, 86, 134, 150; pact with Labour

Name Index

Index by Fiona Barr